Green Alternatives to Globalisation

Green Alternatives to Globalisation
A Manifesto

Michael Woodin and Caroline Lucas

PLUTO PRESS
www.plutobooks.com

First published 2004 by Pluto Press
345 Archway Road, London N6 5AA and
175 Fifth Avenue, New York, NY 10010

www.plutobooks.com

Distributed in the United States of America exclusively by
Palgrave Macmillan, a division of St. Martin's Press LLC,
175 Fifth Avenue, New York, NY 10010

Copyright © Michael E. Woodin and Caroline Lucas 2004

The right of Michael E. Woodin and Caroline Lucas to be identified as the authors of this work has been asserted by them in accordance with the Copyright, Designs and Patents Act 1988.

British Library Cataloguing in Publication Data
A catalogue record for this book is available from the British Library

ISBN   978 0 7453 1933 9 hardback
ISBN   978 0 7453 1932 2 paperback

Library of Congress Cataloging in Publication Data
Woodin, Michael.
  Green alternatives to globalisation : a manifesto / Michael Woodin and Caroline Lucas.
       p. cm.
  Includes bibliographical references.
  ISBN 0–7453–1933–5 — ISBN 0–7453–1932–7 (pbk.)
  1. International economic relations. 2. Globalization—Economic aspects.
3. Economic development. 4. Sustainable development. I. Lucas, Caroline, 1960–   II. Title.

HF1359.W656 2004
338.9'27—dc22

This book is printed on paper suitable for recycling and made from fully managed and sustained forest sources. Logging, pulping and manufacturing processes are expected to conform to the environmental standards of the country of origin. The paper may contain up to 70 per cent post-consumer waste.

10   9   8   7   6   5   4

Designed and produced for Pluto Press by
Chase Publishing Services, Sidmouth, England
Typeset from disk by Stanford DTP Services, Northampton, England
Printed and bound in the European Union by
CPI Antony Rowe, Chippenham and Eastbourne, England

For

Deborah, Talia and Rafael (MW)

Richard, Theo and Isaac (CL)

Contents

Foreword	ix
Acknowledgements	xiii
List of Abbreviations and Acronyms	xv
Introduction	xix

Section One: Assessing the Damage

1.	Globalisation: The Economics of Insecurity	3
2.	Democracy for Sale	17
3.	A World in Decline	33
4.	Globalising Poverty, Inequality and Unemployment	46

Section Two: The Green Alternative

5.	Economic Localisation	67

Section Three: Turning the Tide

6.	Connecting Hearts and Minds	107
7.	Learning From History	117
8.	Storming the Citadels: Sacking Bretton Woods and the WTO	129

Section Four: Applying the Alternative

9.	Local Food: The Global Solution	145
10.	Localising Money	174
11.	A New Context for Multilateralism	200

Conclusion	214
Notes	216
Bibliography	238
Index	251

TABLES

5.1	Creating a General Agreement of Sustainable Trade (GAST)	78
9.1	Average Energy Use of Different Forms of Transport	150

BOXES

Box 1.1	Greens and Growth	12
Box 2.1	GATS	24
Box 3.1	The State of the World: a summary of *GEO 3*	34
Box 9.1	Supermarkets	155
Box 9.2	The 'Development Box'	168
Box 9.3	GM Crops – Myths and Reality	169
Box 10.1	An Underground Currency for London	196

FIGURES

1.1	An environmental Kuznets curve, showing a supposed relationship within any one country between environmental degradation and average income	13
2.1	International trade and the percentage of US and UK voters participating in elections in an era of globalisation	31
3.1	Humanity's growing global footprint	36
3.2	Transport of goods in the EU by mode of transport, 1970–99 (aviation not included)	40
4.1	Unemployment in the EU and US	58
4.2	UK per capita GDP and ISEW (1950–96)	62
4.3	US per capita GDP and GPI	63
4.4	Personal income and satisfaction in the US	63
5.1	Percentage change in household income under Desai's CI proposal	93

Foreword

Mike Feinstein

The unsustainability of our lifestyle as a species cries out for response – both because of widespread environmental degradation that scars our planet, as well as criminal inequities among us that literally rob billions of people of the chance to realize their potential.

These negative trends are not new – in some ways, they've been with us for hundreds if not thousands of years. But our failings today are magnified by the size of our global population, the immense power of our technology and a global economic system that exploits people and planet for short-term profit. This brings about an unprecedented urgency to our time.

Into this moment step Woodin and Lucas with their new book. Visionary yet precise, profound yet full of common sense, Woodin and Lucas carefully dissect the propaganda-laden myths of corporate capitalism that too often lead us to believe 'there can be no other way.'

Even many who instinctively suspect there is something deeply wrong with globalization, often have trouble fully unlearning these myths that we have come to internalize as a result of their almost mantra-like repetition in our daily lives. And even if we have unlearned them in our own lives, we often have difficulty articulating this in concrete terms to others.

To help us with this, Woodin and Lucas bring to bear a sophisticated knowledge of the alphabet soup of economic globalization – WTO, GATS, NAFTA, IMF MAI, and TRIPs – and expose the failings of those institutions in traditional economic terms.

How many of us for example, when hearing a simplistic, jingoistic, yet intuitively attractive saying like 'a rising tide lifts all boats', can succinctly explain why globalization is *not* the answer to poverty? Woodin and Lucas can and do, by giving clear, empirical evidence that the problem is *not* that there is not enough wealth to go around. Rather, the problem is the *way* wealth is created and distributed in the first place.

What about the 'principle of comparative advantage', which suggests that goods should be produced wherever they can be done so most 'efficiently'? This is frequently used to justify economic globalization and at first glance, it also has an intuitive appeal making it hard to argue with.

But Woodin and Lucas demonstrate how the mobility of capital (so coveted by transnational corporations) seeks *absolute profitability* as a basis for comparative advantage, and thus drives down labour, environmental and health and safety standards worldwide.

Such a critique is critical, because it exposes the sheer lunacy of economics based upon unlimited growth on a finite planet – especially an economics that concentrates wealth and power in the hands of the few, while squandering scarce resources at the same time.

But in addition to opposing the status quo, for those of us marching in the streets, debating in the classrooms, or struggling in City Halls and state and national legislatures, we also have to provide a positive alternative. That is where the work of Woodin and Lucas is perhaps most compelling.

Defenders of the status quo often ridicule Green visions as unrealistic 'back-to-nature' fantasies that have little relationship to reality ('those Greens are so against trade, they don't even want to let us eat bananas').

By contrast, Woodin and Lucas propose a sophisticated vision of *economic localisation* that involves reforming monetary, investment and trade policy within an ecological context.

Woodin and Lucas suggest a world where the flow of ideas, technologies, information, culture, money and goods has, as its end goal, the rebuilding of truly sustainable national and local economies worldwide. Embodying what Greens everywhere learn from nature – that we are all deeply interdependent – the emphasis of economic localisation is not on 'competition for the cheapest', but on 'co-operation for the best'.

In such a world – recognizing that democracy, ecology and social justice go hand in hand – control of the economy would also move back from the boardrooms of distant corporations to the peoples and communities that are directly affected by it.

As an activist involved in Green politics, I find Woodin and Lucas's book very inspiring and reassuring. Inspiring, because it demonstrates how problems today, can be turned into solutions tomorrow. Reassuring, because the book itself reflects the increasing maturation of the Green movement over the last three decades. Having been both inside and outside the halls of power, Woodin and Lucas combine the energy of street protest with the policy-making expertise of serving in elected office. The vision and practicality of their recommendations reflect that fact.

One can look around the planet and despair at the immensity of the challenges we face. But just as the current system benefits from a series of self-reinforcing policies and institutions, Woodin and Lucas remind us that a more sustainable and just economy can come into being with similarly synergistic practices.

Acknowledgements

Many people have helped us get to the stage of collecting all these ideas together and setting them out in some kind of order. Most of them are unknown to us. They might have said something at a conference, painted a witty slogan on a placard or penned an article that, in turn, inspired others to think, write or speak until we got to hear of it. We are grateful to you all.

We are, however, particularly grateful to those whom we do know about. Colin Hines has been an extraordinary source of inspiration for many years and owns the intellectual property rights to much of what we have to say. We are also very grateful to Molly Scott Cato for her guidance in Green economics and to James Forder for his patient tutorials in the conventional variety.

Many others have helped us to refine our ideas along the way. They include Steve Dawe, Paul Ingram, Penny Kemp, James Robertson, Lucy Ford, George Monbiot, Spencer FitzGibbon, Justin Wilkes, Darren Johnson and Craig Simmons. Timely literary advice was forthcoming from Emily Miles and Rob Sykes; Xanthe Bevis finished the index and Stig designed the figures. Many thanks also to David Weston, Chris Keene and the excellent folk at WDM Scotland for their ceaseless flow of extremely useful emails.

We are very grateful to Roger van Zwanenberg at Pluto Press for suggesting the book in the first place and to Julie Stoll, our extraordinarily patient editor.

Finally, 'the book' simply would not have been written were it not for the forbearance, inspiration, love and stoicism of our partners and children, particularly over the last 18 months. We hope they think it was worth it.

November 2003

List of Abbreviations and Acronyms

ACP	Africa, the Caribbean and Pacific
AmCham	American Chamber of Commerce
AMUE	Association for the Monetary Union of Europe
AOA	Agreement on Agriculture
ASEAN	Association of Southeast Asian Nations
BSE	bovine spongiform encephalopathy
C&C	Contraction and Convergence
CAP	Common Agricultural Policy
CBI	Confederation of British Industry
CDFI	community development finance initiatives
CEE	Central and Eastern Europe
CI	Citizens' Income
CITES	Convention on International Trade in Endangered Species
CJD	Creutzfeldt-Jakob disease
DfID	Department for International Development
Ebcu	emissions-backed currency unit
EC	European Commission
ECB	European Central Bank
ECOFIN	The Council for Economic and Financial Affairs
ECOSOC	United Nations Economic and Social Council
EIB	European Investment Bank
EKC	environmental Kuznets curve
EMU	European Monetary Union
ERM	exchange rate mechanism
ERT	European Roundtable of Industrialists
EU	European Union
FDI	foreign direct investment
FTAA	Free Trade Area of the Americas
GAST	General Agreement on Sustainable Trade
GATS	General Agreement on Trade in Services
GATT	General Agreement on Tariffs and Trade
GDP	gross domestic product
GE	General Electric
GM, GMOs	genetically modified, genetically modified organisms
GNP	gross national product

GPI	Genuine Progress Indicator
HDI	Human Development Index
HIPC	Highly Indebted Poor Countries
IATP	Institute for Agriculture and Trade Policy
IBRD	International Bank for Reconstruction and Development
IDA	International Development Agency
IGD	Institute of Grocery Distribution
ILO	International Labour Organisation
IMF	International Monetary Fund
IPRs	intellectual property rights
ISEC	International Society for Ecology and Culture
ISEW	Index of Sustainable Economic Welfare
ITO	International Trade Organisation
LDCs	Least Developed Countries
LETS	Local Exchange Trading Schemes
LGA	Local Government Association
LPI	Living Planet Index
LVT	Land Value Tax
MAFF	Ministry for Agriculture, Fisheries and Food
MAI	Multilateral Agreement on Investment
MEAs	Multilateral Environmental Agreements
MEP	Member of the European Parliament
MFN	Most Favoured Nation
MIGA	Multilateral Investment Guarantee Agency
NAFTA	North American Free Trade Agreement
NEF	New Economics Foundation
NFU	National Farmers' Union
NGO	non-governmental organisation
NICs	Newly Industrialised Countries
NIEO	New International Economic Order
NT	National Treatment
OECD	Organisation for Economic Cooperation and Development
OPEC	Organisation of Petroleum Exporting Countries
PFI	private finance initiative
POD	Programme of Obstruction and Deconstruction
POPs	Protocol on Persistent Organic Pollutants
PPMs	Agreement on Process and Production Methods
PPMV	parts per million by volume
PPP	public private partnership

PRGF	Poverty Reduction and Growth Facility
SAP	Structural Adjustment Programme
SGP	Stability and Growth Pact
SMEs	small and medium-sized enterprises
SPS	Agreement on Sanitary and Phytosanitary Standards
TBT	Agreement on Technical Barriers to Trade
TEN	Trans-European Networks
TNC	transnational corporation
TRIMs	Agreement on Trade-related Investment Measures
TRIPs	Agreement on Trade-related Aspects of Intellectual Property Rights
UK	United Kingdom
UN	United Nations
UNCED	United Nations Conference on Environment and Development
UNCTAD	United Nations Conference on Trade and Development
UNDP	United Nations Development Programme
UNEP	United Nations Environment Programme
UNICE	Union of Industrial and Employers' Confederations of Europe
US	United States
WSSD	World Summit on Sustainable Development
WTO	World Trade Organization
WWF	World Wide Fund for Nature
ZSR	Slovak Railway Company

Introduction

GREEN POLITICS AND GLOBALISATION

Reactions to the current wave of economic globalisation vary widely, but its supporters and opponents alike are clear that it is the dominant economic and political process of the age as it tears up long-established assumptions and demands new responses.

Greens see far more harm than good in economic globalisation, an assessment that is shared by many others from across the political spectrum for many different reasons. However, to anticipate a frequent refrain of this book, opposition alone will not reverse such a systematic and powerfully driven tide. If resistance is to be effective it must be driven by an inspiring and coherent alternative. We must move on from opposition to proposition and any political philosophy that aspires to lead the resistance must rise to the urgent challenge of articulating just such an alternative. It is precisely this challenge that motivated our book.

Uniquely, Green politics aims to reconstruct the patterns of human activities and relationships so that they come to respect the natural systems on which they depend and thus guarantee the central goal of sustainability. This goal cannot be achieved until equity and social justice are woven into the fabric of society. There is overwhelming evidence to show that equitable societies are healthier and happier than unequal ones. Equitable societies are also more likely to build sufficient support to undertake the large-scale changes that a genuine commitment to sustainability entails. If people are persuaded that the society in which they live genuinely protects and caters for their interests, they will gain the security that enables them to devote their attention to solving common problems rather than to the narrow fight to 'keep up with the Joneses'. Why, for example, should a young man who earns the minimum wage in a dead-end job be expected to fret about the social and environmental consequences of his choice of mode of transport when there is no decent public transport for him to use and when, at every turn, the message is reinforced that the possession of sufficient wealth to purchase the latest car is the measure of man? Equally, why should we expect the poorest countries to cut greenhouse gas emissions when the richest nations blatantly shirk their disproportionately greater responsibility to do the same?

Green politics seeks not only to protect the natural world, but also to learn from it. It recognises that we are at once part of many interdependent communities of interest, from the local to the global. In a globalised world, even the most mundane activities, such as choosing which shop to use, have implications that reach far beyond the local economy to affect the lives of communities around the world. This situation can only be managed equitably if it is underpinned by genuinely democratic structures at every level. Since these are difficult to achieve at a global level where, in any case, the feedback loops between actions and their consequences are confused and indistinct, Green politics is guided by the principle of subsidiarity. This states that decisions should be made as locally as is appropriate. As we argue later on, some issues like the equitable access to global resources, for example, the atmosphere's ability to absorb emissions of carbon dioxide, can only be settled at a global level. In other spheres, such as trade, the case for doing things predominantly at the global level, where democratic regulation struggles to keep pace with the dominant vested interests, is much less compelling.

This whistle-stop tour of the principles of Green politics attempts to prepare the ground for much of what follows.[1] It also helps to highlight some of the main similarities and differences between our critique of globalisation and those promoted by other sections of the anti-globalisation movement. Together with Greens, many groups on the traditional and hard left blame economic globalisation for growing inequality and global unemployment and for the remorseless drift of power away from elected governments and workers to private corporations and investors. The analysis of the problem is shared, but to Green ears the response of the unreconstructed left is silent on sustainability. It is not sufficient to pursue redistributive policies, enhance workers' rights, boost the public sector and argue for tougher regulation of the private sector, without also directing the more accountable and equitable economy this would create along a path that is as sustainable as possible.

Many environmentalists can also be found marching behind anti-globalisation banners. Greens obviously share their concern about the deteriorating state of the environment. What distinguishes the response of Green politics from that of environmentalism however is that Greens go beyond lobbying the established politicians to clean up their mess. Green politics provides an alternative political philosophy, an economic programme, and an alternative set of politicians to replace the conventional ones and stop the mess being created in the first place.

Green politics is necessarily internationalist. At its heart lies a call to action to tackle urgent global problems. Green politics is therefore helping to identify and mobilise a global community of shared interest. This community is already well aware that the details of the solutions it proposes will vary to meet local conditions, but that the intentions of these solutions are shared, as is the analysis that inspires them. We hope then that, even if this book occasionally becomes preoccupied with details that are specific to Britain or the EU, its intentions and analysis will ring true wherever it is read.

THE BOOK

The book is presented in four sections. Section One examines the theory and consequences of economic globalisation. Chapter 1 looks at the context within which economic globalisation is being driven forward, who is driving it and the flaws in the theory on which their rhetoric is based. Chapters 2, 3 and 4 examine respectively how the process of economic globalisation is radically undermining democratic governance, exacerbating environmental destruction, and widening the gap between rich and poor.

Section Two presents an alternative to economic globalisation: namely economic localisation. It consists of just one very long chapter (Chapter 5) that contains no obvious point at which it might be divided equally into two shorter ones. All is not lost however, as the chapter comes in several short sections which can be read all at once or one at a time, as the reader wishes. The sections explain the main building blocks of economic localisation and then answer some of the principal objections to it.

Section Three explores the strategies that are needed to implement economic localisation. It attempts to deal with those awkward 'ah yes, but how are we going to get there?' questions. Chapter 6 argues that as a precondition for turning the tide of globalisation, people must see the connections between its consequences and the process itself; then they will be prepared to accept an alternative. Chapter 7 asks whether the global institutions that are currently driving economic globalisation could be reformed from within to deliver that alternative. The answer, supported by a brief study of the institutions' history, is 'almost certainly not'; what is required amounts to a revolution from without. Chapter 8 discusses the options for instigating the revolution.

Section Four demonstrates how economic localisation can be applied to provide solutions to some of the most critical issues of our time. The chapters in this section deliberately concentrate on topics that are central to the debate about economic globalisation, yet are the subject of controversy within the wider global justice movement.[2] Thus, Chapter 9 examines agriculture, Chapter 10 argues for the localisation of money and Chapter 11 concludes that prospects for multilateral cooperation would be improved within a context of localisation.

THE AUTHORS

Michael Woodin is one of the two Principal Speakers of the Green Party of England and Wales.[3] He is also the party's Spokesperson on Trade and Industry and wrote its manifesto for the UK general election in 2001. Michael lectures in psychology at Balliol College, Oxford and when not teaching, speaking, or thinking global thoughts, he takes local action as an elected member of Oxford City Council, a position he has held since 1994.

Caroline Lucas is a Green Party Member of the European Parliament (MEP) for South East England. She serves on the Parliament's Trade and Environment committees and was a member of its official delegations to the Seattle, Doha and Cancun Ministerial meetings of the World Trade Organization (WTO).[4] Caroline is also one of the two Principal Speakers of the Green Party of England and Wales. Before her election to the European Parliament in 1999, she was a senior policy adviser at a major development non-governmental organisation (NGO) working on trade and environment issues and served for four years as a member of Oxfordshire County Council.

Section One
Assessing the Damage

Who is driving economic globalisation – and why? What is the theory behind it and what impacts does it have on democratic governance, the environment and the poor?

1
Globalisation: The Economics of Insecurity

> The terrorists deliberately chose the World Trade towers as their target. While their blow toppled the towers, it cannot and will not shake the foundation of world trade and freedom.
>
> Robert Zoellick, US trade representative[1]

In the aftermath of the attacks on the Twin Towers on 11 September 2001, political commentators were quick to pronounce the death of the anti-globalisation movement. On the very morning of the attacks, the *Financial Times* asserted, in what was to have been the first instalment of an upbeat four-part series entitled 'The Children of Globalisation Strike Back', 'one certainty was that anti-globalisation protest was not going away'. The rest of the series was pulled and only published much later in revised form, which included the observation that activists 'who used to relish the rhetoric of revolution and confrontation, are now holding their tongues'.[2]

At the same time, advocates of economic globalisation also seized on the events of 11 September as an opportunity to revitalise their flagging effort to liberalise international trade and investment. The smoke had hardly cleared from the ruins of the World Trade Center before the US trade representative Robert Zoellick and EU trade commissioner Pascal Lamy were pressing for even greater trade liberalisation through the World Trade Organization (WTO), asserting that free trade was an essential means of countering terrorism. In a *Washington Post* column, Zoellick called for a campaign to 'counter terror with trade', arguing that trade 'promotes the values at the heart of this protracted struggle'.[3] The following month, to enthusiastic applause from Californian business leaders, President Bush declared 'We will defeat [the terrorists] by expanding and encouraging world trade.'[4] Developing country delegations at the WTO Ministerial at Doha subsequently complained of being bullied into accepting a new round of negotiations on the grounds that they would be opposing the war on terror if they did not.

Proponents of economic globalisation were also swift to insinuate a link between the terrorists and the global justice movement. On 11 September itself, US Congressman Don Young of Alaska even suggested that there was a 'strong possibility' that the attacks were the work of anti-globalisation protestors. Two weeks later, the Italian Prime Minister, Silvio Berlusconi, asserted that whilst Islam was attacking the West from outside, anti-globalisation protesters were attacking it from within.[5] A leading pro-globalisation columnist in the US wrote: 'While they are not deliberately setting out to slaughter thousands of innocent people, the protestors who want to prevent the holding of meetings like those of the IMF or the WTO are seeking to advance their political agenda through intimidation, which is a classic goal of terrorism'.[6]

Attempts to paint protesters for global justice and Islamic fundamentalist terrorists into the same corner could not be more misconceived or more cynical, for it is the process of economic globalisation itself which is responsible for increasing insecurity. Indeed, there have since been hints from UK and US government sources that this is recognised at the highest levels. The UK's Secretary of State for Trade and Industry, Patricia Hewitt, has argued, 'If we in the West don't create a system of world trade that is fair as well as free ... we will pay a price in increased terrorism and increased insecurity.'[7] Significantly, the CIA has reached a similar conclusion – at least in theory:

> The rising tide of the global economy will create many economic winners, but it will not lift all boats. [It will] spawn conflicts at home and abroad, ensuring an even wider gap between ... winners and losers than exists today ... [Globalisation's] evolution will be rocky, marked by chronic financial volatility and a widening economic divide ... Regions, countries, and groups feeling left behind will face deepening economic stagnation, political instability and cultural alienation. They will foster political, ethnic, ideological, and religious extremism, along with the violence that often accompanies it.[8]

As we detail in subsequent chapters, it is precisely the damaging patterns of economic globalisation, which the rich world is foisting unevenly on the poor, that drives poverty, inequality and environmental degradation. This in turn fuels insecurity and conflict.

In this book we argue for an alternative framework to economic globalisation that will combat inequality and provide space for communities around the world to implement their right to choose appropriate social and economic strategies to meet their own needs. We believe that this, rather than any display of military superiority or war on terror, will create true security. And indeed, it is this vision of security that has inspired millions of people around the world to join the global justice movement, and millions more to demonstrate against the US-led invasion of Iraq, in a globalisation of grassroots protest against the unaccountable projection of Western power across the world. This unprecedented growth of activism and awareness powerfully demonstrates just how greatly exaggerated the rumours of the death of the movement have been.

RESTRAINING THE POWERFUL

If anything is to restrain and democratise the West's power it will be the enormous array of conventions, treaties and agreements by which international relations are regulated. These have grown up over time and now form a complex and fragile edifice that is the nearest thing there is to a global constitution. Rarely are the rules of this constitution enforced however, and when enforcement does occur it is rarely consistent.

UN Security Council resolutions for instance occasionally trigger decisive and effective action, particularly when they coincide with dominant strategic interests, but for the most part they lie scattered, no more than dusty ornaments on the global mantelpiece. A few multilateral environmental agreements have met with success, notably the Montreal protocol on ozone-depleting substances, but most have failed to live up to the expectations they generated. For example, the United Nations Environment Programme (UNEP) estimates that concentrations of carbon dioxide in the atmosphere could double by 2050 despite the UN's Kyoto Convention on Climate Change.[9] Klaus Toepfer, UNEP's executive director, perhaps best described the situation as it relates to environment when he said, 'We now have hundreds of declarations, agreements, guidelines and legally binding treaties designed to address environmental problems and the threats they pose to wildlife and human health and well being. Let us now find the political courage and innovative financing needed to implement these deals and steer a healthier, more prosperous course for planet Earth.'[10] He could equally well have been describing the state of weapons proliferation, development, human rights, or many other policy areas.

If there is one realm of international negotiations that does not fit Toepfer's description, it is trade and international finance. Here, political 'courage', as some would see it, has been found in abundance. They have spawned the General Agreement on Tariffs and Trade (GATT), the WTO, the International Monetary Fund (IMF) and the World Bank. Almost uniquely in international affairs, the regulations of these bodies not only override domestic legislation, but they are also routinely enforced through trade and credit sanctions. Their combined effect is driving the process of economic globalisation.

ECONOMIC GLOBALISATION – WHAT IS IT?

We need a clear definition of economic globalisation from the outset, since many of its advocates and beneficiaries recruit the undoubted benefits that can accrue from constructive international flows of information and technology to excuse the destructive effects of economic globalisation. The former UK international development secretary, Clare Short, typifies this approach. One publication from her department stated, 'globalisation means the growing interdependence and interconnectedness of the modern world.'[11] This woolly, cosy definition allows Short to wax lyrical about the spread of democracy and human rights without understanding that these have very little to do with economic globalisation.

What we mean by the term 'economic globalisation' is precisely defined within international trade theory as the ever-increasing integration of national economies into a giant one-size-fits-all global economy through trade and investment rules and privatisation, aided by technological advances, and driven by corporate power. Even when, due to lexical efficiency or plain laziness, we refer to the process as globalisation without its 'economic' prefix, it is this definition that we are using. It describes a process very different in intent and effect from the mutually beneficial exchange of information, ideas and technology that might be referred to as 'internationalism'.[12]

THE FLAWED THEORY OF GLOBALISATION

The early roots of economic globalisation are based on the principle of 'comparative advantage' that was first developed by Adam Smith in *The Wealth of Nations* in 1776 and later refined by David Ricardo in 1817. It is a 'do what you do best, and trade for the rest' approach, according to which nations should specialise in industries in which they have the greatest 'comparative advantage'. In other words, by mass-producing those goods that make maximum use of factors of production that are locally abundant (whether land, climate, natural resources or labour), countries can gain a price advantage over their competitors. If a country has a significant amount of low-cost labour, for instance, it should specialise in producing and exporting labour-intensive products; if it has a rich endowment of natural resources, it should export resource-intensive products. It will then need to import goods that it needs which other countries have a comparative advantage in producing.

According to Adam Smith, prosperity is maximised by this specialisation because the competition to win export markets reduces prices and increases efficiency through greater productivity and economies of scale. For Smith, what limits prosperity is the size of a market. Specialised production requires larger markets if the full productivity gains and economies of scale are to be realised, hence the imperative that lies at the heart of economic globalisation of establishing 'free trade' within larger and larger markets.

This might all sound good in principle, but in practice it is an ivory tower theory that ignores two crucial features of the real world and the interaction between them. First, trade is rarely conducted between equal partners. In Smith and Ricardo's theory, trading nations are assumed to be equal partners making rational decisions based on objective assessments of the factors of production each has available to it through accidents of history, climate and geography. No weight is given to the power imbalances that exist between traders and producers and between different nations. Throughout the history of international trade, 'comparative advantages' have been created artificially and protected fiercely. Whether through gunboat 'diplomacy', colonisation, slavery, land enclosures, or protective subsidies, dominant trading nations have for centuries expropriated and jealously guarded the factors of production and market access they need to establish their 'comparative advantages' over would-be competitors. This has created the situation seen today, where a few dominant trading nations enjoy comparative advantages in many areas of production, whilst the majority enjoy neither a comparative advantage in anything, nor the power to gain one. Under these conditions, international trade in conducted on vastly unequal terms.

It often serves only to widen the disparity between rich and poor, with women disproportionately affected, and to condemn poorer countries to continuing in their relatively powerless role as low-cost producers of primary goods for Western consumption.

The second feature of today's economic climate that was not anticipated by Smith and Ricardo is the increasing mobility of capital. They both assumed that investors would tend not to invest abroad. Ricardo wrote:

> ... the fancied or real insecurity of capital, when not under the immediate control of its owner, together with the natural disinclination which every man has to quit the country of his birth and connections, and intrust himself with all his habits fixed, to a strange government and new laws, checks the emigration of capital. These feelings, which I would be sorry to see weakened, induce most men of property to be satisfied with a low rate of profits in their own country, rather than seek a more advantageous employment for their wealth in foreign nations.[13]

Based on the assumption that investment would remain at home whilst goods were traded internationally, Smith argued that capital would be guided by 'an invisible hand'[14] of market forces to the domestic industry in the investor's country that enjoyed the greatest comparative advantage, thus aiding global specialisation. Today, however, capital pays scant regard to national boundaries and, rather than seeking national comparative advantage, it seeks *absolute profitability* on a global scale. Developments in information technology, plus a deregulation of controls on capital by nation states, have resulted in around $1.3 trillion now being transferred around the world every day.[15]

Capital deregulation has not occurred by accident; it is one of the favourite prescriptions of agencies like the IMF and the World Bank, in line with another theory that has more to do with ivory towers than the real world: the principle of 'capital advantage'. According to this principle, the liberalisation of capital markets benefits the global economy by easing the allocation of global savings to their most productive uses and by allowing investors to diversify their risks across sectors and countries.

Again, this principle might sound plausible in theory, but it rests on the assumption that investors are able to make rational decisions based on complete information about all the potential investments they could make. This hardly describes the international investment markets where the young men who populate the trading floors slosh millions of dollars around the globe at the click of a mouse, heedless of the social and environmental impact of their actions. Whilst market analysts attempt to provide reliable information to inform the mouse clicks, more often than not, a herd mentality dictates that they simply shadow market trends. This ensures that the markets are inherently unstable and are often driven by dynamics that bear no relation to reality, as was demonstrated in the 1997 Asian financial crisis and the dot.com bubble. Instability is greater when investors are operating in relative ignorance and its impact grows in tandem with liberalisation and the volume of capital involved. It therefore stands to reason that the problems associated with capital market liberalisation will be greatest when investors are moving large volumes of capital into and out of unfamiliar and over-liberalised markets. These are precisely the conditions that occur when countries that have been relatively isolated from the international capital markets are forced to hastily liberalise their capital accounts as a condition of financial assistance from the IMF or the World Bank.

Another claimed advantage of capital liberalisation is that it allows investors to administer healthy 'correctives' to governments whose policies do not favour international investment. Clearly, deregulation does grant additional freedoms to investors, but to claim this as an advantage presupposes that investors' interest coincide with those of the people in whose countries they invest. Once their capital accounts have been liberalised, governments, and particularly those in *comparatively disadvantaged* countries, are forced to lure investment into their economy by obeying the market's correctives and removing restraints on profitability. All too often these restraints are the hard-won regulations that protect workers and the environment, or they are the corporation tax revenues that would otherwise support education, health care, pensions and welfare spending. Women tend to be hardest hit by these cuts in health and welfare spending, since they are often expected to compensate for the loss of public services by providing them themselves.

As one economist concludes, 'When capital is mobile it will seek its absolute advantage by migrating to countries where the environmental and social costs of enterprises are lowest and profits are highest. Both in theory and practice, the effect of global capital mobility is to nullify the Ricardian doctrine of comparative advantage. Yet it is on that flimsy foundation that the edifice of unregulated global free trade still stands.'[16] As if to prove the point, the WTO refers to the theory of comparative advantage as 'arguably the single most powerful insight in economics'.[17]

IN WHOSE INTEREST?

The deep flaws in the theory behind economic globalisation have provided no impediment to the spread of the process itself, they have simply guaranteed that it works to the benefit of the rich at the expense of the poor. Over one quarter of global production is currently exported, in comparison to just 7 per cent in 1950. The average tariff on manufactured goods has fallen from 40 per cent in 1947 to roughly 5 per cent now. The value of cross-border mergers and acquisitions nearly quadrupled between 1993 and 1997, when this form of international concentration of ownership accounted for 59 per cent of all foreign direct investment.[18] There is plenty of evidence to show that the beneficiaries of this massive expansion in international trade are the transnational corporations (TNCs) that control it. For example, 51 of the top 100 economies in the world are TNCs.[19] Just 500 TNCs control 70 per cent of international trade and a mere 1 per cent of TNCs control half of the world's foreign direct investment. And whilst the global economy typically grows at 2 to 3 per cent every year, large corporations have an 8–10 per cent growth rate.[20]

It is hardly surprising then that it is the TNCs and their lobbying organisations that are driving the process of economic globalisation by pushing governments to sign up to free trade deals. The International Chamber of Commerce spearheaded the GATT Uruguay Round. The US Business Roundtable of TNCs, together with Canada's equivalent, the Business Council on National Issues, promoted the North American Free Trade Agreement (NAFTA). In the EU, the European Roundtable of Industrialists (ERT) led the adoption of the European Single Market and Single Currency.

Indeed, the ERT has been one of the main political forces in the European Union for over a decade. Founded in 1983, it consists of around 45 highly influential heads of industry from European multinational companies, with a combined turnover approaching £400 billion. Its unprecedented access to decision makers at both European and national levels has given it enormous influence over the EU's political agenda, and ensured that policies are introduced which increasingly favour the agenda of large corporations and promote economic globalisation.

GLOBALISATION'S BRAINWASHED CULT

The TNCs' intense lobbying appears to have had a hypnotic effect on world leaders. It is not too surprising that two former director generals of the WTO came to regard globalisation as no less inevitable than gravity. According to Mike Moore, former director general of the WTO, 'Globalisation is with us. It cannot be uninvented.'[21] Similarly, for his predecessor, Renato Ruggiero, trying to stop globalisation is 'tantamount to trying to stop the rotation of the earth'.[22] However, this 'there is no alternative' cult of the inevitable even seems to have engulfed the leaders of the 'free' world. Speaking to the World Trade Organization on 18 May 1998, then US President Bill Clinton stated that globalisation is 'not a policy choice, it's a fact'. The following day, UK Prime Minister, Tony Blair, provided a close variation on the theme. For him globalisation was 'irreversible and irresistible'.

Of course it suits some to suggest that the status quo cannot be changed, but it's clear that part of the intention of these descriptions of globalisation is to try to stop us from analysing the phenomenon; to suggest that anyone attempting to examine its driving forces and effects is wasting their time. However we agree with one such 'time waster' who wrote: 'To suggest that interrogating the policies and processes, the economic philosophy and the currently dominant paradigm of this system is tantamount to trying to stop or reverse inexorable cosmic laws is a crude political device that should find no acceptance amongst serious analysts.'[23]

Indeed, globalisation is not driven by irrefutable economic laws; it is not governed by inevitable market forces. It is not some natural law of the universe, like gravity and it has not happened by accident. Globalisation has been driven over the past three decades by the world's leading business and government elites. They have agreed and deliberately pushed forward common aims, including economic integration, deregulation, and an economic philosophy based on free trade and international competitiveness.

The shameful fact is that governments have so little control over economic globalisation precisely because they have systematically abrogated their powers, handing them over to unaccountable bodies like the WTO. And when people complain about the effects of globalisation, conventional free-trade politicians who respond by wringing their hands and saying 'so sorry, it's not our fault, there's nothing we can do' are frankly not telling the truth. These politicians have already made a deliberate choice to adopt the rules and logic of free trade. Just as those decisions have been made in the past, so different decisions can be made for the future, and new trade and investment rules can be adopted to reinforce those new choices.

Significantly, the *Economist* magazine recognised this in its editorial of 21 September 2000: 'The protestors are right that the tide of 'globalisation', powerful as the engine driving it may be, can be turned back ... International economic integration is not an ineluctable process, as many of its most enthusiastic advocates appear to believe. It is one ... of many possible futures for the world economy; others may be chosen, and are even coming to seem more likely.'

In the remainder of this section we present the evidence to show that economic globalisation is the wrong future for the world economy. But first, we will set out the principles of Green economics, which we believe must be the foundation for any economic future if it is genuinely to be both equitable and sustainable.

GREEN FUTURES

If, in a latter-day version of the challenge once issued to Rabbi Hillel,[24] the essence of Green politics had to be explained whilst standing on one leg, the reply would be 'equity, ecology, democracy'. This response readily translates into three guiding principles of Green economics. First, the economic system must respect the dynamics and limits of the earth's natural systems on which it depends (see Box 1.1). Second, economic policy must pursue equity and social justice as an overriding aim. Third, the economy must be democratically regulated to ensure that production is driven by need rather than by profit, and that the methods of production are consistent with the first two principles. This should be achieved both through formal channels of democratic accountability and by maximising the contact between producers and consumers.

BOX 1.1 Greens and growth

Green politics can trace part of its origins to the Club of Rome's 'Limits to Growth' hypothesis, first mooted in 1974.[25] This stated that it is dangerously self-defeating to pursue perpetual economic growth within the earth's closed ▶

---

systems because such growth will consume all available non-renewable resources or, if that could be postponed through increased efficiency, produce so much pollution and waste as to render all further production impossible. The time-scales suggested in *The Limits to Growth* report were unduly pessimistic, but its basic point that limits to growth do exist remains a crucial insight.

Herman Daly, a former employee of the World Bank, was one of the first Green economists to develop an economic model based on this insight. He called for 'steady-state' economies, which pursue the betterment, or development, of human society without increasing the throughput of resources.[26] More recently, the term 'sustainable development' was coined in an attempt to express the same idea, although its impact has since been diluted through over-use.

Critics of these approaches argue that conventional economic growth is necessary to solve environmental problems. According to their arguments, which are summarised by the environmental Kuznets curve (EKC) shown in Figure 1.1, environmental degradation increases as a country starts to get richer, but is reversed as the country becomes rich enough to clean up its act. This implies that there is little point worrying about environmental degradation in developing countries, as it will be reversed later on.

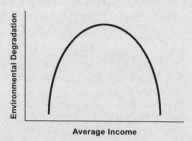

Figure 1.1 An environmental Kuznets curve, showing a supposed relationship within any one country between environmental degradation and average income

The main problem with EKC theory is that it is flatly contradicted by the empirical evidence. Deforestation and sulphur dioxide emissions had been touted as the best examples of environmental degradation that is reliably reversed as development proceeds.[27] However, the relationship between a country's level of income and deforestation varies from one continent to another,[28] and emissions of sulphur dioxide have been shown to decrease steadily over time, regardless of income.[29] Crucially, other forms of environmental degradation such as the production of solid wastes and atmospheric carbon emissions have increased continuously as income grows.[30]

Another problem with EKC theory is that it assumes that the environmental problems created at early stages of development can be reversed later on. Clearly, this is not always possible, for example, when natural resources are depleted at an unsustainable rate, or when persistent, toxic, chemicals are dispersed into the environment.

Greens therefore reject the head-in-the-sand 'growth is good for the environment' theory and insist instead that environmental and economic policies should be integrated at every stage of development.

One of the best ways to encourage the integration of economic and environmental policies is to reject economic indicators that ignore the environment and other factors conventional economics struggles to recognise. Economists normally assess a country's performance by looking at the annual change in its gross domestic product (GDP). However, GDP, like the closely related gross national product (GNP), is merely a gross tally of the financial value of all products and services bought and sold, with no account taken of hidden costs or distinction made between transactions that add to or diminish well-being. Or, as US Senator Robert Kennedy put it:

> The Gross National Product includes air pollution and advertising for cigarettes, and ambulances to clear our highways of carnage. It counts special locks for our doors, and jails for the people who break them. GNP includes the destruction of the redwoods and the death of Lake Superior. It grows with the production of napalm and missiles and nuclear warheads ... and if GNP includes all this, there is much that it does not comprehend. It does not allow for the health of our families, the quality of their education, or the joy of their play. It is indifferent to the decency of our factories and the safety of our streets alike.'[31]

Even the creator of GDP, Simon Kuznets, accepted the limitations of the indicator when he said, 'The welfare of a nation can scarcely be inferred from a measurement of national income.'[32]

Other indicators have been devised that take the broader welfare of a society into account. The Index of Sustainable Economic Welfare (ISEW) attempts to measures the true state of people's well-being by correcting GDP over a range of issues, such as income inequality, environmental damage, and the depletion of environmental assets.[33] The Genuine Progress Indicator (GPI) does a similar job.[34] The UN Development Programme (UNDP)'s Human Development Index (HDI) combines per capita GDP with life expectancy at birth, adult literacy and educational enrolment.[35]

We use these indicators in this book whenever we can, and the 'development' we advocate is an increase in the activities that cause growth of ISEW, GPI or HDI, but not necessarily of GDP.

The contrast between Green economics and capitalism, the driving force of economic globalisation, could not be more stark. Capitalism is a system that seeks unprecedented privileges for capital and disproportionate rewards for its owners. It directly violates all the basic principles of Green economics. First, capitalism has only one means of generating sufficient profit to fund the returns that the owners of capital demand: economic growth. And as the owners of capital are rewarded, so their investments expand and their demands increase. Under capitalism, growth must therefore be perpetual, despite the finite limits of the planet. Second, as a direct consequence of capitalism, wealth accumulates in the hands of the owners of capital and is denied to others. Wage demands must be contained if profits are to be protected and the poor majority is to be kept pliant to the demands made of it by the capitalist system. Capitalism thus both creates and thrives on inequality. Finally, under capitalism, the opportunity for profit is created by distancing producers from consumers. The biggest rewards are generated for those who manage to extract value by meeting demands that individuals cannot meet for themselves or have met for them free of charge by friends or family. When distances between consumers and producers are not very large, profits will tend to be reasonable. If the butcher sells meat to the baker he will bear in mind, when calculating his mark-up, that he will need to visit the bakery in the morning to buy his bread. Should the candlestick maker be discovered to be oppressing her apprentice, word is likely to spread round the town and her trade will suffer. As distances increase so does the potential for unreasonable and ill-gotten profit and in an increasingly globalised economy, it is the TNCs that are most able to exploit the growing distances.[36]

Clearly, the Green future for the world's economy would directly confront these failings and, defined in these terms, is firmly 'anti-capitalist'. However, labels are to some extent unhelpful, and some Greens might feel uncomfortable hanging one that says 'anti-capitalist' around their neck. We do not share this particular nervousness, but we do recognise that identity is an important part of radical politics, and if the label 'anti-capitalist' carries too much intellectual baggage for some, we can avoid it. It is far more important to identify the central demands of Green economics than to insist on unanimity over a label for what it is not.

Nestling amongst the intellectual baggage is a confusion over the relationship between capitalism, states and markets. If we do label Green economics 'anti-capitalist', does that imply the creation of a command economy, with no role for markets or private ownership? The short answer is 'no'. The longer answer is that Green economics clearly seeks to deny capital those freedoms and privileges it currently enjoys at the expense of local communities and the environment. It also seeks to prevent the expansion of those privileges, as currently proposed at the WTO and elsewhere. In order to achieve the principal aims of Green economics, governments need to adopt a more assertive regulatory and fiscal role than they do at present, for example, by using environmental taxation to internalise costs that are currently 'hidden' from the market.[37] The need to bring producers and consumers together would increase the proportion of public and cooperative forms of ownership. Within this framework however, markets would serve to distribute goods and services.

David Korten unpacks and makes sense of some of the baggage with his insightful distinction between capitalism and market economies.[38] As described by Adam Smith, market economies are place-based and consist of small, locally owned enterprises that are geared to meet the needs of the community and function within an ethical framework that enjoys its support. Capitalism, on the other hand, is an economic system under which a few reap the benefits of the productive assets, despite the fact that their productivity depends on the labour of the many. For Korten, the 'relationship of capitalism to a market economy is that of a cancer to a healthy body. Much as the cancer kills its host – and itself – by expropriating and consuming the host's energy, the institutions of capitalism are expropriating and consuming the living energies of people, communities and the planet. And like a cancer, the institutions of capitalism lack the foresight to anticipate and avoid the inevitable deathly outcome.'[39]

Smith's place-based and ethically supported markets have a place in the world's Green economic future. The cancer of capitalism, as Korten describes it, does not.

2
Democracy for Sale

> Governments should interfere in the conduct of trade as little as possible.
> Peter Sutherland, former Director General of GATT.[1]

Writing in 1998, Larry Elliott and Dan Atkinson likened the end of the twentieth century to its beginning:

> Just as the profound political and economic changes of the pre-1914 age challenged all the certainties of the mid-Victorian world, leading to revolutions in art, design, music and literature, so the twentieth century is ending with a search to find out where the modern phase of globalisation is supposed to be leading us all: a world in which the question of production is solved once and for all, and all nations share in universal peace and prosperity? Or a soulless, standardized materialism in which the greed of the favoured few and a system skewed in favour of the rich and powerful drive the planet to the brink of extinction?[2]

If Elliott and Atkinson distil the question, the IMF pretends to know the answer:

> Globalisation leads to economic growth and higher incomes. No country has benefited for any length of time from closed-door policies, and the countries that have achieved most prosperity have embraced globalization, together with the policies that make it work. Outward-oriented policies brought dynamism and prosperity to much of East and Southeast Asia. This experience shows that globalization offers extensive opportunities for truly worldwide development.[3]

The protesters who brought the WTO to a standstill in Seattle in 1999, and have dogged its every movement ever since, point to a different answer. Their chorus of protest, at first sight baffling and splendid in its diversity, might well have been inspired by several tens of thousands of activists happening across the following definition in the dictionary of the International Society for Ecology and Culture (ISEC):

> Globalisation
> Noun 1: the process by which governments give away the rights of their citizens in favour of speculative investors and transnational corporations.
> 2. The erosion of wages, social welfare standards and environmental regulations for the sake of international trade.
> 3. The imposition worldwide of a consumer monoculture. Widely but falsely believed to be irrevocable. See also financial melt-down, casino economy, Third World debt, and race to the bottom.[4]

That we agree more with the protesters than with the IMF will surprise no one, but in this chapter and the two that follow we present the evidence that backs our judgement.

WHO'S IN CHARGE?

The first charge against globalisation in the ISEC's definition is that it is a 'process by which governments give away the rights of their citizens in favour of speculative investors and transational corporations'. By exploiting differences in social and environmental standards between countries in order to maximise profits, TNCs are creating global production systems over which governments have ever less control. Power is shifting away from governments and politicians and being invested instead in transnational corporations and institutions. We now live in a world where corporations are taking over from the state, where business appears more powerful than politics, and where commercial interests are paramount.

There is plenty of evidence to back up these assertions. Multinationals are now as big as many nation states – 300 TNCs now account for 25 per cent of the world's assets. Individual companies now have more wealth than whole countries. Mitsubishi is the 22nd largest economy in the world, General Motors the 26th, Ford the 31st. Each is larger than the economies of Denmark, Thailand, Turkey, South Africa, Saudi Arabia, Norway, Finland, Malaysia, Chile and New Zealand, to name but a few. Corporate sales account for two-thirds of world trade and one-third of world output, while as much as 40 per cent of world trade now occurs within multinational corporations.[5]

THE RACE TO THE BOTTOM OF INTERNATIONAL COMPETITIVENESS

Their economic dominance gives TNCs huge amounts of power. Their unprecedented strength and mobility means that they are increasingly able to play one state off against another in the search for ever lower standards and cheaper locations to base business. Governments are becoming trapped in a regulatory 'race to the bottom' to achieve international competitiveness. Under economic globalisation, democratic efforts to ensure corporations pay their fair share of taxes, provide their employees with a decent standard of living, or meet environmental targets are met with the response that such measures could undermine their international competitiveness – followed closely by a threat to relocate to countries with less stringent controls.

The implication is, as Hans Tietmeyer, former president of the German Bundesbank, has said, that, 'Politicians have to understand that they are now under the control of the financial markets and not, any longer, of national debates.'[6] The sorry tale of Oskar Lafontaine, the former finance minister of Germany, is a case in point. Revenue from corporate taxes in Germany has fallen by 50 per cent over the past twenty years despite a rise in corporate profits of 90 per cent. In 1999, Oskar Lafontaine dared to attempt to raise the tax burden on German firms. He was simply blocked by a group of companies all of which threatened to relocate investment or factories to other countries if government policy did not suit them. Their threat was successful – and it was Lafontaine who was relocated, out of the government.

Poll after poll shows that people want more money to be spent on improving basic social needs such as health, education and pensions. One recent poll in the UK found that 62 per cent of voters said they would support plans to fund public services by rises in taxation.[7] The priority of the corporate rulers is the opposite: to minimise taxation. Between 87 per cent and 92 per cent of people think that the government should protect the environment, employment conditions and health – even when it conflicts with the interests of multinationals.[8] If international competitiveness is the be-all-and-end-all of government policies, then it will be curbs on public expenditure and the lowering of environmental and labour standards that are the future, not the democratic wishes of the majority.

CORPORATE RULE

We are witnessing a 'slow motion coup d'etat',[9] a process of political osmosis by which power is seeping out of increasingly flaccid national governments to swell the already turgid TNCs and international trade and finance institutions. Any resistance to the coup from conventional politicians ceased long ago. They have become its willing accomplices and the distinction between government and big business is becoming increasingly blurred.

Political parties and governments appear to be available for hire. In July 2003, more than 500 centre-left leaders and thinkers including Gerhard Schröder, Tony Blair and Bill Clinton attended a 'progressive governance' conference. The event was paid for by British Airways, Citigroup, PwC, KPMG and 'that great supporter of progressive causes, the sultan of Brunei'.[10] In his ground-breaking book on the corporate takeover of Britain, *Captive State*, George Monbiot notes the irony of the 1999 Labour Party Conference where the meeting on holding government and companies to account was sponsored by the lottery company Camelot. The meeting on renewing democracy and rebuilding communities was financed by Tesco, whose out-of-town superstores are widely blamed for shattering the economic heart of local communities. When Lord Whitty, an environmental minister, was asked by the BBC whether the exhibitors at the conference were buying access to ministers, he replied 'You don't buy access to ministers. You buy access to the whole party.' We assume he was trying to reassure us.[11]

Several recent corporate donations to the governing parties in the UK and US have directly benefited the donors. In 1997, Bernie Ecclestone, the head of Formula One racing, gave a £1m donation to the British Labour Party. Less than a year later the Labour Party, now in government, used its anti-smoking health minister, Tessa Jowell, to argue that Formula One should be exempt from a tobacco advertising ban. There was an echo of the furore that surrounded the Ecclestone case in 2002 when PowderJect won a £32m government contract to supply smallpox vaccines without going through the usual tendering process. Its chief executive, Paul Drayson, had previously donated £50,000 to the Labour Party. In perhaps the most infamous case to date, the US government lodged a complaint at the WTO against the EU's preferential tariffs for Caribbean bananas just a few days after Clinton's ruling Democratic Party received a $500,000 donation from Chiquita, a US-based banana-producing TNC.

The enmeshing of government and corporate interests extends beyond the level of political 'donations'. In Britain, numerous senior business executives have been appointed to advisory and regulatory bodies, some to ministerial positions in the House of Lords. Very often these captains of industry have passed through the 'revolving door' to find themselves responsible for regulating areas that directly affect the industry they have just left. Monbiot catalogues more than forty of these appointments. One highly representative example is Lord Simon of Highbury, the former chairman of BP and vice-president of the ERT who became a minister responsible for 'competitiveness in Europe', including some aspects of European energy policy.

If these were simply unconnected appointments or just particular instances of individual companies buying favours, the situation would not be so serious, but they are symptomatic of a much wider democratic malaise. The corporate world is able to achieve so much influence over governments because of the constraints of globalisation, yet the trade and investment agreements that now give corporations such a hold over governments were promoted by the corporate lobby in the first place. And each time power has been ceded to the TNCs they have used it to extract further concessions.

PROTECTING PROFIT

Corporate interests share a common, perverse outlook that makes the globe first, and foremost, a common market and source of capital. From this corporate perspective, democracy and laws that support the environment, citizens' health and safety, the sustainable use of land and resources and so on, are protectionist barriers to trade that must be countermanded by the rules of global free trade. From any other perspective, they are valued safeguards on unfettered economic activity.

Thus, according to the official rhetoric, the multilateral rules governing global free trade are all that stands between us and a return to destructive protectionism. Yet, the corporate interests driving trade and investment liberalisation have ensured that the rules serve a protectionism of a different kind, one that protects corporate profits from any attempts by citizens and governments to preserve those things of value that are threatened by free trade. For example, WTO 'like product' rules render it illegal to discriminate between imports of similar products on the basis of the way in which they were produced. They therefore prohibit discrimination between GMOs and non-GMOs, or between imports of clothes made with child labour and those made in decent conditions, or between meat and dairy products made through the appalling mistreatment of animals and those made with high animal welfare standards. Governments are now unable to exercise their responsibility to protect their citizens from products that damage the global environment, or from foods made with appalling animal welfare standards. By giving up the right to condition investment in a country on certain societal standards, or to make the entry of products into domestic markets dependent on compliance with national rules, governments have deliberately eroded the leverage they once held over corporate behaviour on behalf of the people.

NAFTA SETS THE SCENE[12]

The North American Free Trade Agreement (NAFTA) is the testing ground for some of the most audacious instances of the corporate colonisation of the democratic domain. As one commentator put it, 'NAFTA is where US industry uses Canada and Mexico for target practice to test trade weapons they will take international through the WTO.'[13]

NAFTA's investment chapter (Chapter 11) gives unprecedented protection to corporate investors against government regulation under the guise of the 'national treatment' principle. This gives foreign investors the right to equivalent treatment to domestic producers, in theory, as a defence against the state seizure of private property during nationalisation, as happened in 1938 when Mexico nationalised its foreign oil refineries. In practice however, most 'investor-to-state' cases have had little to do with the seizure of property. Instead, corporations from all three NAFTA countries, Canada, the US and Mexico, have used Chapter 11 to challenge a wide range of national, state and local policies on the environment and public health (some examples are covered in the next chapter of this book) that they believe threaten their profitability. Foreign investors have also attempted to overturn federal procurement laws and domestic judicial decisions using NAFTA.

Cases brought against governments under NAFTA go through the investor-to-state dispute resolution mechanism, and are heard in secret by a three-member tribunal. If a corporation wins its case, it can be awarded unlimited cash compensation from public funds for a loss of profits even though it has effectively evaded the domestic laws and court system.

In a direct assault on the democratic rights of the Canadian people, the American parcel delivery company UPS is claiming $160m in damages against the Canadian government's provision of a publicly owned mail delivery service. UPS argues that public funding for Canada Post constitutes an unfair subsidy to a domestic service provider at the expense of foreign competitors. In another case, Loewen, a large Canadian group of funeral companies, lost a lawsuit filed against them by the O'Keefe family of Mississippi after negotiations for the purchase of the family's funeral business turned sour. Loewen lost the case and damages of $500m were awarded against them. The Supreme Court of Mississippi refused to waive the requirement that Loewen deposit a bond to the value of 125 per cent of the damages to preserve their right of appeal and Loewen then reached an out-of-court settlement with the O'Keefes for $175m. Loewen has attempted to re-run the case by launching a NAFTA complaint against the US on the grounds, amongst other things, that the judge had failed to provide due protection to foreign investors because anti-Canadian testimony had been heard in the court case. According to the court transcript, the founder of the Canadian funeral chain, Ray Loewen, was characterised as a foreigner, a 'gouger of grieving families', an owner of a large yacht, a racist, a customer of foreign banks, and greedy besides. Loewen are claiming $725m from the US government.

In a preliminary decision, NAFTA accepted jurisdiction for the case, arguing that the Mississippi trial court's award of damages against Loewen and the State Supreme Court's requirement that Loewen post a $625m bond fell within the definition of 'measures' that should not be unfairly applied to foreign investors under NAFTA Article 201. The tribunal also ruled that the US government was ultimately responsible for the rulings of a judge and jury in Mississippi.[14]

Regardless of the eventual outcome in this case, the preliminary decision in *Loewen's case against the US* sets a dangerous precedent. It appears to install NAFTA as the ultimate judicial authority in signatory countries, with powers to reverse the effect of court decisions and punish governments for the actions of juries and the judiciary. Even though NAFTA is not formally empowered to set aside laws, decisions of this type are bound to tempt governments into pressuring the judiciary to respond to commercial imperatives when they are in conflict with the law. Moreover, the level of damages awarded in

NAFTA decisions has already provoked warnings from states and municipalities that their ability to govern is being compromised.[15]

NAFTA's Chapter 11 was the inspiration for the Organisation for Economic Cooperation and Development's (OECD) Multilateral Agreement on Investment (MAI), which was derailed in 1998 by an unprecedented wave of semi-coordinated cyber-protest from NGOs and individuals. Many of NAFTA's key features, such as national treatment for foreign investors, have been recycled into the General Agreement on Trade in Services (GATS – see Box 2.1). And, if the Bush administration gets its way, the NAFTA model of democracy and investor rights will be exported to another 33 countries in the Americas and Caribbean under the Free Trade Area of the Americas agreement by the end of 2005.

BOX 2.1 GATS

GATS is the latest WTO trade agreement. It bears all the hallmarks of its predecessors, yet is far wider in scope. It aims to open 160 service sectors to foreign investment by 2005.[16]

How does GATS work?

GATS includes 'basic obligations' and 'specific commitments'. The basic obligations will automatically cover all service sectors. Specific commitments will apply only to those sectors that governments decide to 'commit' to these rules during the negotiations. Most WTO members have only committed a small number of their services, particularly tourism, hotels and restaurants, computer-related services and value-added communications. In large part due to public pressure, they have been more reluctant to offer services with a high level of public sector provision. For example, the European Commission (EC) specifically excluded health, social services and education from its initial list of offers.

By contrast, the EC has made wide-ranging demands of developing countries, asking them to commit many sectors including postal services, environmental services and telecommunications. As Oxfam's Kevin Watkins put it, developing countries 'have been presented with a list of demands that will make even hardened privatisers in the World Bank wince'.[17]

The main rules of GATS

Most Favoured Nation Rule – This is a basic obligation, binding on all sectors, that says that the best treatment given to any foreign provider must be given to all like providers. For example, if a single foreign provider of higher education gains degree-granting authority, then all foreign providers of higher education must have the same opportunities to seek degree-granting authority.

▶

In practice, this will make it far more difficult to reverse commercialisation, as governments would face opposition from many providers, not just one.

National Treatment – This is a specific commitment that dictates that foreign providers must be treated identically to national ones. It would prevent research or development subsidies to local companies, or assistance to local business run by directors from a local community.

WTO disputes panels have interpreted these two rules very strictly in the past and any policies that have *unintended* effects on trade will be vulnerable to future rulings under GATS. For example, government subsidies to non-profit childcare providers could be judged to discriminate against foreign firms in situations where most for-profit providers are foreign and most non-profit providers are local.

Market Access – This specific commitment prevents countries imposing limits on the number of service providers. Countries can only specify particular conditions by listing them as country-specific exceptions when a sector is committed. Exceptions can only be changed after three years and by compensating any affected service providers. This will make it difficult to address any new problems that arise, for example, unexpected environmental impacts or a scarcity of resources. India's former ambassador to GATT stated that 'the developing countries have lost the flexibility of modifying their policy in the light of future experience ... even if it is assumed that they benefit by importing services.'[18]

Domestic Regulations – The basic thrust of this specific commitment is that any national, regional or local regulation of the quality of services will have to be vetted to ensure it does not have *unnecessary* impact on international trade nor 'constitutes unnecessary barriers to trade in services', an issue the WTO will resolve should disputes arise.

No escape?

According to the GATS text, not even essential public services like education and health are exempt. They are seen as lucrative commodities, to be traded on the international market for the benefit of private companies and shareholders, rather than the public interest. Although GATS officially excludes 'public services', its definition of them in Article I.3 is extremely narrow. It applies only to sectors that are provided neither on a commercial nor competitive basis. Thus, a largely publicly run sector could be exempt from this exclusion if it already contains a private element. Private finance initiatives (PFIs) and private schools, for example, could in principle bring large parts of the UK's National Health Service and education sectors under GATS. In many advanced market economies, liberalisation of the public sector is already advanced and private providers will exert continuing behind-the-scenes pressure on governments to commit any uncommitted sectors. Unless anti-GATS campaigners can

▶

keep up their momentum, GATS is likely to have a 'lock-in' effect, making any reversal of liberalisation, and the privatisation to which it often leads, effectively impossible.

GATS, democracy and development

Local authorities and governments will be restrained from regulating for fear of legal challenge under GATS. A UK local authorities' report voices fears that 'the current negotiations at the WTO may have far-reaching consequences for local authorities in terms of their powers and freedoms, particularly in respect of procurement, regulatory activities and land-use planning.'[19]

As several developing countries have pointed out,[20] GATS will have a particularly catastrophic effect on the South. As in all WTO processes, developing countries lack bargaining power and are under intense pressures to liberalise. The GATS negotiations do not recognise that developing countries often have far less institutional capacity than the North to implement effective regulation, and are in a relatively weak bargaining position with foreign TNCs.

Developed and developing countries also have a huge difference in export capacity. Western TNCs already dominate many service sectors. The EU alone has 26 per cent of world trade in services, and the US vastly dominates the export market. The overwhelming benefits of service sector liberalisation will go to the existing strong services industries in developed countries, leaving developing countries unable to compete.

Service sector liberalisation will almost inevitably lead to privatisation in developing countries as their public services and domestic companies will be ill equipped to compete with incoming TNCs. Privatisation, particularly in developing countries, has failed to deliver to the poorest and most needy, whilst channelling benefits to the richest sections of society. Cross-subsidisation, which keeps public sector prices for basic services artificially low for certain categories of user, will be impossible under privatisation. The charity Save the Children has called for a 'health check' on GATS, arguing that trade liberalisation has had 'devastating effects on children's nutrition and basic health ... Instead of adding extra capacity, the increased involvement of the private sector threatens to undermine public services by drawing away key personnel and "cream skimming" the most profitable consumers.'[21] In June 2002, a decision to privatise two Peruvian state electricity companies to Belgian company Tractebel sparked violent demonstrations and Colombian trade unions have protested against water privatisation following price rises and huge increases in unemployment and poverty in other privatised sectors.

GATS will have a disproportionate effect on women, who make up roughly 80 per cent of the work force in the service sector. Women are over-represented in low-skilled jobs and suffer poor conditions of employment. For example, women in the EU are often paid between 15 and 33 per cent less than men for doing the same job. Private involvement in the public sector, as seen in the UK's PFIs, has already been shown to push down wages, reduce job security and lead to job losses, particularly for the lowest paid, many of whom are

▶

women. Experience also shows that public sector conditions of employment are not protected for new employees when jobs are transferred to the private sector. Women are also the main users of health and education services, so will be more affected by any reductions in the quality of service that result from GATS.

The European Commission has admitted that 'GATS is first and foremost an instrument for the benefit of business.'[22] Service industry lobby groups have been particularly influential in drafting the agreement. A former WTO official stated, 'Without the enormous pressure generated by the American financial services sector, particularly companies like American Express and Citicorp, there would have been no services agreement.'[23] The European Services Forum has had regular access to the European Commission's GATS negotiating committee, while the European and national Parliaments and wider civil society have barely been consulted at all. Only a few MEPs, including one of the authors of this book, have had access to documents listing the requests made by the EU to other countries. Before they could see the papers, they had to sign a document committing themselves never to reveal the contents of the documents to anyone, not even their fellow MEPs; to keep the papers in 'a metal box and locked by key', and shred them when they had read them. GATS' cursory references to social, environmental and other vital issues of public interest is hardly surprising when set against this background of farcical secrecy and privileged access for industry.

Lack of assessment

In common with all other WTO agreements, there has been no assessment of the impact of GATS. Former US trade representative Jeffrey Lang admitted that there is 'overwhelming uncertainty about the meaning of the provisions of GATS ... So little is known about their origin and intention that it may be years before we discover the impact of these provisions.' But, he added, 'I do not advocate pausing in the movement forward to accomplish some kind of ecclesiastical exercise of figuring out what these provisions mean. That can only aid and abet those who want to frustrate progress.'[24] Perhaps because we do not share his definition of progress, we take the opposite view. The movement 'forward' must be halted unless and until we know that GATS will not have the effects we fear. Such a pause will indeed not be 'some kind of ecclesiastical exercise'; it is the minimum precaution necessary to protect the basic rights of the overwhelming majority who inhabit the margins of the global economy.

A SHORT TRIP TO CORPORATE CONTROL

The protection of intellectual property rights (IPRs) provides yet another example of the moulding of trade rules to protect corporate profit against the interests of the people. This extraordinarily controversial issue was put on the Uruguay Round agenda by a group of 13 major companies, including General Motors and Monsanto. In the negotiations that followed, 96 out of the 111 members of the US delegation working on intellectual property rights were from the private sector. Many developing nations, by contrast, cannot afford to support permanent representatives at the Geneva-based WTO. Little surprise then that the final agreement, TRIPs (the WTO Agreement on Trade-related Aspects of Intellectual Property) does far more to serve corporate interests than provide the minimum protection for IPRs needed to spur innovation.

The South[25] suffers many problems that could be reduced or solved by the application of patented technology, but it only accounts for 2 per cent of global research and development. Developing countries are therefore overwhelmingly net importers of patented technology and stand to lose out as patent protection is increased.[26] The South also holds a vast reservoir of indigenous knowledge and the bulk of the world's unexplored genetic resources. Governments in the South have traditionally been reluctant to issue patents for living organisms, traditional agricultural methods and remedies, holding them to be commonly owned resources. However, TRIPs has dramatically widened the range of products and processes for which WTO member governments must offer patents to include agricultural chemicals, pharmaceuticals, micro-organisms, traditional remedies, plant varieties and seeds, including those that have resulted from generations of crossbreeding. The agreement also introduced protection for individual patents that is far stronger than that offered by the existing legislation in most countries. Under TRIPs, patents give monopolistic rights for 20 years, compared, for example, with 17 years under previous US legislation. Consequently, TRIPs has opened large sections of the natural world and indigenous cultures to privatisation and commercial exploitation, and has increased the incentives to TNCs to engage in such exploitation. The depressingly predictable results are that poor people are being denied the benefit of commonly owned indigenous resources and their access to patented goods and knowledge is being undermined.

One shocking example concerns the treatment of HIV/AIDS. Ninety per cent of the estimated 40 million people living with HIV and AIDS live in the developing world. By increasing the protection for the patents of pharmaceutical products, TRIPs makes it much harder for people in the South to gain access to cheap anti-AIDs drugs. TRIPs outlaws practices such as licensing the manufacture of cheaper generic versions of patented drugs, as Brazil has done, importing patented products from countries where they are sold more cheaply (parallel importing), or forcing patent holders to license production by local manufacturers in return for royalties. Governments can sidestep these rules by declaring a national emergency, but they run the risk of being challenged by the affected patent holders, who have to be compensated if their complaint is upheld at the WTO.

In 1997, Nelson Mandela's South African government passed the Medicines and Related Substance Control Amendment Act, which aimed to make medicines more affordable, mainly by allowing parallel importing of patented drugs and lower-cost generic products to be substituted for brand-name drugs. A group of 39 pharmaceutical companies, backed by the US, challenged the law in February 1998 and the South African government felt forced to delay its implementation until the case was resolved. Global public opinion finally forced the companies to abandon their action in April 2001. In the intervening three years, 400,000 South Africans died of AIDS.

Even Dr Supachai Panitchpakdi, the director general of the WTO, has cited TRIPs as 'one of the glaring examples of the pressure coming from the corporate sector on governments that ultimately resulted in some agreements being forced on countries that we have to try to prevent'.[27] He has however since backed away from his pledge, made in the same speech, to introduce a code of conduct to limit corporate influence on future trade negotiations.

THE DECLINE AND FALL OF DEMOCRATIC GOVERNANCE

Governments have systematically ceded far greater powers to the WTO and the other multilateral trade organisations than have ever before been granted to an international body. The WTO's powers now extend into a large number of areas where domestic legislation used to be the rule, raising new threats to national governance and to parliaments' freedom to legislate. Its powers extend beyond trade issues to cover investment policy, patent law and, thanks to GATS, who provides some of our essential services. The non-tariff 'barriers' to trade, which are increasingly the focus of the WTO's attention, are often part and parcel of the body of domestic laws and regulations that different nations have democratically adopted. As the scope of the WTO's agreements expands and increasingly impinges on domestic policies and transboundary issues such as environmental protection, the WTO is evolving from a technical negotiation forum, driven by trade ministries, towards a more politically charged organisation concerned with overall governance of global economic policy. Moreover, the WTO operates without effective democratic scrutiny. It has legislative powers, in that it can pass its own laws; executive powers, in that it can implement them, and judicial powers, in that it can penalise those countries that violate them. It threatens to supplant democratic governance.

STRUCTURED INTO SUBMISSION

Not everyone agrees with us. The IMF's considered view is that 'globalization does not reduce national sovereignty. It does create a strong incentive for governments to pursue sound economic policies.'[28] The IMF plays a big part in offering developing countries 'incentives' to pursue what it would see as 'sound economic policies'. As the guarantor of last resort of international finance, controlled by its major shareholders (the G7 and the rest of the EU control 57 per cent of the voting power at the IMF), it is called in to assess the creditworthiness of its 'client' countries. Invariably, the rescheduling of existing loans or any new lending has been conditional on the client country adopting a Structural Adjustment Programme (SAP), which forces it to liberalise trade and investment, devalue its currency, privatise state-owned enterprise, liberalise its labour markets, gear its economy to the export market and cut public spending to eliminate budget deficits. In short, the IMF's loan 'conditionalities' means a client must globalise or be starved of any further international help.

So far, more that one hundred countries with a combined population of four billion people have been 'structurally adjusted'. The results have been disastrous. SAPs have impoverished millions of people around the world. In one study, Professor Michel Chossudovsky, one of the foremost experts on the IMF, presents examples from different regions of the world of the effects of IMF and World Bank reforms. He details how these reforms have caused or worsened a wide range of social and economic disasters, including famine in Somalia, economic genocide in Rwanda, the postwar economic destruction of Vietnam, economic crises in Brazil and Peru, the drug economy in Bolivia, the 'thirdworldization' of the Russian Federation, and the violent disintegration of the former Yugoslavia.[29] Another authoritative critic of the IMF is Joseph Stiglitz, Nobel Prize-winning economist and former chief economist at the World Bank. In his view, the IMF's 'excessively rapid financial and capital market liberalisation was probably the single most important cause of the crisis' that hit East Asia in 1997–98.[30]

The IMF offers a distinctive variety of unreduced national sovereignty to its victims. It's the 'you're free to do anything you like, as long as you do what we tell you' variety – just one short step from direct colonial rule. The so-called democracies of the developed world fare little better. Their submission to corporate will is not forced on them by the IMF, it is adopted 'voluntarily' at the behest of the corporate interests who stand to benefit. In some parts of the world, economic globalisation causes the stillbirth of democracy, elsewhere the patient is stronger and must be smothered step by step. Whatever the method, the outcome is much the same.

HANDS UP FOR DEMOCRACY

If the turnout in British and US elections is anything to go by, the electorate clearly recognises that power is shifting away from elected governments. Many factors determine the turnout in any one election. The spectacular fall in voter turnout between the 1997 and 2001 general elections in the UK for example had a lot to do with the predictability of the result. Nevertheless, as Figure 2.1 shows, the

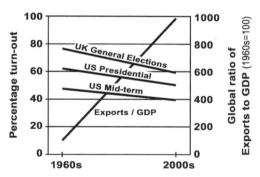

Figure 2.1 International trade and the percentage of US and UK voters participating in elections in an era of globalisation

Sources: UK elections: Butler, D. and Kavanagh, D. (2002), *The British General Election of 2001*, Basingstoke: Palgrave. US elections: Center for Voting and Democracy (2002), *Early 9/11 Political Returns In: Primary Turnout Trending Towards Record Low*, Washington, DC: CVD. Export Data: WTO (2001), *International Trade Statistics 2001*, Washington, DC: WTO. Table II.1 <http://www.wto.org/english/res_e/statis_e/its2001_e/section2/ii01.xls>.

Note: Voter turnout data is the average for all relevant elections within the given decade (for the 2000s the UK general election of 2001 and the US presidential election of 2000 are used). The ratio of the value of global exports to global GDP is derived from annual indexed data (1990=100 in both cases) and scaled such that the average ratio for the 1960s is 100. For the raw data see columns C and R of Table II.1 of WTO, International Trade Statistics, 2001.

period of rapid globalisation during the last part of the twentieth century has coincided with a marked fall in voter participation in the US and UK.

The corporate dominance of political life that comes with economic globalisation poses a grave threat to democracy, possibly the greatest threat it has faced since the Second World War.

3
A World in Decline

> To attract companies like yours ... we have felled mountains, razed jungles, filled swamps, moved rivers, relocated towns ... all to make it easier for you and your business to do business here.
> Advert placed by the Government of the Philippines.[1]

The global environment has deteriorated rapidly during the last few decades of accelerating globalisation. Almost without exception, environmental indicators have shown a dramatic decline. Despite the Kyoto protocol, atmospheric concentrations of carbon dioxide, the chief greenhouse gas, are growing at an exponential rate. For 400,000 years they fluctuated in a narrow band between 260 and 280 ppmv (parts per million by volume). They now stand at 370 ppmv, 30 per cent higher than previous peak values in interglacial periods.[2] The last systematic survey of rainforest destruction was undertaken in 1990. It revealed that an area the size of England and Wales was being lost every year and it is feared that the rate of destruction has increased since then.[3] Global consumption of fresh water is doubling every twenty years. In 25 years' time, two-thirds of the world's population will suffer from water shortages.[4] Twelve per cent of bird species and about a quarter of all mammal species, 1,130 in total, are threatened with extinction.[5]

Significant policy initiatives have reversed a few damaging environmental trends. For example, the Montreal Protocol on Substances that Deplete the Ozone Layer cut global consumption of ozone depleting substances by 85 per cent between its adoption in 1987 and 2000.[6] Legislative action during the 1990s also reduced the amount of pollution entering rivers in the EU, leading to national reductions in concentrations of phosphorus in river water averaging 30–40 per cent.[7]

These success stories are few and far between, however, and are overshadowed by the unremitting bleakness of the overall picture. In 2002, UNEP published *Global Environment Outlook 3 (GEO 3)*, a major report that charts the 30 years of environmental degradation that has taken place since the first World Environment Conference was held in Stockholm in 1972.[8] A summary of the report's stark conclusions is reproduced in Box 3.

Several attempts have been made to distil this mass of environmental information into a comprehensible single indicator.

Box 3.1 The state of the world: a summary of GEO 3

Recent human impacts on the atmosphere have been enormous, with anthropogenic emissions a prime cause of environmental problems. Emissions of almost all greenhouse gases continue to rise.

Ground-level ozone, smog and fine particulates have emerged as significant health risks, triggering or exacerbating respiratory and cardiac problems, especially in vulnerable people such as children, the elderly and asthmatics, in developed and developing nations alike.

Overexploitation of many of the surface water resources and great aquifers upon which irrigated agriculture and domestic supplies depend has resulted in more and more countries facing water stress or scarcity. About 1200 million people still lack access to clean drinking water and some 2400 million to sanitation services. The consequences include the deaths of 3–5 million people annually from water-related diseases.

The earth's biological diversity is under increasing threat. The extinction rate of species is believed to be accelerating. Habitat destruction and/or modification are the main cause of biodiversity loss but invasive species are the second most important pressure.

There has been a sharp global trend towards increasingly intense exploitation and depletion of wild fish stocks. Numerous fisheries have collapsed and others are threatened with overexploitation.

Land degradation continues to worsen, particularly in developing countries where the poor are forced onto marginal lands with fragile ecosystems and in areas where land is increasingly exploited to meet food and agricultural needs without adequate economic and political support to adopt appropriate agricultural practices.

Many remaining forest ecosystems have been degraded and fragmented. Since 1972, extensive forest monocultures have been established in the developing world but these do not replace the ecological complexity of natural forests.

Crop and livestock production has contributed to the large increase in reactive nitrogen in the global biosphere, contributing to the acidification and eutrophication of ecosystems.

With almost half of the world's population living in less developed countries, urban areas and megacities, infrastructure and municipal services are inadequate to accommodate millions of the urban poor. Urban air pollution and deteriorating water quality are having major health, economic and social impacts.

An increase in the frequency and intensity of natural disasters over the past 30 years has put more people at greater risk, with the greatest burden falling on the poorest communities.

Whilst it is always possible for sceptics to question the methodology and reliability of the data that produces these indicators, they tell a consistently grim tale.

WWF's Living Planet Index (LPI) is one example that attempts to measure the state of global biodiversity. It is derived from scientific estimates of the population sizes of individual wild species, calculated as a percentage of their size in 1970. The mean value of the index is calculated as an average of all the species included in the assessment. The index includes 319 temperate and tropical forest species (mostly birds), 217 species of marine animals and 194 inland water and wetland species. In 2002, the LPI recorded that 35 per cent of the world's biodiversity was lost between 1970 and 2000.[9]

Ecological Footprinting is another method of deriving a single indicator of environmental sustainability. An ecological footprint is the area of land or water that is needed to support human activities, or to absorb the waste and pollution they cause (for example, the area of forest required to absorb the carbon dioxide emitted by the burning of fossil fuels). The footprint of a city, region, nation or even the whole world, can then be compared with the size and productivity of the area it has available (its ecological capacity) to see whether the current level of economic activity is sustainable. A recent study found that human activities demanded 70 per cent of the earth's ecological capacity in 1961, reached 100 per cent in the 1980s, and 120 per cent in 1999 (see Figure 3.1).[10] Humanity's footprint is now bigger than the planet on which it depends. Our 'ecological overshoot' is eroding the natural capital of future generations.

IS GLOBALISATION DESTROYING THE ENVIRONMENT?

Just because two things happen at the same time does not mean one causes the other. So, is it unfair to blame economic globalisation for the rapid destruction of the global environment? The clear answer from UNEP is 'no'. In *GEO 3*, UNEP predicts what the world might look like in 2032 under four different scenarios. Their 'Markets First' scenario is one in which

> ... most of the world adopts the values and expectations prevailing in today's industrialized countries. The wealth of nations and the optimal play of market forces dominate social and political agendas. Trust is placed in further globalization and liberalization to enhance corporate wealth, create new enterprises and livelihoods,

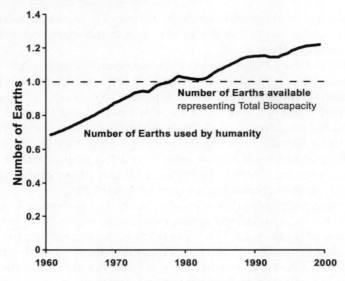

Figure 3.1 Humanity's growing global footprint

Source: Wackernagel, M. et al. (2002), 'Tracking the ecological overshoot of the economy', *Proceedings of the National Academy of Science*, 99, pp. 9266–71.

and so help people and communities to afford to insure against – or pay to fix – social and environmental problems. Ethical investors, together with citizen and consumer groups, try to exercise growing corrective influence but are undermined by economic imperatives. The powers of state officials, planners and lawmakers to regulate society, economy and the environment continue to be overwhelmed by expanding demands.

'Markets First' is the business-as-usual scenario which continues the economic trends we have already examined. Its outcomes also bear an air of familiarity. By 2032, there is continued and rapid growth both of greenhouse gas emissions and the mean global temperature. Over 70 per cent of the earth's land surface is affected by the impacts of roads, mining, cities, airports and other infrastructure. This disrupts the breeding patterns of wildlife and wipes out species, particularly in coastal areas where most human settlement is concentrated. Forests have continued to disappear at an alarming rate and 10 per cent of cultivated land is lost through soil degradation. Meanwhile, more than half the world's people live in severely water-stressed areas, including 95 per cent of people in the Middle East, and 65 per cent in the rest of Asia and the Pacific. Progress in eliminating absolute poverty has been slow under the trickle-down theory that 'Markets First' relies on. Although the percentage of people facing hunger has reduced, growth in the world's population ensures that the actual number remains the same.

UNEP explores alternative scenarios in *GEO 3* ('Policy First' and 'Sustainability First') that make far greater progress by tackling the reduction of poverty and hunger head-on as policy objectives.

UNEP deliberately constructed 'Markets First' to be a continuation of the current policies and power balances that are driving economic globalisation. The fact that it worsens the environmental trends that are already in evidence obviously suggests, at the very least, that globalisation has already helped to set them in train.

WHY GLOBALISATION IS DESTROYING THE ENVIRONMENT

So why is globalisation worsening the environmental crisis? Like all good questions, this one can be answered at several different levels.

Clash of the paradigms

At the most general level, as Martin Khor, the director of Third World Network, has pointed out, globalisation is driven by a set of values that directly contradicts and undermines the 'sustainable development paradigm'.[11] Khor argues that the 1992 UN Conference on the Environment and Development in Rio (UNCED) was an example of international relations based on the sustainable development paradigm. In his words, its approach was

> ... that of consensus-seeking, incorporating the needs of all countries (big or small), partnership in which the strong would help the weak, integration of the environment and development concerns, the intervention of the state and the international community on behalf of public interest to control market forces so as to attain greater social equity and bring about more sustainable patterns of productions and consumption.[12]

By contrast, globalisation's free market liberalism springs from a very different paradigm in which market forces are to be unfettered. Freedoms are to be granted to investors and the right to profit protected. Governments and the international community are not to intervene in the market on behalf of the environment or the poor, as the market will ultimately provide the best solutions to these problems. In this approach, the strong and 'efficient' are the winners. Losers are not to be cushioned or compensated. They must fend for themselves and learn to be more efficient.

We have already seen that, even on their own terms, the economics of globalisation are flawed and if left unchecked lead inevitably to unassailable concentrations of market power. Added to this, the market has found no way of pricing the environment, not even its direct contribution to human well-being, let alone the intrinsic value of its existence. Without 'artificial' interventions in the market, natural capital is priced at no more than the cost of extracting it and the cost of pollution is hidden, unable to exert any economic force. Not all hidden costs can be internalised through environmental taxation and additional regulation will generally be required. But one thing is certain: a genuinely free market will inevitably take environmental goods for granted until they are gone.

Khor characterised the period since Rio as a 'dramatic clash' between the two paradigms, which the sustainable development paradigm is losing heavily, as the failure of the Johannesburg World Summit on Sustainable Development (WSSD) has since testified. Bretton Woods and the WTO are beating the UN hollow. Arguably, the Kyoto protocol is the acme of achievement of the sustainable development paradigm. It embodies a consensus-based solution to the global environmental problem of climate change and employs the 'Common but Differentiated Responsibility' approach that demands more of developed than developing nations. However, it excludes aviation, the fastest growing sector of greenhouse emissions, lacks any enforceable compliance mechanism and could only gain sufficient support by adopting targets that fall pitifully short of the level of action that is required. Even so, the US, which produces 25 per cent of global greenhouse emissions, was able to abandon the protocol for the sake of its international competitiveness without fear of sanction; the protocol will collapse altogether if Russia fails to ratify it. By contrast, the bastions of the free trade paradigm – the IMF, the World Bank and the WTO – are between them able to grant or withhold credit, impose trade sanctions, override domestic legislation and effectively take over the running of a country's economy – small wonder sustainable development is losing out.

There is even mounting concern that free trade's armoury could be mobilised to strike down the trade-related provisions of Multilateral

Environmental Agreements (MEAs) that protect the ozone layer (Montreal protocol), control the dumping of toxic waste overseas (Basle Convention) and ban trade in endangered species (Convention on International Trade in Endangered Species of Wild Fauna and Flora (CITES)).[13] At the very least, the free trade imperative already exerts a 'chilling' effect on the negotiation of new MEAs.

Global chilling

The free market paradigm 'chills' (in trade jargon) or stifles (in English) environmental innovation. It creates a climate that makes governments wary of introducing environmental and social safeguards either because of threats from foreign investors to relocate to other jurisdictions where the obligations are less onerous, or for fear of WTO action against regulations on the grounds that they are non-tariff barriers to trade.

For example, just the threat of WTO action, brandished by an infant formula company, persuaded the Guatemalan government to backtrack on its compliance with the World Health Organization's ruling on breast milk substitutes. Similarly, it was enough for the US and Canada simply to threaten to bring a WTO challenge against EU proposals to ban the import of fur products from animals trapped in cruel leghold traps to make the EU back down, despite the fact that these traps are banned in 60 countries including the EU. Indeed these 'chilling effects' can sometimes be even more powerful than the direct impact of formal dispute resolution. In the US, the Maryland state senate rejected a bill banning contracts with firms doing business in Nigeria after the State Department testified that the legislation would violate international trade rules. Yet campaigners in Maryland, who were promoting the legislation to highlight the persecution of Nigeria's Ogoni people, had based it word for word on anti-apartheid legislation that had been successfully adopted by Maryland in the 1980s.[14] More generally, it is also becoming apparent from more recent environmental treaty negotiations, including the Protocol on Persistent Organic Pollutants (POPs), that concern to ensure compliance with trade rules is proving to be a barrier to the inclusion of trade provisions and bans in MEAs, however justifiable, to stop environmentally damaging activities.[15]

Unpicking progress

The aim of the MEAs is, obviously enough, to protect the global environment. The free trade paradigm not only undermines this aim because the rules of its client organisations limit the effectiveness of the trade-related aspects of the MEAs, but also because it contributes directly to the environmental damage that the MEAs seek to reverse.

Take climate change, for example. Transport produces 20–25 per cent of global emissions of carbon dioxide (CO_2), the leading greenhouse gas. Globalisation is producing a rapid rise in international trade and, therefore, the overall level of freight transport. This trend is already well advanced in the European Union, whose Single Market reforms prefigured much of the current global trade liberalisation agenda. Here, total tonne kilometres roughly doubled between 1970 and 1999, with a near three-fold increase in road freight (see Figure 3.2).[16]

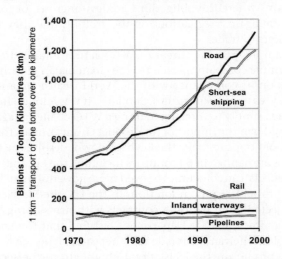

Figure 3.2 Transport of goods in the EU by mode of transport, 1970–99 (aviation not included)

Source: European Commission (2001), *White Paper. European Transport Policy for 2010:Time to Decide*. Brussels: EC <http://europa.eu.int/comm/energy_transport/en/lib_en.html>.

Aviation is the most environmentally damaging form of freight transport, and is growing even more rapidly. For example, UK imports of fish products by plane grew by 240 per cent between 1980 and 1990. Over the same period, airborne imports of fruit and vegetables to the UK grew by 90 per cent. UK air freight (imports and exports) grew by about 7 per cent a year in the 1990s, and it is expected to increase at a rate of 7.5 per cent a year to 2010. By weight, fruit and vegetables account for the largest category of any UK airfreighted imports.[17]

The transportation of kiwi fruit by air from New Zealand to Europe results in 5kg of CO_2 being pumped into the atmosphere for every 1kg of fruit carried. Importing apples from South Africa to Europe, rather than producing locally within a 30km radius of their selling point, results in 600 times more production of nitrogen oxide.[18]

The liberalisation of trade and investment has also led to a rapid increase in the transport associated with industrial production. Corporations are now more likely to locate various phases of production at different sites around the world. Thus when Otis Elevator introduced an advanced elevator system, it contracted out the design of the motor drives to Japan, the door systems to France, the electronics to Germany, and small gear components to Spain. All of these components were then shipped to the US for final assembly, before being exported around the world.[19]

In 1997, the OECD predicted that by 2004, global freight transport would increase by 70 per cent from 1992 levels.[20] If, as likely, this prediction turns out to have been accurate, then this one development alone will have approximately doubled the extent of the cuts in carbon dioxide emissions that are required for the Kyoto protocol targets to be met.

The Convention on Biological Diversity came into force in 1993 following the Rio summit, yet global biodiversity is declining at an alarming rate. This is due in no small part to surging worldwide demand for internationally traded products. For example, consumption of fish has increased by 240 per cent in forty years; 70 per cent of the world's commercially important fisheries are now classified as either fully fished, overexploited, depleted or slowly recovering.[21] Global consumption of timber has increased three-fold in the last thirty years.[22] Together with the unsustainable harvesting of internationally traded cash crops such as soybeans, coffee and bananas, this has led to widespread loss of biologically diverse original-growth forest. Mining and other infrastructure developments such as roads and ports are also major causes of habitat loss. Often these have been supported by international bodies such as the IMF, the World Bank and the European Union as part of their drive to increase the availability and ease of transport of internationally traded goods and commodities.

Trade rules, OK?

The major multilateral trade agreements contain a raft of rules that are designed to remove obstacles to trade. Many of these have been used to overturn environmental regulations. For example, in just the first five years of the WTO's existence there was a systematic rollback of US environmental policy.[23]

The US Clean Air Rule was weakened following a successful challenge at the WTO in 1995 by Venezuela in defence of its oil industry. The WTO decided that the way the US Environmental Protection Agency enforced the rule discriminated against foreign oil refiners.

Former US President Clinton voluntarily stripped the Marine Mammal Protection Act of clauses that had banned the use of the purse seine methods of tuna fishing, which kills millions of dolphins, in order to avoid the embarrassment of an enforceable WTO ruling in support of a previous, but non-enforceable GATT judgment. The basis of the GATT judgment in this case was the 'like product' rule, which held that all tuna are alike, no matter how they are caught. According to GATT, the preservation of dolphins did not merit an exception to this rule because placing a ban on the use of purse seine nets was not the only way to protect dolphins and was not therefore 'necessary'.

A similar WTO 'like product' judgment stands against the US Endangered Species Act that protects sea turtles from shrimp fishing. Until 1989, when the Act required shrimpers to fit relatively inexpensive 'Turtle Excluder Devices' to their nets, 55,000 turtles were killed each year. The Act prevented 97 per cent of these deaths. According to the WTO however, the Act was 'designed' to interfere with trade and deprive the WTO Agreement of its 'object and purpose'. The Panel also ruled that because these regulations were unilaterally imposed on US trading partners, the law deprived the WTO of its object and purpose in establishing a multilateral trade regime, regardless of the non-trade-related objective that was being pursued and despite the fact that the Act did not discriminate between domestic and foreign fisheries.[24]

EU environmental regulations have also fallen foul of the WTO. The most widely reported case is the WTO judgment against the EU's ban on the import of beef produced from cattle treated with growth hormones.[25] The EU had banned the sale of beef from cattle treated with artificial hormones and had applied the ban in a non-discriminatory way to both domestic and imported beef products. In 1990, 90 per cent of US cattle were treated with hormone implants to make them grow larger and faster. In 1989, the EU reacted to concerns that residual traces of the growth hormones in beef and dairy products pose a carcinogenic risk to humans, especially to pre-pubertal children, by invoking the precautionary principle, which is recognised in EU law-making, to support its ban. Spurred on by Monsanto, the manufacturers of some of the leading hormone treatments, biotech and pharmaceutical lobby groups set to work on both sides of the Atlantic to get the ban lifted and, when they failed, the US took the case to the WTO. The EU defended the ban under the SPS (the Agreement on Sanitary and Phytosanitary Standards), which aims to protect human and animal health, and produced a scientific report outlining the health risks. The report acknowledged that 'the available data do not enable a quantitative estimate of the risk'.[26] The WTO rejected the EU's case and effectively overturned the precautionary principle by ruling that the EU's scientific case was unproven. The WTO met the EU's refusal to lift the ban by authorising the US to impose trade sanctions worth $116.4m on a variety of unrelated EU goods.

NAFTA is in many ways a forerunner of the WTO. Indeed it was the experience of a year of NAFTA that finally convinced those US environmentalists who had supported that agreement to oppose Congress's 1994 implementation of the GATT Uruguay Round, which set up the WTO. Their change of heart was prompted partly by the way the unprecedented investor-to-state rights that corporations gained under NAFTA's Chapter 11 have been used to challenge public health and environmental policies. For example, the California-based Metalclad Company was awarded $16.7m against a Mexican municipality after it was denied a permit to operate a toxic waste dump in an area that had been officially declared an 'ecological zone'. In 1997, Canada was forced to repeal its law banning MMT, a petrol additive and suspected neurotoxin. MMT's manufacturer, the US-based Ethyl Corporation, brought the case and was awarded $13m in compensation for lost profits. Canada's Methanex Corporation has filed a similar complaint against the state of California. Methanex makes another fuel additive, MTBE, which is a known animal carcinogen and suspected human carcinogen. It is highly soluble in water, very difficult and costly to clean up, and has already polluted 10,000 Californian groundwater sites.[27] Methanex's case rests partly on the grounds that former California Governor Gray Davis was influenced in issuing an executive order banning MTBE by legal campaign donations from a competing company.

Exceptions that prove the rules

Despite the overwhelming evidence, the WTO vigorously denies the charge that its rules systematically undermine the environment. In its view, 'there is a lot of misunderstanding of recent WTO disputes involving government environmental or health regulations.'[28] It claims to have ruled against environmental regulations, not because they seek to protect the environment, but because they 'treated foreign suppliers less favourably than domestic suppliers, or discriminated among foreign suppliers or were more trade restrictive than necessary to achieve the desired environmental objective'.[29] In its ruling on the US Clean Air case, the WTO clarifies the extent of governments' freedom to protect the environment with this revealing exercise in doublethink: 'WTO Members were free to set their own environmental objectives, but they were bound to implement those objectives only through measures consistent with [WTO] provisions.'[30]

Apologists for the WTO can point to a number of clauses and agreements that, on the face of it, permit 'exceptions' to trade-promoting rules in order to protect human, animal or plant life. The SPS Agreement allows such exceptions in relation to food and food safety laws. Article XX of GATT widens the scope of potential exceptions so that they can be applied generally, to any regulation or law that would otherwise fall foul of the WTO, if it can be shown to be 'necessary' to protect human, animal or plant life or health, or 'relate' to the conservation of 'exhaustible natural resources'. Indeed, the existence of such clauses allows the WTO to claim that it 'has not made any rulings that limit the rights of governments to make laws to protect their environment or to safeguard their citizens from safety or health risks'.[31]

However, Article XX states that any exceptional measures must be: 'subject to the requirement that such measures are not applied in a manner which would constitute a means of arbitrary or unjustifiable discrimination between countries where the same conditions prevail, or a disguised restriction on international trade'.[32]

In practice, successive WTO dispute panels have used this widely cast and overriding caveat, together with the requirement that an exceptional measure must be 'necessary', to dismiss defences of WTO-incompatible environmental policies. Indeed, to date, only one such defence has succeeded. In a dispute where Canada sought to overturn a French ban on asbestos, France successfully argued that the ban was 'necessary' as no procedures can eliminate all health risks to those handling the material.

As each defence has been dismissed, so the scope of potential health and environmental safeguards against WTO rules is diminished. Perversely, the rules that at first appeared to offer some protection have been turned around to become rules that allow the WTO to, in effect, maintain, 'Well, if it (say, consuming traces of growth hormones, breathing polluted air or killing millions of dolphins) really was a problem, we would have let you stop it. We didn't. Therefore it can't be a problem.' And so, free trade's assault on the environment is reinforced.

4
Globalising Poverty, Inequality and Unemployment

> The WTO is often promoted as a 'rules-based' trading framework that protects the weaker and poorer countries from unilateral actions by the stronger states. The opposite is true: the WTO, like many other multilateral international agreements, is meant to institutionalise and legitimise inequality.
>
> Waldon Bello.[1]

The debate whether or not liberalisation of trade and investment is the best way to reduce inequality, boost employment and help the poor is the most keenly contested corner of the argument between the proponents and opponents of economic globalisation. However, some facts are incontestable.

The gap between rich and poor, both within and between countries, is widening[2] to the extent that even the IMF has admitted that globalisation 'is clearly not progressing evenly'.[3] A recent study that compared the relative purchasing power of the poorest and richest households across the globe (covering about 84 per cent of the world's population) found that the poorest 10 per cent have only 1.6 per cent of the spending power of the richest 10 per cent. The richest 1 per cent of households receive as much income as the poorest 57 per cent. The richest 10 per cent of the US population (around 25 million people) have a combined income greater than that of the poorest 43 per cent of the world's people (around 2 billion people); and the richest 25 per cent of the world's households receive 75 per cent of the world's income.[4]

The income gap between rich and poor has accelerated during the current period of rapid economic globalisation. The richest fifth of the world's population had an income 30 times greater than that of the poorest fifth in 1960, rising to 60 times greater in 1990, and 74 times greater by 1997. In 1820, Western Europe's per capita income was three times that of Africa's; by the 1990s, it was more than 13 times as high.[5] Inequality is also rising within countries, particularly China, states in Eastern Europe and the former USSR, and in OECD countries, especially Sweden, the UK and US. This trend has accelerated since 1980.[6]

Economic globalisation is not, according to the IMF, to be blamed for the growth of inequality. Indeed, it is the lack of it that does the damage. They state: 'Countries that are integrating more slowly are seeing slower growth and more poverty.'[7] However, wage inequality has increased in almost all developing countries that have undertaken rapid trade liberalisation. Most often this has occurred because of declining industrial employment of unskilled workers and large absolute falls in their real wages, of the order of 20–30 per cent in Latin America for example. By the beginning of 1999, there were some 150 million people unemployed worldwide and up to 1 billion under-employed – a third of the world's labour force. Not since the Depression of the 1930s have things been so bad. In the words of then International Labour Organisation (ILO) Director-General Michael Hansenne, 'the global employment situation is grim, and getting grimmer.'[8] He was right: by 2003 the global unemployment total had reached 180 million.[9] The situation is worst of all for developing countries and Eastern Europe. However, even in the developed world, pressure to reduce real wages and downsize or 'casualise' labour forces has been a hallmark of policy since the late 1970s.

In 1997, the UN Conference on Trade and Development (UNCTAD) concluded that this dramatic increase in global inequality is no simple coincidence, but that it is being caused by economic globalisation.[10] By 2002, UNCTAD was of the opinion that further rounds of globalisation had done little to improve the situation. They stated, 'few of the countries which pursued rapid liberalization of trade and investment and experienced a rapid growth in manufacturing exports over the past two decades achieved a significant increase in their shares in world manufacturing income.'[11] This is because the developing nations' role in the manufacturing process tends to be limited to the provision of cheap labour for assembling imported components, with most of the value-added income going to the foreign-based TNCs that control the production process.

Countries are forced to compete with each other to win and retain private foreign direct investment (FDI). As they rush to create the low-debt, low-tax, deregulated environments that investors demand, job-creating public spending is squeezed, replaced instead by inducements to potential investors: corporate welfare is climbing above human welfare on governments' agendas. Financial deregulation eases mergers and acquisitions, together with the job losses they inevitably bring. And just as investors are free to come, so they are free to go. Actual or threatened relocation of industries to less regulated, lower-waged economies is exerting downward pressure on jobs and labour standards throughout the world.

Measures of absolute poverty also reveal a grim picture. Of the world's 6 billion people, 2.8 billion – almost half – live on less than $2 a day,[12] and more than 1.2 billion – a fifth – live on less than $1 a day, with numbers having increased during the 1990s in most regions of the world apart from India and China.[13] Figures such as these led Joseph Stiglitz, the former senior vice-president and chief economist of the World Bank, to declare in 1999, 'we are not winning the fight against poverty',[14] a frank admission for a senior official of an organisation whose mission statement is 'a world free of poverty'.[15]

Poverty, of course, has many dimensions. It is not simply a measurement of income, but an assessment of well-being, measured in terms of access to health, education, resources, assets and entitlements. Policy makers routinely overlook the broad evidence that women bear the brunt of this 'capacity-based' poverty.[16] Yet trade and investment liberalisation inevitably affect men and women differently since they shape the economic and social factors on which their incomes and resources depend in a manner that both reflects and exacerbates existing gender inequalities. Worldwide, women face an oppressive division of labour and, more often than men, lack access to and control over assets and resources. This is the case both for intangible resources like information and influence, and productive resources, including land, equipment and credit. While globalisation may have brought increased formal industrial employment for some women, the terms of that employment are often very poor. There is growing evidence that women tend to suffer more from the impact of low income, precarious labour conditions and long hours, and that their unpaid work both in the informal economy and in social reproduction is unrecognised and undervalued.[17]

MORE OF THE SAME?

Despite the overwhelming evidence that poverty remains, in the World Bank's words, 'a global problem of huge proportions',[18] that inequality has ballooned during the most rapid period of economic globalisation, and UNCTAD's authoritative opinion that this is no

Globalising Poverty, Inequality and Unemployment 49

mere coincidence, advocates of globalisation continue to insist that more and stronger doses of the same medicine will cure the patient. Even if some of them do now accept the overwhelming evidence of growing inequality, they hold doggedly to the belief that globalisation is the best route out of poverty. This view is well summarised in the words of UK Prime Minister, Tony Blair:

> If the poorest countries can be drawn into the global economy and get increasing access to modern knowledge and technology, it could lead to a rapid reduction in global poverty – as well as bringing new trade and investment opportunities for all. But if this is not done, the poorest countries will become more marginalized, and suffering and division will grow. And we will all be affected by the consequences.[19]

The logic of this position is simple. It goes like this. Economic growth increases incomes, including those of the poor. Economic globalisation is the best way to boost growth. Thus, globalisation is the best way to reduce poverty, QED. And if logic is not enough, two World Bank economists, David Dollar and Aart Kraay produced a paper in 2000 entitled 'Growth is Good for the Poor', which attempted to prove that the logic is reflected in reality.[20]

In their paper, Dollar and Kraay analysed 370 observations of income levels and economic growth from 125 countries over four decades. They found that incomes rise as growth takes place and that on average the income levels of the poorest fifth of the population rise at about the same rate as overall per capita income. The authors conclude that 'growth generally does benefit the poor and that anyone who cares about the poor should favor the growth-enhancing policies of good rule of law, fiscal discipline, and openness to international trade' and that 'globalization is good for the poor.'

Dollar and Kraay's paper has been seized on by those who wish to dismiss critics of globalisation. The *Economist* learned from this study that cutting inflation and reducing public spending disproportionately help the poor and concluded that 'globalisation raises incomes, and the poor participate in full.'[21] Reacting to Dollar and Kraay's study, Martin Wolf, a leading pro-globalisation columnist in the UK, opined 'protesters against the World Bank and the IMF are in effect seeking to deny the poor the benefits of a liberal world economy.'[22]

DOES GROWTH BENEFIT THE POOR?

On the surface, Dollar and Kraay's study directly contradicts our view that globalisation is part of the problem, not the solution. However, in this case the surface is a particularly thin veneer and quite unrepresentative of what lies beneath.

On a technical level, the accuracy of the findings has been questioned. It is very difficult to measure the income of the poorest fifth of the population in any country, and particularly so in developing countries. Since, as Green economist Richard Douthwaite pointed out,[23] the income of the poorest fifth of the population is only a tiny fraction of total national income – 4.2 per cent in the US, for example – relatively small changes in income distribution that might be missed due to inaccurate sampling (the authors admit 'for most countries, only one or a handful of observations are available') will impact disproportionately on the section of the population that are of chief interest in the study. Moreover, the study says nothing about the distribution of income within the poorest fifth of the population.

A second and more profound challenge to Dollar and Kraay's work arises from the fact that measures of GDP and income relate only to the monetarised part of an economy. For large numbers of the world's poorest people, particularly women, only a relatively small proportion of the household economy will take place within the formal economy. As development takes place, income might rise, but so will the proportion of monetary transactions. Put another way, migrant shanty-town dwellers, cast off the land by 'development' of their country's agricultural sector, now must buy all their food and fuel rather than producing it for themselves; they must also pay rent and fares for the first time. Although they might receive higher incomes from their sweatshop jobs than they did as subsistence farmers in their villages, they might easily be much worse off. We cannot tell without a detailed social investigation. However, it must be added that this criticism applies equally to any study that uses monetary income as the sole measure of economic well-being.

Third, there is the question of whether absolute poverty is all that matters. Dollar and Kraay's main claim is that the incomes of the poor and the rich grew at the same percentage rate as growth took place. Even if we accept these findings on face value, despite the reservations we expressed above, this means that the absolute, rather than relative gap between the incomes of the rich and poor will always get wider. To some this is of no consequence; all that matters is that as incomes increase the number of people living below the absolute poverty threshold decreases: in the words of Martin Wolf, 'bemoaning the magnitude of global inequality, as opposed to the low standards of living of large parts of the world, is just empty rhetoric.'[24] In the view of others, including ourselves, 'a significantly more equal world is likely to be more stable, peaceful and possibly more prosperous ... We should be concerned with both absolute and relative gaps, for both relate to important ethical values, both are relevant to feelings of disempowerment and deprivation.'[25] A 'more of the same' globalisation prescription will leave the poor feeling even more disempowered and deprived in relation to the rich, and regardless of whether the Dollar and Kraay thesis is correct, we need to take urgent measures to reduce *relative* poverty. We look at what these measures should be in the next chapter.

IS GLOBALISATION THE BEST WAY TO BOOST GROWTH?

Earlier we summarised the logic of Dollar and Kraay thus: 'Economic growth increases incomes, including those of the poor. Economic globalisation is the best way to boost growth. Thus, globalisation is the best way to reduce poverty.'

So far we have looked at the first statement and found it wanting; what about the second statement and the conclusion it seems to support? Dollar and Kraay do not present any evidence in their study to suggest that economic globalisation promotes growth; in stating, 'globalization is good for the poor' they simply *assume* that it does. The evidence however suggests otherwise.

The Cambridge economist, John Eatwell, has drawn together a wide collection of data that suggest that conventional economic growth has slowed as capital liberalisation has become more widespread. Of a sample of 57 of the world's richest countries, 47 experienced lower rates of growth of per capita GDP in the period 1982–91 than the average for 1960–71, an era of fixed exchange rates and tight capital controls. The later period was also marked by a decline in investment as a proportion of GDP and large increases in the rate of unemployment.[26]

More recently, Mark Weisbrot, Dean Baker and their colleagues at the US Center for Economic and Policy Research have drawn up a 'globalisation scorecard'.[27] They compared the period from 1980 to 2000 – the era of Reaganite neoliberal globalisation when the drive for capital deregulation, privatisation and the lifting of barriers to international investment was at its height – with the period from 1960 to 1980. During this earlier period, virtually every developing nation was progressing along the lines of the 'Import Substitution Model', by which locally owned industry was built through government investment and high tariffs.

They discovered that the poorest countries went from a growth rate of 1.9 per cent annually in the 1960–80 period to a decline of 0.5 per cent a year between 1980 and 2000. The middle group of countries did worse, dropping from annual growth of 3.6 per cent to just under 1 per cent after 1980. The world's richest countries also showed a slowdown.

They also looked at per capita income rates – a more useful measure of individual poverty. During the earlier era of increasing national government control and ownership (1960–80), per capita income grew by 73 per cent in Latin America and by 34 per cent in Africa. Today, by contrast, more than 80 countries have per capita incomes lower than they were during that period. In Latin America, growth in incomes has come to a virtual halt, increasing by less than 6 per cent over 20 years. African incomes have declined by 23 per cent.

Using the UNDP's Human Development Index (HDI), Weisbrot and his colleagues found that between 1980 and 2000 there was a 'very clear decline in progress'. A similar picture emerges for life expectancy. Only the richest countries showed a higher rate of improvement in the past 20 years than in the period between 1960–80, and since 1985 life expectancy has been falling in 15 African nations. Among middle-income and poor countries, progress in reducing child mortality and raising school enrolments was also faster before 1980.

These conclusions have since been reinforced by the 2003 *Human Development Report*, which states:

> For many countries the 1990s were a decade of despair. Some 54 countries are poorer now than in 1990. In 21, a larger proportion of people is going hungry. In 14, more children are dying before age five. In 12, primary school enrolments are shrinking. In 34, life expectancy has fallen. Such reversals in survival were previously rare. A further sign of a development crisis is the decline in 21 countries in the human development index ... This too was rare until the late 1980s, because the capabilities captured by the HDI are not easily lost.[28]

Indeed, only four countries experienced a fall in HDI during the 1980s. Even the IMF has admitted that 'in the recent decades, nearly one-fifth of the world population have regressed' – arguably 'one of the greatest economic failures of the twentieth century'.[29]

However, never slow to shoulder a burden in defence of the World Bank's party line, Dollar and Kraay have responded with a study that looks at the economic performance of a group of developing countries they regard as 'globalizers'. Their conclusions appear to show considerable linkage between globalisation and economic growth: 'Their [the globalising nations'] growth rates have accelerated from the 1970s to the 1980s to the 1990s, even as growth in the rich countries and the rest of the developing world has declined. The post-1980 globalizers are catching up to the rich countries while the rest of the developing world is falling farther behind.'[30]

As with their previous paper, Dollar and Kraay's conclusions have already gained widespread currency as further proof of globalisation's philanthropic intent. Yet, once again their view of the world has run into criticism. The Harvard economist, Dani Rodrik, has analysed their study and finds fault with their method of selecting globalising countries.[31] These were selected using two criteria: rapidly reducing tariffs and a high ratio of external trade to GDP. Rodrik argues that a high volume of international trade relative to GDP is an outcome outside the direct control of policy makers that says as much about a country's size and position in relation to other countries as it does about its intention to globalise. It should therefore not be mixed with the level of tariffs, a direct policy measure, to select globalisers. Even so, Rodrik finds that if Dollar and Kraay's own data are applied, using their stated criteria, a different group of globalisers is generated to the group they selected. He implies that Dollar and Kraay have fixed the outcome of their study and finds that his 'no-tricks' set of globalisers grew on average at a significantly slower rate during the 1980s and 1990s than they did during the 1960s and 1970s. He delivers a forthright verdict on Dollar and Kraay: 'The authors' claims regarding the beneficial effects of trade liberalization on poverty have to be seen as statements based on faith rather than evidence.'[32]

CAUSE AND EFFECT

Of course, the fact that economic globalisation has occurred at the same time as progress in tackling poverty has suffered a reverse does not prove that one factor caused the other. But the fact that nearly all countries experienced slower growth and declining improvements in human development at the same time does suggests a common underlying cause. As Mark Weisbrot and his colleagues put it, 'at the very least, the burden of proof ... [is] squarely placed on those who claim success – by any available measure of human well-being – for the last two decades of the experiment in globalization.'[33]

Studies certainly reveal no evidence of a link between financial liberalisation and higher investment and growth. If anything, the evidence indicates a positive relationship between capital controls and growth of per capita income.[34] The only clear pattern is that countries have dismantled their trade restrictions as they have grown richer. Today's rich countries, with few exceptions, embarked on economic growth strategies behind protective barriers but now display low trade barriers.

This is certainly true of the East Asian 'Tigers' who are often held up as examples of what can be gained by engaging in the world economy. However, their development strategies were very different from those being prescribed to poor countries today. Countries like Taiwan, South Korea and Malaysia had to abide by few of the current rules during their formative growth period in the 1960s and 1970s and faced far less pressure to open their borders to capital flows. They underwent rapid industrialisation and achieved large reductions in poverty by adopting strategies based on import substitution and the export of high-tech goods manufactured by foreign-owned TNCs. They used many innovative mechanisms to ensure they benefited from the FDI on which this strategy depended. The mechanisms included high-tariff and non-tariff barriers, large-scale public ownership of banking and industry, patent and copyright infringements, restrictions on capital flows, trade-balancing requirements that linked an investor's imports of components and raw materials to the value of the exports of their finished product, and 'local content' regulations that required a certain proportion of components to be sourced locally. Together, these mechanisms helped to raise income from capital-intensive exports, develop locally owned support industries, and bring in new technology while still managing to protect local entrepreneurs' preferential access to the domestic market. For example, Malaysia's local content policy enabled it to build a 'national car' in conjunction with Mitsubishi, which has about 80 per cent local content and a 70 per cent market share.[35] It would be impossible to replicate these strategies today without breaking the rules of the WTO or IMF.[36]

The same can also be said of India and China. They have recently achieved remarkable increases in per capita GDP, which together have offset the increases in absolute poverty in the rest of the world, yet they have done so by adopting policies far removed from those prescribed by the Washington consensus.

As Rodrik concludes elsewhere,[37] 'the globalisers have it exactly backwards: integration may be the result, but it is certainly not the cause, of economic and social development.'

TRADING IN POVERTY

It is because they have it 'exactly backwards' that the WTO and other international financial institutions insist incessantly that greater integration into the world economy is the only way for the world's poorest countries to develop. In recent years, this unswerving faith in integration has spread to political leaders and policy makers around the world. Such integration is more than just lowering barriers to trade and investment, however. Countries must now comply with a long list of admission requirements, from new patent rules to more rigorous banking standards, and undertake complex institutional reforms that took today's industrialised countries generations to achieve and were only undertaken from an established position of strength.

This is bad news for the world's poor. More than fifty countries now have per capita incomes lower than they were a decade or more ago and it is often countries that are highly 'integrated' into the global economy that are becoming even more marginal. For example, the number of people living in poverty in Sub-Saharan Africa has continued to grow in spite of the fact that exports from the region have reached nearly 30 per cent of GDP, compared to just 19 per cent for the OECD industrialised countries.[38]

Indeed, there is no better illustration of the dangers of following the misconceived prescriptions of economic globalisation than the devastating situation in Russia. Ten years after liberalisation of the Russian economy began in 1989, the UNDP reported that inequality had doubled, wages had fallen by almost half, and male life expectancy had declined by more than four years to 60 years.

Blind adherence to the integrationist faith leads governments in poor countries to divert human resources, administrative capabilities and political capital away from more urgent development priorities such as education, public health and institutional reform. It leads to ever-greater dependence on the whims of international market forces and leaves less space for the development of economic strategies based on more stable and controllable domestic investors and institutions.

There is a high price to be paid for obeying the dogma of globalisation, and as the World Bank now recognises, it is paid disproportionately by the poor:

> The costs of adjusting to greater openness are borne exclusively by the poor, regardless of how long the adjustment takes. In addition, the consequences of terms of trade changes are far greater for the poor than for the middle or wealthy classes. The poor are far more vulnerable to shifts in relative international prices, and this vulnerability is magnified by the country's openness to trade.[39]

CURBS ON PUBLIC SPENDING

Government spending on public services such as education, healthcare, housing, welfare and public transport is a vital defence against poverty; it is also a major source of employment. Yet strict curbs are being imposed on public spending as, in rich and poor countries alike, governments strain to meet the dictates of global markets and financial institutions and to attract private investment to their national economies.

The Structural Adjustment Programmes imposed by the IMF on debtor countries provide the most extreme examples of this. Following the 1979 hike in oil prices and the increase in US interest rates in the early 1980s, many indebted countries found themselves unable to meet their debt repayments. The commercial lenders increasingly refused to extend their loans to any debtor country unless the IMF would certify that its economy was being 'soundly maintained' and 'restructured', in other words, that the country had subjected itself fully to the neocolonialist strictures of an SAP.

The effect of SAPs on employment has been dramatic. Public sector workers have been sacked, domestic producers have lost their jobs to more 'efficient' importers, and earnings and employment from exports have failed to materialise because most SAP countries are encouraged to produce the same range of agricultural and mineral exports and prices have plummeted.

The IMF has hailed Senegal's rate of economic growth as proof of the efficacy of its market-oriented reforms. Yet, between 1991 and

1996, under IMF tutelage, unemployment in Senegal grew from 25 per cent to 44 per cent. During 1998, an average of 8000 South Koreans lost their jobs every day due in large part to the conditions attached to a $58bn structural adjustment loan.[40] Throughout the 1990s, Argentina was another poster child for reform, IMF-style. It brought down trade and investment barriers faster than most other countries in Latin America. It liberalised its capital account more radically, privatised everything that wasn't nailed down, and tied its hands further by pegging the value of its currency to the US dollar. Yet its debt-fuelled consumer boom went bust in 2001 when it ran out of assets to sell to service its debts, and its exports, priced in dollar-pegged pesos, became uncompetitive. The IMF's response was to grant further 'aid' packages, based on public spending cuts. By December 2001, unemployment reached 25 per cent, the country was in open revolt against the political establishment, and three presidents left office within ten days. Industrial production declined by 20 per cent in the first quarter of 2002, and jobs continued to be lost at the rate of 80,000 a month in the first six months of the same year.[41]

SAPs are not restricted to the developing world. The European Union too has been living with one of its very own since the early 1990s in the shape of the Maastricht convergence criteria, and now the Stability and Growth Pact of European Monetary Union (EMU). The convergence criteria made entry to the Single Currency conditional on restricting a nation's total public debt to 60 per cent of GDP and its annual budget deficit to 3 per cent of GDP. Additional inflation and interest rate criteria also applied. Once the euro had been introduced at the beginning of 1999 the Stability and Growth Pact came into force. Under the pact, the European Central Bank (ECB) can fine euro-zone countries if their annual budget deficits exceed its limit of 3 per cent of GDP (see Chapter 10). The immediate aim of these deflationary monetarist targets is to lock an inherently diverse collection of national economies into a uniform framework tight enough to establish the euro as a strong and credible currency. The wider aim of EMU, as we see it, is to 'Europeanise' the member states' national economies as a staging post towards globalisation, and to mould them to the demands of the international investors. No matter the aims, the results have been utterly predictable. Widespread government cutbacks to meet the convergence criteria created record levels of unemployment in the EU at a time when it fell considerably in the US. In 1983, the EU and US had virtually the same unemployment rate. By the time the euro was introduced on

1 January 1999, unemployment in the EU stood at around 11 per cent; in the US it had halved to less than 5 per cent (see Figure 4.1).[42]

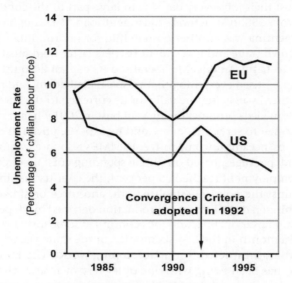

Figure 4.1 Unemployment in the EU and US

Source: Eurostat <http://europa.eu.int/comm/eurostat/>.

It is not just the formal rules of institutions such as the IMF and ECB that restrict the public spending of governments that fall under their influence; the logic of the liberalised global economy forces them to 'choose' to restrict it for themselves. If FDI is to be won, governments must compete to reduce company taxation and offer the biggest inducements to inward investors. If exports markets are to be expanded, governments must subsidise the exporters.

For example, it has been estimated that each job in the British defence industry is supported by a £13,000 annual subsidy in the form of export guarantees, support for R&D and sales promotions.[43] The state of California and the city of Anaheim are reported to have spent $880m on roads and other infrastructure projects to persuade Disneyland to stay.[44] Production of the European Airbus Industry's A3XX airliner was confirmed in 2000 only after the British government stumped up a quarter of the £2bn initial investment required from British Aerospace who won the contract to make the wings. The total investment to create each job on this project is roughly £100,000.

By contrast, the investment required to create each job in arguably less glamorous but certainly greener sectors of the economy, such as energy efficiency, conservation, public transport and recycling can be as little as £10,000 and rarely exceeds £40,000.[45] This growing corporate welfare agenda is reducing the supply of public money that can be invested in direct service provision, which would almost always provide far more employment per tax-dollar invested.

RELOCATION

It is not too difficult to see why governments that set out on the path of economic globalisation soon lock themselves into a spiralling corporate welfare agenda. Companies will simply relocate if they do not. In February 2002, James Dyson, inventor of the bagless vacuum cleaner, announced that his manufacturing operation would relocate from the English town of Malmesbury to Malaysia, with the loss of 800 jobs in the UK. Only three years earlier, this plucky British inventor who battled with sceptical banks and investors for 15 years to bring his product to market, had urged Britain to become 'a powerful manufacturing nation making wonderful products'.[46] Another highly symbolic example of job losses through relocation occurred when the last producer of cloth caps, the headgear of choice for generations of working-class men in parts of northern Britain, transferred from Leeds to China. Disastrous as these relocations are for the workers who lose their jobs, they are portents of many more job-destroying events to come, as governments sacrifice domestic industries to the WTO agenda.

There is now a huge new WTO member on the global stage: China. Its 900 million well-educated workers earn about 25 cents an hour, compared with more than $2 an hour in Malaysia. With technology transfer and automation, China will potentially be able to beat OECD competition and dominate the markets in Europe and the rest of the North in a huge range of goods. Shougang Steel, for example, has already become so expert in computerised production techniques that it won a contract to install the control systems for a US steel maker.[47]

On the surface, this might look like a 'good thing' for the countries that receive the relocating companies, yet the profits of foreign-owned TNCs are rarely reinvested in the host economies and globalisation offers no security for workers in these developing countries. This is because they are constantly forced to compete with other workers from even poorer countries. General Electric provides a relevant case study. It has slashed its US workforce by almost half since 1986 through automation, downsizing, out-sourcing and plant closures. It has globalised its operations by shifting production to low-wage countries, but even there the jobs remain precarious. GE recently closed a factory in Turkey to move it to lower-wage Hungary. It has since threatened to close a factory in Hungary and move it to India.[48] Often just the threat of relocation alone is enough to undermine the workforce's expectations of better wages and conditions and their ability to bargain for them. As the British Trades Union Congress puts it: 'The current form of globalisation, with the international rules and policies that underpin it, has brought poverty and hardship to millions of workers, particularly those in developing and transition countries. They have seen an erosion of their working conditions, wages and job security in a time of unprecedented wealth and technological capability.'[49]

What is more, job-rich 'indigenous' industries in the host countries are often undermined by cheap imports at exactly the same time as FDI is creating new, insecure employment in highly automated and job-sparse industries. For example, China's membership of the WTO will unleash a flood of cheap food imports, particularly from the US. This will further disadvantage the rural majority, many of whom will be forced to join the 100 million who are already looking for work in urban areas. This recipe for ever-lower Chinese wages at a time of export emphasis will further devastate its developing world competitors and lock them with China into a self-defeating spiral to the bargain basement of the global economy. As one commentator put it: 'In the "race to the bottom", China is defining the new bottom.'[50]

China is already capturing Northern textile markets from poor competitors such as Bangladesh. How long before Dyson moves from Malaysia to China as well?

GLOBALISATION ISN'T WORKING

Globalisation is not just creating global underemployment; it is also setting in train large-scale changes to the pattern of employment both within and between countries. In many developing countries, millions of rural workers have been forced off the land and are migrating to the shanty-town margins of the urban economy. Traditional industrial areas in the North are acclimatising to their post-industrial future and the original Asian miracle, Japan, is adjusting to the trauma of prolonged deflation, the result of years of over-intensive production.

One response to these changes, aided by the increased flow of information unleashed by globalisation, is for workers to up sticks and seek work abroad. In 2000, an estimated 185 million people were living for twelve months or more outside their country of birth or citizenship, up from 120 million in 1990.[51] However, economic globalisation has delivered a striking mismatch between the freedoms enjoyed by capital as it roams the planet seeking the best return and the privileges granted to workers. The debate about migration in most industrialised countries is now dominated by anti-immigrant sentiment. In Europe, right-wing parties are growing and it seems only a matter of time before armed guards and warships patrol the eastern frontier the Mediterranean to keep the migrants out.

In a few areas of high inward migration that suffer from under-investment in public services such as schools and health care facilities, there are genuine problems that require sensitive handling, but the stereotype of foreign workers taking 'our jobs' and soaking up benefits is well wide of the mark. Studies have repeatedly found that migration is a net generator of wealth. Dani Rodrik argues that 'even a marginal liberalization of international labor flows would create gains for the world economy' of the order of $200bn, far larger than prospective gains from trade negotiations, and with the benefits going into workers' pockets.[52] Moreover, migrant workers, legal and illegal, head for economies where labour is in short supply. The foreign workers on the building sites of London and the South-East of England are not depriving British brickies of a job; they are helping to combat severe labour shortages, easing inflationary pressure, and keeping interest rates low for everybody with a mortgage or other form of debt. If governments accept this in private, they dare not admit as much in public.

As we argue in later chapters, the ideal solution to the global labour market's problems would be to foster vibrant local economies that can provide plentiful and rewarding employment in every part of the world. This would surely be the solution preferred by those who are currently forced to leave their home communities to search of work. However, this is no excuse for the hypocrisy that seeks freedoms for the goods and capital of the North, but denies those same freedoms to the workers of the South. Enforced economic migration is a direct product of the inequality, poverty and under-employment that are the fruits of economic globalisation. If politicians in the North do not like it, they had better stop blaming the victims and start addressing the root causes instead.

THE POOR GET POORER, WHAT ABOUT THE RICH?

It would be easy to assume that rich countries in some way benefit by imposing liberalisation, together with the poverty, inequality and unemployment it brings, on poor countries. Yet, even in a narrow sense, as measured by GDP, this assumption is questionable. In the second half of the twentieth century, the UK's GDP trebled in real terms and post-tax per capita income in the US roughly quadrupled between the 1940s and 1990s, but, as we have seen, the rate of growth in rich countries slowed as globalisation advanced. Moreover, these gains in wealth have not been matched by improvements in well-being. As Figure 4.2 shows, the UK's ISEW (see Box 1.1) peaked in the early 1980s and declined during the period of rapid economic globalisation that has occurred since then. The same is true for GPI in the US (see Figure 4.3). Strikingly, despite the massive accumulation of personal wealth in the US, the percentage of the population that claims to be 'very happy' has not increased (see Figure 4.4).

Under economic globalisation, the rich have become richer at the expense of the poor, but it is hard to see how they have benefited from it.

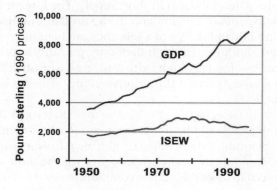

Figure 4.2 UK per capita GDP and ISEW (1950–98)

Source: Jackson, T., Marks, N., Ralls, J. and Stymme, S. (1997), *Sustainable Economic Welfare in the UK – a pilot index 1950–1996*, London: New Economics Foundation.

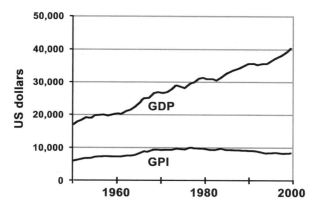

Figure 4.3 US per capita GDP and GPI

Source: Redefining Progress <http://www.rprogress.org/projects/gpi>.

Figure 4.4 Personal income and satisfaction in the US

Source: Myers, D.G. and Diener, E. (1996), 'The pursuit of happiness', *Scientific American*, 274, 54–5.

Section 2
The Green Alternative

The bottom line is that a planet of finite resources and increasingly unmet social needs cannot sustain an economic system that is driven by corporate interests and is based on ever-increasing free trade and international competitiveness. This system can and must be replaced by an alternative that challenges its insistence that all economies be contorted to the end goal of international competitiveness, and its emphasis on beggar-your-neighbour reduction of controls on trade and investment. Economic localisation is just such an alternative. It involves a better-your-neighbour supportive internationalism where the flow of ideas, technologies, information, culture, money and goods has, as its end goal, the rebuilding of truly sustainable national and local economies worldwide. Its emphasis is not on competition for the cheapest, but on cooperation for the best.

5
Economic Localisation

> As mutual aid is replaced by dependence on external markets, people begin to feel powerless to make decisions in their own lives.
>
> Helena Norberg-Hodge[1]

The street protests in Seattle that brought the 1999 WTO Ministerial in that city to a juddering halt sparked an unprecedented bout of soul-searching amongst the leaders of the free trade world. Apparently for the first time, they realised that they faced significant opposition. To their surprise, their opponents numbered far more than the tens of thousands of activists on the streets, but included millions of people around the world who would never contemplate placing themselves in the line of tear-gas fire, but quietly applauded those who did.

The response has been a scrambled attempt to appease, if not the protesters themselves, then at least their armchair sympathisers. Statements from the World Bank and IMF began to echo more obviously some of the anti-globalisation movement's concerns. The trade round initiated at the 2001 WTO Ministerial in Doha has been dubbed the Development Round – a reflection of the WTO's anxiety that developing nations should at least appear to be getting a better deal from trade liberalisation. In the run-up to the 2002 Johannesburg summit on sustainable development, EU leaders began to worry publicly that failure there to agree a clear plan of action to help the poorest counties meet basic development goals would scupper future trade talks. EU Development Commissioner Poul Nielson's view was that 'If Johannesburg fails, we will probably see very negative effects in the global trade arena. Doha would have a very difficult start indeed if this were the background.'[2]

It is always easier to agree that there is a problem, than to agree what to do about it. Simply condemning the latest acronymic outrage, be it MAI, GATS or TRIPs is straightforward. The urgent and more demanding challenge now facing critics of economic globalisation is to capture the momentum of the protests and move from opposition to proposition, to articulate a coherent political alternative. If we fail to meet this challenge the momentum of the protests will be lost, dissipated amongst the globalisers' face-saving proposals for minimal reform.

Clare Short, the former secretary of state for international development in Tony Blair's cabinet is a prominent face-saver. One of the key policy commitments in her department's White Paper, *Eliminating World Poverty: Making Globalisation Work for the Poor*, was to 'support continuing reductions in barriers to trade, both in developed and developing countries, and work to improve the capacity of developing countries to take advantage of new trade opportunities'.[3]

This is presumably what she meant by 'globalisation with a human face'. To Greens, this sounds worryingly like a wolf with a sheep's face or Dracula with a first aid kit. It is a 'more of the same only a bit fairer' agenda that tinkers at the margins of the glaring inequalities caused by the current global trade and investment systems, rather than challenging their fundamentally destructive foundations. This is about as far as reformers within the pro-globalisation establishment are allowed to go.

Adding a few environmental clauses here or a social clause there will not alter the fundamental nature of the beast. The bottom line is that a planet of finite resources and increasingly unmet social needs cannot sustain an economic system that is driven by corporate interests and based on ever-increasing free trade and international competitiveness. Indeed as we have already seen, the drive for international competitiveness is one of the greatest obstacles to achieving higher social and environmental standards and the whole raft of Green policies that are needed for a more sustainable society. As soon as proposals like this are suggested, corporations put the brakes on by claiming it will reduce their competitiveness, and threatening to relocate.

Greens believe therefore that, rather than trying to make dog-eat-dog economic globalisation a little bit kinder and a little less ruthless, it can and must be replaced by an alternative that challenges its insistence that all economies be contorted to the end goal of international competitiveness, and its emphasis on beggar-your-neighbour reduction of controls on trade and investment.

Economic localisation is the antithesis to economic globalisation. This involves a better-your-neighbour supportive internationalism where the flow of ideas, technologies, information, culture, money and goods has, as its end goal, the rebuilding of truly sustainable national and local economies worldwide. Its emphasis is not on competition for the cheapest, but on cooperation for the best.

Several leading anti-globalisation theorists and campaigners have recently promoted economic localisation,[4] but one of the clearest statements of its basic principles pre-dates the current debate by several decades. In a famous lecture in 1933 entitled 'National Self-Sufficiency', John Maynard Keynes said: 'I sympathise, therefore, with those who would minimise, rather than those who would maximise, economic entanglement between nations. Ideas, knowledge, art, hospitality, travel – these are the things which should of their nature be international. But let goods be homespun whenever it is reasonable and conveniently possible, and above all, let finance be primarily national.'[5]

Economic localisation actively discriminates in favour of more local production and investment whenever it is, as Keynes said, 'reasonable and conveniently possible'. However, 'local' will not always mean national, as Keynes supposed. The New Economics Foundation defines local as

> ... a relative term. It means different things to different people and depends on context. For example, your local TV Station is likely to be further away than your local corner shop. For some of us local refers to our street. For others it means our village, town, city or region. However we think of it, 'local' usually connects to a group of people and the things they depend on – whether shops, health services, schools or parks. Think of local as that surrounding environment and network of facilities that is vital to our quality of life and well-being.[6]

Thus, in applying localisation, what constitutes the 'local' will differ from one place to another and from one product to another in accordance with the principle of trade subsidiarity, which is explained later in this chapter.[7] The precise mix of policies that should be adopted will vary accordingly. Some countries are big enough to aim for increased self-reliance within their own borders, while smaller countries would look first to a grouping of their neighbours. Sometimes 'local' will be a region or community within a large nation state.

Over a period of time, there would be a transition away from dependence on international export markets, with countries racing each other round a downward spiral of social and environmental standards, and towards the national provision of as many goods and services as is feasible and appropriate. Long distance trade would then be reduced to its original purpose: supplying what cannot easily come from within one country or geographical grouping of countries.

In his groundbreaking book, *Going Local*, Michael Shuman of the Washington-based Institute for Policy Studies, describes the localisation process as one that 'does not mean walling off the outside world. It means nurturing locally owned businesses, which use local resources sustainably, employ local workers at decent wages, and serve primarily local consumers. It means becoming more self sufficient and less dependent on imports. Control moves from the boardrooms of distant corporations and back to the community where it belongs.'[8]

Economic localisation provides a political and economic framework for people, local government and businesses to rediversify their own economies. It does not mean a return to overpowering state control – merely that governments provide the policy framework to promote rediversification. Crucially, this will increase community cohesion, reduce poverty and inequality, improve livelihoods, promote social provision and environmental protection and provide an all-important sense of security.

Economic localisation has the developmental advantage of enabling poorer countries to protect their infant industries and food production systems from ruthless and often devastating competition from cheap imports, thus allowing them to develop diverse and resilient local economies that respond to local needs. It has the environmental advantage of no longer requiring the transportation of so many goods over unnecessary distances. It has the democratic advantage of promoting an increase in national and local control of the economy and allowing people to decide for themselves the direction in which they wish their economy to develop, and the potential – at least – for the benefits of that economy to be shared out more fairly.

Economic localisation is an ambitious agenda that, just like economic globalisation, will take time and political will at every level from the local to the international to implement. And just like economic globalisation it will only come about through the determined implementation of a set of interrelated and self-reinforcing policies. We examine the policies for localisation in more detail below.

THE BUILDING BLOCKS OF ECONOMIC LOCALISATION

Localising money

Rapid liberalisation of investment is key to economic globalisation, but it has created a global casino economy that deals a double blow to local economies. On the one hand, local economies have to distort themselves to conform to the demands of global finance. On the other, their stability is undermined by moment-to-moment fluctuations in the international financial markets that have no basis in real economic activity. The scale of this problem is illustrated by the exponential growth in the value of cross-border financial transactions. Their total value in 1980 was $80bn; by 1999, their daily total reached $1500bn, yet 90 per cent of these transactions were entirely speculative rather than productive, and aimed at exploiting differences between exchange and interest rates.[9]

Localisation demands that investment seek the development of stable local economies, based on sustainable patterns of production and consumption – not the quickest short-term return and the fattest Christmas bonus for traders in London and New York. This requires controls on capital flows and tax evasion, including off-shore banking centres, and measures to limit the destabilising effect of short-term speculative currency transactions.

The WTO is seeking to liberalise investment, so that governments have even fewer rights to attach conditions to inward investment. By contrast, we must build international agreement to an alternative localist code of investment and procurement. This would allow governments to prefer local investors and discriminate between inward investors on the basis of social and environmental criteria. Governments should be able to insist on measures that maximise the benefits of inward investment, such as prohibiting the excessive repatriation of profit and specifying the minimum proportion of labour and content that should be sourced locally.

Most financial crises in the last ten years were triggered when currency speculators seized on localised shocks to investor confidence and magnified them into full-blown crises. Faced with the speculators' vulture-like, concerted selling of their currency, central banks are forced into major devaluations, often following expensive but unsuccessful interventions in foreign exchange markets in defence of their currency.

Currency crises have severe human costs. Devaluation increases a country's debt burden and capital investment takes flight from the stricken economy. Populations are hit by widespread job losses and reduced wages. The prices of essential commodities rise and vital public services are cut. Those already at the margins of the economy – the poor, women, children and the elderly – inevitably suffer most. Nearly ten million people lost their jobs in the South-East Asia crisis.

A Tobin-like tax on speculative currency transactions would help dampen the impact of the foreign exchange markets.[10] Levied at just 0.05 per cent, it would raise between US $50–100bn a year, more than the current global aid budget. These revenues could be placed in a multilateral fund administered by the UN to promote sustainable development in the poorest countries. However, at this rate it would do little to halt the stampede of transactions seen during currency crises. To overcome this problem the German economist, Paul Bernd Spahn, suggested a variation of the Tobin tax whereby a very low default rate is set, but a much higher surcharge rate is imposed for transactions involving a particular currency if that currency's value changes suddenly by a large amount. The surcharge rate would be set sufficiently highly to remove the profitability of speculative attacks on the currency, and would operate in a similar way to the New York Stock Exchange's circuit-breaker mechanism.[11]

Controls on international currency trading and investment flows should be complemented at the local level by policies that support smaller, locally based banks and loan schemes, credit unions, local bond issues, and local exchange and trading schemes. Known collectively as Community Development Finance Institutions (CDFIs), these measures help to retain wealth and exchange within a community. They provide insulation from the turbulence of global financial markets and a secure source of finance, often on favourable terms, which can help generate local employment and training opportunities or be used to finance community infrastructure. CDFI-based schemes foster direct links between investors, producers and consumers, and are characterised by their long-term commitment to the communities in which they operate. This helps to strengthen and democratise those communities by increasing the mutual interest between partners within the local economy, as well as the accountability they bear to each other for the social and environmental impacts of their activities. The CDFI sector is playing an increasingly important role in the UK, particularly in run-down urban areas where more traditional lenders are reluctant to tread. Between 1998 and

2001, the assets controlled by the sector in the UK grew by 30 per cent to £500m.[12]

Recently, the New Economics Foundation has proposed that the principles of the CDFI sector be extended to provide an alternative to the stock market as a vehicle for the investment of pension contributions. Mutually managed 'peoples' pension funds' would be established to collect employers' and employees' contributions and use them to develop the local public infrastructure, such as schools, hospitals and public transport systems. Once completed, the new facilities would be leased to the government for a long fixed term at an agreed rent, providing both the necessary income to the fund and a sound alternative to the private finance initiative.[13]

Site here to sell here: controlling the TNCs

TNCs enjoy economic power that is out of all proportion to their importance as employers. Just 500 corporations control 70 per cent of world trade and the value of the combined sales of the world's 200 largest TNCs exceeds the combined global economy except the biggest nine countries. Yet these 200 companies employ just 0.75 per cent of the global workforce,[14] and many of them are busy 'downsizing' by shedding jobs.[15] Nevertheless, because of the number of jobs involved in each plant, the threat of relocation holds powerful leverage over governments.

The urgent need for a tighter regulatory framework for TNCs is illustrated by the effect they have on the environment. TNCs produce more than half of the global greenhouse emissions from the industrial sectors that have the greatest impact on global warming. They have virtually exclusive control of the production of CFCs and their replacement gases. TNCs dominate the extraction and trading of natural resources that threaten global forest, water and marine resources together with the people who depend on them, just six TNCs produce 63 per cent of mined aluminium for example and 20 companies account for the production of 90 per cent of all pesticides. TNCs manufacture the majority of the most persistent and polluting chemicals – the chlorine-based PCBs, dioxins and DDT.[16]

Tellingly, all previous efforts to regulate TNCs at the international level have failed. In 1993, attempts to finalise a Code of Conduct on TNCs were formally killed off and the UN Centre on Transnational Corporations itself was closed down. UNCTAD's Code of Conduct on Technology Transfer and its Set of Principles on Restrictive Business

Practices have been marginalised by developed countries who do not want to see them come into effect.

Economic localisation would give governments the leverage to hold TNCs to account by encouraging countries or regional groupings of countries to adopt 'site here to sell here' policies for manufacturing and services, which would make access to a given market dependent on a company being based in that country or regional grouping of countries. Under this policy, an inventory of imports would be drawn up with a view to identifying those goods and services that should be produced within the domestic market area. Over a transitional period, incentives would be offered to producers to set up within the domestic market. These incentives would vary in detail, but could include a mixture of direct government subsidies and import tariffs placed on the selected goods. The aim would be that by the end of the transitional period, local producers would dominate the domestic market for the selected goods.

The principle of trade subsidiarity states that distance between production and consumption should be as short as reasonably possible. Clearly then, in accordance with this principle, the size of the 'domestic' market area adopting 'site here to sell here' policies for a particular good would vary depending on the type of good and the size of the potential market. Thus, market areas for goods and services that are relatively easy to produce, such as staple food crops, should be the most localised. Goods that depend on highly capital-intensive production, such as cars and computer chips, could in principle also be manufactured on a very localised basis, but in practice this would be highly inefficient and their 'domestic' market area would therefore need to be larger, perhaps even the size of the EU. Market areas for these products would initially need to be larger still in regions where market volumes are relatively low, for example, computers in Africa. Nevertheless, production standards should ensure that the repair and recycling and, in some cases, elements of the assembly of these products can take place on a more localised basis. There are some products that simply cannot be produced in certain localities, such as tropical food crops. For obvious reasons, these should be excluded from the import substitution programme and traded according to fair trade principles. An additional consideration is that it would be less energy-efficient to transport some mineral resources that are extracted in relatively few locations to producers scattered around the world than it would be to distribute their end products to a number of far-flung markets; bauxite and aluminium provide examples. Locating processing near to the few points of extraction might therefore be the best option in these cases, a decision that will be aided once the environmental costs of transport have been internalised (see the next section of this chapter 'Taxes for localisation').

This programme would reduce the leverage of TNCs' threats to relocate when higher social or environmental standards are proposed. TNCs would no longer be able to play the trump card of international competitiveness as an excuse not to be bound by better working, environmental or tax regimes, giving governments greater power to regulate TNCs' activities and to ensure that their presence benefits the local economy. Governments would also be able to insist that companies meet higher labour standards and levels of transparency, for example, by producing rigorous annual reports on the social and environmental impact of their activities. In a speech to the Confederation of British Industry (CBI) in October 2000, Tony Blair called on the UK's largest companies to voluntarily produce reports on their social and ethical performance by the end of 2001. Only 79 of the top 350 companies had met his request by that deadline.[17] Clearly voluntarism is not enough. With a few pioneering exceptions, TNCs have rarely accepted responsibility for the social and environmental impacts of their activities unless publicly shamed into doing so by NGOs. Under localisation, such exceptional campaign successes would become the rule.

There would be drawbacks to the 'site here to sell here' approach if it were introduced inappropriately and in isolation from the other elements of the localisation agenda. Producers would be relatively insulated from competition; prices might rise, and choice and innovation might decline. However, this simply serves to emphasise the interactive and mutually reinforcing nature of the localisation agenda. As the other parts of this section demonstrate, under economic localisation, local competition policies would be reinforced to prevent monopolies and cartels forming; weakening IPRs would spur local innovation; environmental taxation would remove the hidden subsidies that many products currently enjoy, and a more progressive tax and benefit regime would help to offset the effect of any price increases.

Taxes for localisation

By reducing the power of the TNCs and making investors, producers and consumers much more directly accountable to each other, the policies already outlined will help to create sustainable local economies. However, this shift will be given extra impetus by an overhaul of taxation that internalises the hidden costs of the current production and distribution systems.

Energy derived from fossil fuels should be taxed in proportion to the carbon content of the fuel used and aviation fuel's exemption from excise duty should be ended. The use of other polluting resources should also be taxed and 'Eco-taxes' should replace value-added tax (VAT) or sales taxes. The level of Eco-tax levied on any product should reflect the health and environmental impacts of its full life cycle. These taxes could be introduced at relatively low rates, but be increased steadily according to a pre-arranged timetable, as suggested in von Weizsäcker's Ecological Tax Reform proposal.[18] This would provide powerful incentives for technological improvements in energy and resource efficiency. Crucially, it would also reflect the environmental impacts of transport more directly in its cost, which would help to localise patterns of production and consumption and cut down on the unnecessary transportation of goods that could be produced nearer to the point of consumption. Developing countries that are currently dependent on exporting rare mineral resources would experience an additional benefit. Typically, they retain only a very small proportion of the value of the raw material, with the bulk of the benefit of its exploitation going to the more industrialised countries where the value-added processing takes place. If transport were properly priced, areas near to the point of extraction of a mineral resource would become more favourable as locations for its industrial processing, as raw materials are normally considerably bulkier and heavier than the products that are derived from them.

Ecological taxes have the potential to raise a great deal of revenue, but their aim is to curb pollution so the revenue they generate should decline over time. This means they will be an ideal way of funding any transitional costs involved in introducing localisation. However, research has predicted that they would yield lasting economic benefits beyond their obvious environmental effects, particularly if their introduction is matched by a reduction of taxes on employment. One study modelled the effect on the UK economy from 1997 to 2005 of introducing a package of ecological taxes and using the revenues to reduce taxes on employers (that is, National Insurance Contributions). This reduced all the main sources of waste and pollution by 10–20 per cent and generated 700,000 new jobs.[19]

There are two potential pitfalls that must be avoided when introducing ecological taxes. First, indirect taxes have a relatively greater impact on poorer people. For example, a tax on domestic energy levied at a uniform rate will consume a greater proportion of the income of a poor household than that of a rich household. The same is true for any system of indirect taxation, such as VAT or sales taxes, but this causes a particular problem when the tax is levied on a basic commodity such as domestic heating. There are several ways of avoiding this problem. Households could be granted a basic allowance of domestic energy tax-free, for example, or a means-tested benefit could be introduced, funded from ecological tax revenues, to offset the regressive effect of Ecological Tax Reform. The problem will disappear as more sustainable, and therefore lightly taxed, alternatives to fossil fuel energy become readily available. Governments can help to bring this about by switching their subsidies from the fossil fuel economy to the new green industries.

Second, imports from economies that impose lower levels of ecological taxes will unfairly undercut the price of domestically produced goods. As discussed below, international trade rules should be amended to allow countries, or regional groupings of states, to impose import tariffs to prevent this, providing they accept the terms of a Green Marshall Plan as described in the next section but one.

Rewriting the rules

Under localisation, international trade will continue, but only when it provides for the most efficient distribution of goods after all external costs have been internalised and does not undermine the diversity and resilience of the traders' local economies. Similarly, FDI will in some cases have a role to play in the transition towards sustainable and self-reliant local economies. In other words, goods and money will still move around the world. Therefore, the need for the agreement and enforcement of international rules to govern these movements will be as great as ever, but the current rules must be rewritten so that their end goal is to rebuild diverse and sustainable national and regional economies everywhere. Existing WTO rules must be radically overhauled so that they incorporate the goal of economic localisation and permit the introduction of the policies outlined in the rest of this chapter. A leading localisation campaigner, Colin Hines, has suggested one set of reforms to the key provisions of the 1994 version of GATT and other trade agreements that together make up the rules of the WTO.[20] Taken together, these reforms would create a General Agreement of Sustainable Trade (GAST). They are summarised in Table 5.1.

Table 5.1 Creating a General Agreement of Sustainable Trade

	Current rule	Amended under GAST rules to:
GATT Article I Most-Favoured Nation (MFN) Treatment	The MFN rule requires WTO members to treat products from all other members equally favourably. Discriminating between foreign producers is prohibited. This rule threatens trade-related environmental conventions (for example, the Montreal protocol, CITES and the Basle Convention), which require less favourable treatment of countries that fail to meet their obligations under these conventions. The MFN rule also prohibits special trading relationships that support development programmes in poorer nations, such as the EU's former preferential tariffs for bananas produced by African, Caribbean and Pacific (ACP) countries.	*Provided it is not at the expense of domestic goods and services, states shall give preferential treatment to goods and services from other states which respect human rights, treat workers fairly and protect animal welfare and the environment.*
GATT Article III National Treatment	The National Treatment rule requires that imported and locally produced goods be treated equally. Thus, under WTO rules, it is unlawful for governments to favour domestic products above imported goods.	*Trade controls that increase local employment with decent wages, enhance protection of the environment, and otherwise improve the quality of life are encouraged. States are urged to give favourable treatment to domestic products and services which best further these goals.*
GATT Article III Process and Production Methods	The rule on Process and Production Methods (PPMs) makes it unlawful to discriminate against goods because of concerns about the damaging or unethical processes that may have been used to produce them. This makes it impossible to protect domestic producers with high environmental or animal welfare standards (for example, producers of free-range eggs) from unfair competi-	*Members are permitted and encouraged to make distinctions between products on the basis of the way they have been produced in order to further the aims of sustainable development.*

Table 5.1 *continued*

	Current rule	Amended under GAST rules to:
	tion from imports produced with lower standards (for example, producers of eggs from battery cages).	
GATT Article XI Elimination of Quantitative Restrictions	This Article prohibits quantitative controls on exports or imports through quotas or bans. This can create serious environmental and social problems, for example, when a country wants to place an export ban on unprocessed resources like timber, or an embargo against the export of agricultural commodities when suffering food shortages, or a prohibition against trade in endangered species, or a ban on the export of hazardous wastes to less developed countries.	*Quantitative restrictions should be permissible. For those products which are imported, preferential access should be given to goods and services going to and coming from other states which, in the process of production, provision and trading, respect human rights, treat workers fairly and protect animal welfare and the environment.*
GATT Article XX General Exceptions to WTO Rules	In theory, this allows the adoption or enforcement of measures to protect public morals, to protect human, animal and plant life or health, or the conservation of finite natural resources that would otherwise contravene WTO rules, provided they are not arbitrary or unjustifiably restrictive. In practice, it has been interpreted extremely narrowly, and has failed to offer the protection it promises. With only one exception, the WTO has struck down every single domestic environmental, health, or safety law that it has reviewed as an illegal trade barrier.	*Article XX exemptions should allow trade interventions for a wide range of purposes that further sustainable development, for example, sanctions against human rights violations; tariffs for the maintenance of environmental, food, health and animal welfare standards, and enforcement of treaties on environment and labour rights.*
The Agreement on Technical Barriers to Trade (TBT)	In international trade law, all environmental standards and regulations are, prima facie, considered technical barriers	*All international environmental and social standards and regulations are considered as effectively creating a floor*

80 Green Alternatives to Globalisation

Table 5.1 continued

	Current rule	Amended under GAST rules to:
	to trade. The TBT agreement is detailed and complex, but reduced to bare bones, it establishes: • An international regime for harmonising environmental standards that effectively creates a ceiling – but no floor – for environmental regulation • A detailed procedural code for establishing new laws and regulations that would be difficult for even the wealthiest nations to meet. The TBT rules have emerged as important new weapons for challenging government regulatory initiatives at the WTO.	*for governing the conditions for trade between parties. Any country with higher levels should experience positive discrimination in terms of trade. Poorer countries for whom such standards are at present too expensive should receive financial support to help them improve their standards, and once they have set a future date for such improvements, should experience positive discrimination in trade terms.*
The Agreement on Sanitary and Phytosanitary Standards (SPS)	The SPS agreement is very similar to the TBT, but deals with food and food safety issues including pesticides and biotechnology. Like the TBT, the SPS has been used to roll back regulatory initiatives that are unpopular with large corporations. The text of the SPS appears to permit the use of the precautionary principle, but WTO rulings have not recognised this principle as a justifiable basis for regulatory controls (for example, the ruling against the EU ban on the import of beef produced with growth hormones). The SPS Agreement also seeks to delegate 19 decisions about health, food and safety from national governments to international standard-setting bodies such as the Codex Alimentarius – an elite club of Geneva-based	*All laws and regulations that concern food and food safety, including pesticide regulation and biotechnology, are considered as effectively creating a floor for governing the conditions for trade between parties. Any country with higher levels should experience positive discrimination in terms of trade. Poorer countries for whom such standards are at present too expensive should receive financial support to help them improve their standards, and once setting a future date for such improvements, should experience positive discrimination in trade terms. The 'precautionary principle' is a justifiable basis upon*

Economic Localisation 81

Table 5.1 *continued*

	Current rule	Amended under GAST rules to:
	scientists. Codex is inaccessible to all but a handful of TNCs and business associations capable of maintaining delegations in Geneva. Codex standards often fall substantially short of those established by jurisdictions closer and more responsive to the interests and views of consumers and health advocates.	*which to establish regulatory controls affecting trade when the risks warrant action, even in the face of scientific uncertainty about the extent and nature of potential impacts.*
The Agreement on Trade-Related Intellectual Property Rights (TRIPs)	TRIPs subjects an entire domain of domestic law to WTO regulation. It compels all WTO members to adopt and implement patent-protection regimes, virtually providing US and European TNCs with WTO-enforceable global patent rights. The common rights of indigenous communities to genetic and biological resources are ignored. This facilitates the appropriation of the genetic commons by corporate interests, which can then demand user rents from the communities who are the rightful 'owners' of the genetic resource.	*Global patenting rights should not override the rights of indigenous communities to genetic and biological resources that are held in common. For products, fees should be able to be levied to cover the cost of development, plus a reasonable level of profit, but such patenting rights must have a limited timeframe and fully reimburse the parties whose knowledge contributed to the patented entity. Patents on life are prohibited.*
The Agreement on Trade-Related Investment Measures (TRIMs)	TRIMs set rules for investment in the production of global goods and services. This investor-rights agenda is based on the same principles as NT and MFN rules that are common to all WTO Agreements, but goes much further in two critical ways. First, it gives individual investors the same rights as nation states by allowing them to seek enforcement directly against nation states. Secondly, under the heading 'Performance Requirements' domestic investment regulation	*No individual investor may invoke international enforcement mechanisms against investment regulations of nation states. The implementation of domestic investment regulations shall not be constrained by trade rules, provided that the former improve social and environmental regulations domestically.*

Table 5.1 continued

	Current rule	Amended under GAST rules to:
	is constrained, even when applied only to domestic investors.	
The Agreement on Agriculture (AOA)	The vision expressed by this WTO Agreement is of an integrated global agricultural economy in which all countries produce specialised agricultural commodities, and increasingly supply their food needs by shopping in the global marketplace. Protective barriers to foster indigenous farming, for example, are not allowed; neither are subsidies to support poorer farmers.	*Protective barriers should be introduced to enable countries to reach maximum self-sufficiency in food, where feasible, with long-distance trade limited to food not available in the country or region.*
General Agreement on Trade in Services	See Box 2.1	See Box 2.1

A key element of the GAST is that trade will be regulated by fair trade rules similar to those that are currently adopted voluntarily within the fair trade movement to guarantee decent wages, working conditions, environmental standards and fair prices for producers and consumers. One way of enforcing such rules would be for a successor to the WTO (see Chapter 8) to withdraw the international trading licence of any company that is found to have breached the rules.[21]

A Green Marshall Plan

Many trade theorists parade their belief in trickle-down economics by arguing that international trade is the best, or in the extreme, the only means of redistributing wealth between nations.[22] They thus regard elements of localisation as unjust, inasmuch as they would reduce the opportunities for poor countries to export to rich countries: rich areas that undertook localisation would remain rich, while poor areas would remain poor. To prevent this injustice arising, localisation must demonstrate that trade is not the only means of transferring resources from rich to poor countries. In other words, the developed world must radically reorient its approach to development aid and debt so that sufficient resources are transferred to the South to give it the opportunity to create the resilient, self-reliant local economies that will lift its people out of poverty.

Since the mid-1980s, aid to the South has been dwarfed by the costs of debt servicing. By the end of 1999, when the landmark Jubilee 2000 campaign reached its climax, for every £1 received in aid, £9 was repaid in debt service. Even the debt charges to the very poorest countries matched aid pound for pound. Repeated pledges have been made to increase aid, notably at the 1992 Rio Earth Summit; rarely have they been kept. OECD aid in 1992 totalled $61bn, in 1993 it fell to $56bn and it has continued to decline since then.[23] In 2000, development aid was just 0.39 per cent of donor countries' GNP. Only Denmark, the Netherlands, Norway, Sweden and Luxembourg exceeded the UN target of 0.7 per cent of GNP.[24] Subsequent international meetings, such as the Monterrey Conference on Financing for Development and the Johannesburg Summit on Sustainable Development, both held in 2002, have produced plenty of rhetoric on the need for greater international effort to eradicate poverty, but little by way of new concrete proposals.

Pledges on debt have met with a similar degree of success. The 52 poorest countries owe well in excess of $300bn of unpayable debt. Despite an unprecedented wave of public protest under the Jubilee 2000 banner at the turn of the millennium, just $30bn has been cancelled. Only half of that total is covered by the Highly Indebted Poor Countries (HIPC) initiative, which was adopted by the IMF and the World Bank in 1996 to provide a 'lasting exit' from unsustainable debt burdens for the world's poorest countries. The G7 nations have committed themselves to cancel a further $33bn once the debtor nations have reached 'completion point' by satisfying the World Bank and IMF they have complied with the prescribed Poverty Reduction and Growth Facility (PRGF). PRGFs have replaced SAPs and are a slight improvement in that they insist on poverty reduction as a condition of debt relief, but like SAPs they impose deflationary, austerity-driven economic reforms and orientate HIPC countries' economies towards export markets. In return, the first 22 HIPC countries to reach Completion Point can expect no more than an average 48 per cent reduction in their debt service payments between 2001 and 2005 and, according to Jubilee Research, all of them will still carry unsustainable debt burdens.[25]

This situation is an outrage, not only because it denies hundreds of millions of people access to basic necessities such as clean water, primary health care and basic education, but also because the 'debt' the South owes shrinks into total insignificance when compared with the indebtedness of the North. For centuries the North has expropriated resources and labour from the South and it continues to accumulate a huge 'ecological debt'. The North consumes far more than its fair share of the earth's resources, and causes far more pollution and environmental degradation per head of population than the South.

It is not easy to put a price on global environmental goods, but some facts are clear. According to the reinsurance giant Munich Re, the number of climate-related 'hydro-meteorological' disasters quadrupled during the 1990s compared to the 1960s. During the same period, economic losses associated with such disasters increased eight-fold. The financial services initiative of UNEP estimates that the extra economic costs of disasters attributable to climate change are running at over $300bn annually and will cost developing countries up to £6.5 trillion in the next 20 years.[26] The industrialised world is overwhelmingly responsible for climate change, yet 96 per cent of all deaths caused by natural disasters attributed to global warming occur in developing countries.[27] Another way of assessing the North's debt to the South involves calculating a per capita greenhouse gas budget, based on a sustainable level of global emissions. Industrialised countries emit more than the combined per capita budgets of their population and 62 times more per person than the least developed countries. In a typical year in the 1990s, the value of the G7 economic output based on this carbon debt has been calculated to be in the region of $13–15 trillion. At the same time the indebted poor countries had a carbon credit that could be valued at three times their conventionally calculated foreign debts.[28]

The concept of 'third world' debt must be turned on its head. The North must fund a UN-sponsored Green Marshall Plan as rapidly as possible to repay its debt and rescue the developing nations from the economic and ecological calamity it has inflicted on them.

The cancellation of conventional 'third world' debt would be the starting point for the Green Marshall Plan. Not only would this free debtor countries to devote more resources to essential public services, but crucially, it would also reduce their need for foreign exchange earnings and allow them to diversify their economies away from over-reliance on export markets. In the interim for as long as conventional debt remains, poor debtor states should be free to restrict debt servicing to 10 per cent of their annual export earnings and spread payments over longer periods at fixed interest rates. UN-classified 'middle income' states, which do not qualify for relief under the HIPC initiative, should be able to make payments in their own currency, so reducing their reliance on volatile export markets.

A bankruptcy procedure should be introduced as a back-up, allowing countries to hold their creditors at bay should their debts become unmanageable. The additional risks this would present to lenders would help to discipline their behaviour. In the past, lenders often lured debtor nations into accepting unmanageable loans to fund unsuitable projects. Typically they did this either for political motives, such as buying allegiance to the West in the Cold War, or because they ignored the potential impact of events beyond debtors' control, such as external economic shocks and large-scale natural disasters. In other cases, the rulers of debtor countries were corrupt enough not to need to be lured, but accepted the loans willingly for personal gain.

Traditionally, the argument against sovereign nation bankruptcy is that it would deny debtor nations access to global finance because lenders would fight shy of debtors with poor track records, but recent evidence does not support this view. In 1998, Russia defaulted on its debts amid dire warnings that it would become the pariah of the markets. But free of the burden of debt, devaluation made its exports competitive, and rising oil prices earned it valuable revenue. Within three years, it was able to borrow again and capital started to flow back into the country. Once Russia began to look profitable, the markets quickly forgot its past; they wanted a piece of the action. Frequently, when countries should be given space to rebuild their economy to meet local needs behind the protective barrier of bankruptcy, they are forced instead to accept emergency bail-outs from the IMF. More often than not this extra money goes straight to the rich Western lenders at the head of the queue of creditors, or sustains exchange rates at an artificially high level, giving the rich an extra window of opportunity to get their money out of the country. In the longer term, the bail-outs add to the debt burden.

Even the IMF has begun to take the idea of bankruptcy seriously, but true to form it proposes to adopt the role of judge, jury and executioner, giving itself the right to grant or deny bankruptcy or a standstill on debt, and to design the restructuring requirements that would be imposed as a condition of its agreement. Given that the IMF is a major creditor, its conditions would inevitably be unbalanced in favour of the creditors rather than the debtors.

ead the insolvency procedure must be conducted by an *ad hoc* under the aegis of the UN.²⁹ The panel should include one ~sentative each of the creditors and the debtor nation together th an independent 'judge', jointly appointed by the other two .embers. The procedure should be based on Chapter 9 of the US :riminal code, which applies to states, cities and other public bodies, rather than Chapter 11 that applies to companies. Crucially, Chapter 9 not only gives taxpayers and employees a right to be consulted about the bankruptcy arrangements, but also a veto on any plan that emerges. Chapter 9 insolvency plans are only considered feasible if the debtor emerges from the reorganisation with reasonable prospects of financial stability and economic viability, and US law ensures that creditors cannot prevent municipalities from delivering vital services – something which debtor nations have been prevented from doing all too frequently, and with dire consequences.

Debt cancellation would merely stop the ongoing and unjust extraction of wealth from the South; it does nothing to make reparations for the North's historic exploitation of the South. Thus, a second element of the Green Marshall Plan would involve a dramatic increase in development aid as a transitional measure to help poor countries develop the diverse local economies that will be their engines of future sustainable development. It would be all too easy to argue that increased aid from the rich world 'would merely trap the poor nations in patronage, dependency and blackmail' and that 'their people would neither respect themselves nor expect to be respected by outsiders',³⁰ but to do so lets the North off an enormous hook scot-free. The transfer of resources from North to South under the Green Marshall Plan would not be regarded as charity, but as rightful compensation borne of the North's overwhelming moral obligation to the South.

Nevertheless, safeguards must be provided against the dangers of patronage and dependency. Under the terms of the UN Green Marshall Plan, payments would made according to an agreed and time-limited timetable and would be targeted on projects that would help to reduce the need for aid in the future by eradicating poverty and establishing greater local self-reliance. Projects should be planned and led by the local community and should aim in particular to boost local food and energy security and make basic health care, education and family planning universally available. There is no place for tied aid-for-trade deals or the funding of damaging large-scale projects, such as large dams and nuclear power stations.

As a third element of the Plan, the North should transfer to developing countries free or at least at-cost, the knowledge, IPRs and environmentally sound technologies they need to create sustainable local, national and regional economies.

Finally, a robust emissions-trading scheme should be introduced as part of a new international treaty to cut greenhouse gas emissions, based on the Contraction and Convergence (C&C) model. Under the C&C model each country would be allocated the same per capita allowance for greenhouse gas emissions. The per capita allowance would be reduced over time so that total global emissions would contract to an environmentally sustainable level. Initially, industrialised countries would vastly exceed their total budget. For example, the US hosts approximately 4 per cent of the world's population, yet produces a quarter of global greenhouse gas emissions. The C&C model sets a time limit for countries to converge on the per capita allowance and permits them, within limits, to complete the element of convergence that they cannot achieve through technological innovation and energy conservation by purchasing surplus emissions budget from other countries. Thus, given the 1990s estimate of the value of the industrialised countries' annual output that was dependent on emissions in excess of their budget ($13–15 trillion), very substantial sums of money would flow to the least developed countries with the greatest emissions budget surpluses.[31]

It is hard to imagine that the North would adopt the substantial obligations contained in the Green Marshall Plan voluntarily. For this reason, the ability of a developed country to adopt the trade- and investment-related localisation measures that would restrict access to its markets, such as the 'site here to sell here' provisions or import tariffs and quotas, should be conditional on its compliance with the terms of the Green Marshall Plan. Similarly, payments to the South under the plan would be conditional on recipient countries honouring their commitments under international agreements to respect human rights, protect the environment and eliminate corruption.

Democracy for localisation

Many of the failings of economic globalisation stem from the fact that the global market it is creating completely outstrips the reach of any meaningfully democratic structures that might regulate it. From those who regard this as a problem comes a variety of responses. At one end of the spectrum reformist critics of globalisation argue that since economic globalisation is inevitable, we should direct our efforts not at reversing it, but at ensuring that democratic globalisation keeps pace with it; reform will only be possible once the global institutions that regulate the global economy are fully democratic. All effort should therefore be directed towards that end. The argument at the other end of the spectrum is that nothing short of complete autarky, a retreat into total and isolated local self-sufficiency, will serve as an adequate defence against the democratic deficit that exists at the international level.

In his recent book, *The Age of Consent,* George Monbiot assesses the merits of two approaches that lie close to the ends of the spectrum in the following terms:

> In the absence of an effective global politics ... local solutions will always be undermined by communities of interest which do not share our vision. We might, for example, manage to persuade the people of the street in which we live to give up their cars in the hope of preventing climate change, but unless everyone, in all communities, either shares our politics or is bound by the same rules, we simply open new road space into which the neighbouring communities can expand.[32]

This line of reasoning draws Monbiot to the political globalisation end of the spectrum and the conclusion that, 'by first rebuilding the global politics, we establish the political space in which our local alternatives can flourish.' Accordingly, he proposes to remedy the democratic deficit that lies at the heart of the global institutions largely by relying on the 'moral authority' of a new, democratically elected, world parliament to call them to account. In a similar vein, the fairness of trade and the good conduct of private corporations are to be guaranteed at the global level through the agency of a Fair Trade Organisation.

Proposals that world trade rules should be fair and that global institutions should be genuinely democratic are not new and, naturally, we agree with them. However, it would in our view be both unnecessarily restrictive and slightly naïve to believe that action at the global level alone will be rapid and successful enough to justify postponing local action until after that success.

Action at the local level will of course be reinforced if it is supported by global agreements. Nevertheless, to return to the enlightened car-free residents, given sufficient democratic empowerment at the local level their street need not simply become new road space for the neighbouring communities to occupy. The residents could, for example, persuade their local council to close their street to through-traffic and turn it into a homezone, creating space for children to play and trees to grow. Of course, one car-free street will not prevent climate change, but the children who live in it will have more fun and less asthma, the residents will gain a pleasant shared space in which to get to know each other and their local shops and bus services will benefit. Crucially, it will set an inspiring example for others to follow – one that might even spread sufficiently for the rate of growth of transport-related greenhouse gas emissions to be slowed in advance of the global treaty that finally combats climate change. It would be unduly restrictive to prevent the residents from reclaiming their street until after that treaty had been ratified.

Equally, to rely on creating truly democratic global institutions as the only defence against the injustices of economic globalisation demonstrates extraordinarily courageous optimism in the face of all available experience. It relies on the assumption that there is nothing inherent in the nature of global negotiations and the institutions they create to dictate that they should have been so comprehensively captured by the dominant economic interests – it has just turned out that way so far, and could equally turn out different in the future. This assumption might be valid, but it is not one we would choose to make. Such is the diversity of human society and the global environment on which it depends that truly representative democracy, let alone the participative variety, can only work very imperfectly at a global level. It is therefore no accident, for example, that the one-size-fits-all rules of the IMF and WTO ride roughshod over the world's intricate pattern of cultural and economic variations, just as thoroughly as the economic activities they propagate trample its fragile ecosystems.

George Monbiot's proposal for a global parliament illustrates the difficulties of operating democratically at the global level. Rightly, he suggests that people, rather than states should be represented in the parliament, which should not become too large to operate efficiently. The world is therefore to be divided into 600 constituencies, each containing 10 million voters who elect a single member of the parliament. Two problems immediately become apparent. First, one person cannot accurately represent the diversity of opinions and interests of 10 million people and, second, the 600 members of the parliament would be easy targets for corporate lobbyists. These problems do not rule out the proposal, but they certainly caution against expecting too much of it.

Nevertheless, Monbiot has high hopes for the influence the parliament would have over the global institutions and world leaders. He asserts: 'We have every reason to believe that, if properly constituted, our parliament, as the only body with a claim to represent the people of the world, would force them to respond.'[33] Regrettably, recent history does not bear out such optimism. The European Parliament, for example, is the only body that can claim to represent the people of the European Union, yet it hardly has a distinguished track record of 'forcing' European leaders to respond in those areas of EU policy where it has only its moral authority to rely on.

Localisation therefore draws some inspiration from both ends of the spectrum. Autarky is rarely advanced with any seriousness; it ceased to be a realistic option many centuries ago. But achieving greater self-determination by relying less on markets over which one has little control is a central goal of economic localisation. Equally, localisation contends that democratising the global institutions is indeed urgent and necessary, but there is much that could be done more locally to right the wrongs of economic globalisation in advance of the dawning of the age of perfect global democracy.

This is not an argument against maintaining a multilateral approach to international trade or for abandoning any attempt to improve the democratic health of global society (Chapters 8 and 11 deal with some of these issues). Advocates of economic localisation do not advocate withdrawal from the international stage, but they do recognise that, no matter how much it is improved, global society will never reflect the full diversity of its component parts as successfully as national or local society. Global democracy should therefore only be relied upon to solve those problems that cannot be better resolved more locally, such as the equitable allocation of the right to emit greenhouse gases. Except in a small minority of cases, the fair distribution of goods is not one such problem. There are only a very few goods, such as climate-specific agricultural products and rare mineral resources, that can only be sourced from a few geographically specific locations. Thus, a major advantage of economic localisation is that it will shift the balance of economic control towards a level where democratic institutions enjoy greater prospects of imposing socially and environmentally sensitive regulations on the market. It would also allow economic blocs such as the EU, which are powerful enough to stand up to the corporate interests that drive globalisation, to take the lead in progressing such regulations in advance of global consensus.

However, for the shift towards more diverse local economies to be effective and equitable, local democratic involvement must be increased to keep pace with the reinvigorated power of the local economy. Localisation must avoid replicating the democratic deficit that lies at the heart of globalisation. There is no precise prescription for increasing democratic involvement. Each community and society has a different starting point and this will determine what needs to be done, but there are two glaringly obvious disincentives to democratic involvement in the UK and the US.

First, elections in these two great 'democracies' do not produce the right results. In the US presidential election in 2000 the winning candidate, George W. Bush received half a million fewer votes than his Democrat opponent, Al Gore. The UK general elections in 1951 and in February 1974 similarly managed to award more seats to the party that came second in the popular vote. Whilst it is relatively uncommon for 'losers' in UK and US elections to win, the winners rarely deserve the full spoils of victory that are heaped on them. The UK general election of 2001 provides a typical example. Tony Blair's Labour Party received a minority of the votes cast (40.7 per cent), but won a large majority of the seats in the House of Commons (62.5 per cent). Thanks to the first-past-the-post voting systems used in the UK and the US, the same systematic distortions of the democratic will are repeated in local elections.

Apart from routinely handing undiluted executive power to parties that achieve only minority support, the first-past-the-post electoral system forces the major parties to compete for the votes of the same narrow band of centre-ground swing voters. It also effectively denies minority voices political representation. This can only be achieved when a party can muster more votes than any other in one particular area. Altogether, this is a recipe for a stultifying and unrepresentative political consensus that alienates its critics and only responds to new challenges clumsily and tardily. It is just such a consensus that has depressed voter turnout, allowed neoliberalism in the Anglo-Saxon model to flourish, denied its critics access to parliaments and driven them onto the streets. Proportional voting systems must be introduced if economic localisation is to be introduced first to the mainstream political debate, and subsequently as a series of agreed and well-planned policy initiatives.

A second problem for democratic involvement in both the US and Britain is that political parties are heavily reliant on private corporate donations and, as outlined earlier, these large donations have frequently been associated with related policy changes. If the views of people, rather than corporations, are to be decisive in shaping local economies, political parties must be funded primarily by public money and in proportion to the support they receive at elections.

Aside from reforms to the political system, there are steps that could be taken to give individuals and local communities more direct power in the running of their local economies. One such is to introduce a Citizen's Income (CI). This is a non-means-tested payment to every citizen, working or not, set at a level to cover basic needs without removing all motivation to take paid employment which, in its full form, would replace state pensions, tax-free allowances and all benefits. CI aims to abolish the poverty trap and free people to choose the type of work and hours they want as their circumstances change. CI thus stands to increase the power of individuals in the labour market, but also to help build cohesive and resilient communities by providing a basic wage for carers and community volunteers, who currently go unpaid.

The proposal remains controversial because it would be expensive to introduce the full form of CI that replaces all benefits. However, some years ago the eminent economist Meghnad Desai provided a costed example of a partial CI scheme for the UK.[34] He based his model on the levels of income and benefits that were current in 1997, which now seem rather meagre, but his calculations serve to illustrate the principle of CI. His proposed scheme provided a CI of £50 per week to every citizen, with a non-means tested supplements up to the Minimum Income Guarantee (£62.50 per week at the time) for people aged 65 and above. The proposed CI replaced job-seekers' allowance (unemployment benefit), income support, family credit and state pensions. Housing, disability and council tax benefits, which depend directly on the personal circumstances of entitled individuals, were not replaced by the CI and were still to be claimed separately. Desai showed that his proposal could be funded by raising the basic rate of income tax from 23 per cent to 35 per cent. Because much of this tax increase would be offset by CI payments to those in work, only the richest 30 per cent of households would be less well off by an average of less than 4 per cent, whereas poorer households would gain considerably (see Figure 5.1). Desai's proposals would help to reverse some of the recent growth in income inequality, and their redistributive effect could be enhanced if the CI scheme was funded by raising the basic rate of income tax by a smaller amount and increasing the higher rate to make up the difference.

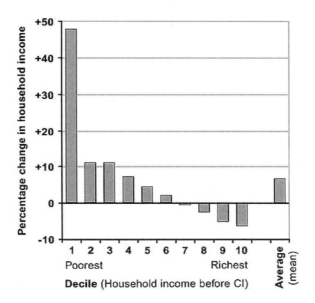

Figure 5.1 Percentage change in household income under Desai's CI proposal

Source: Desai, M. (1998), 'A basic income proposal', Paper 4 in *The State of the Future*, London: Social Market Foundation.

Another means of vastly increasing democratic control over local economies would be to introduce a tax on the value of land, the most basic commodities of all local economies. A land value tax (LVT) would be at a fixed percentage of a site's value. One study has suggested if set at 4 per cent a LVT in the US could generate enough revenue to replace all other forms of taxation.[35] Given the power to vary the level at which the tax is set according to the economic, social and environmental desirability of different land uses in their locality, local councils and the communities they represent would gain a significant influence over the local economy.

Protecting innovation

In the relatively protected environment that localisation will create, it would be easier for producers, left unchecked, to establish monopolies, cartels or corrupt, patronage-based networks of production and distribution. This could reduce the choice and quality of products available, inflate prices and lead to wasteful production methods, as sometimes occurred both under the Soviet-style economies and the 'crony capitalism' of some newly industrialised countries (NICs). To avoid this, localising economies will need to introduce tough local competition policies and offer incentives to new market entrants.

International treaties to ease the transfer of technology and information would also ensure that localisation's reduction in international competition would not result in a loss of innovation. Indeed, localisation will reduce the profit companies can expect from the global exploitation of their intellectual property. This will have two very important effects. First, companies are likely to reduce their R&D effort. Although this might initially appear to be a 'bad thing', it will place the onus for research funding more firmly on governments, resulting in research that is driven more by public interest than potential profit and greater public ownership of the outcomes.

Second, TNCs will fight less hard to retain IPRs when they have less to gain from them. Currently, TNCs are fiercely resistant to any erosion of IPRs and have promoted the TRIPs agreement to prevent this. As we have already seen, TRIPs is blocking the transfer to developing countries of beneficial technologies, such as drugs to treat AIDS and replacements for CFCs, and preventing the emergence of domestic industries that could exploit them. Some IPR protection is necessary to provide an incentive for innovation, but the balance is currently tilted too far in favour of private corporations against the public good.

Import and export controls

The policies already outlined in this chapter will go a long way to ensure that international trade rediscovers its original purpose of providing for the equitable exchange of 'exotic' goods, and no longer undermines local economies, harms the poor nor destroys the environment. For example, eco-taxes will reduce wasteful long-distance trade and 'site here to sell here' policies will produce incentives for the diversification of local economies. However, countries that set out to gain a competitive advantage by adopting lower social and environmental standards could undermine these policies. There are two ways around this problem. The first would be to do nothing until the higher standards can be agreed and applied globally. The second is to allow different regions of the world or groupings of countries to move towards economic localisation as quickly as they want. To achieve this, localising economies must be permitted to negotiate the introduction of safeguards, such as import tariffs and quotas, to protect the enhanced standards they wish to adopt from exports that are subsidised by the maintenance of lower standards in the exporting countries. Quotas will be particularly important in cases where tariff systems fail to reflect fully the varying external costs imposed by different producers. Similarly, the effort to diversify the local economy would be undermined if too much reliance were placed on export markets. To guard against this possibility, localising economies should end export subsidies and introduce export tariffs and quotas.

These proposals of course constitute very great heresy in the current era of free trade orthodoxy. Critics are swift to label them 'anti-trade' or 'protectionist' and assert that they would return international trade relations to the state that precipitated the Depression of the 1930s. Moreover, their argument continues, quotas and tariffs would deny developing countries the access to Northern markets they need to lift them out of poverty. We tackle these arguments head-on towards the end of this chapter, but for the moment and specifically in relation to import and export controls there are three points to make.

First, under economic localisation, the introduction of tariffs and quotas would be phased and whenever possible, negotiated internationally – just as is their removal currently under the WTO. This will be important not only to give 'home' producers time to reorient to the domestic market, but also to build international confidence in the collaborative, rather than competitive, nature of localisation. Localisation aims to protect many social and environmental assets that currently bear the brunt of globalisation's external costs, but it is not protectionist in the traditional sense.

Second, as part of the overall localisation agenda, the introduction of import quotas and tariffs would be conditional on the compliance with a UN-sponsored Green Marshall Plan, as detailed above. Not only would this combat poverty and improve economic security in the South, it would benefit the rich nations by helping to build a more genuinely secure world.

Third, the hypocrisy of the developed world, which currently preaches free trade but maintains extensive systems of export subsidies and selectively impedes imports from the South, must be countered by a commitment to fair trade principles. Fair trade does not, however, automatically imply more trade. International trade rules are vital and should always be fair, but we must expose for what it is, the intellectually craven and engrained assumption that rules can only work in one direction: to liberalise trade. The creation of vibrant and sustainable local economies requires rules that *reduce* international trade to a fairly traded exchange of those goods that should not be produced more locally once all external costs have been internalised.

The proposal for a 'Development Box' in the WTO's Agreement on Agriculture is an example of one such rule. This idea, put forward by a group of least developed countries (LDCs), would allow poor countries to restrict imports that would otherwise compete with, and unfairly undermine the production of locally produced staple crops. This would protect the livelihoods of their small farmers and improve their local food security by increasing domestic food production for local consumption (see Chapter 9).

Within the framework of economic localisation, the tariffs and quotas needed to regulate trade would not be perceived as a narrow, protectionist measures. Rather they would be seen as elements of an internationalist project designed to help all parts of the world achieve greater food security and self-reliance and to replace market-dependence with resilient and socially responsive local economies.

DRIVING REFORM

Economic localisation requires substantial reform. Even though Seattle forced reform onto the agenda, localisation might seem far-fetched, heretical even, when looked at as a whole. However, it involves no more than the bringing together of a series of individual reforms under a single banner, each of them a logical response to the failings of globalisation. Packaging the reforms together and giving them a name will help to drive the process of reform in at least three ways. First, the label 'economic localisation' makes sense of the reforms and emphasises their mutually reinforcing effect. Second, it gives the anti-globalisation movement something to be in favour of, and a much-needed focus for its diverse demands. Third, it provides a timely challenge to the many reformist critics for globalisation who see it as a force for good that simply needs a bit more of a 'human face'. Localisation provides a stick to prod them into following through the logic of their argument and 'come out' as full-blown opponents of economic globalisation.

In short, economic localisation provides a rallying point and a foundation for a constructive opposition to economic globalisation. The alternative is to appease the globalisation agenda that is set by and serves corporate interests. In turn, those interests simply use appeasers to reinforce the impression that economic globalisation, like gravity, is inevitable. We believe the struggle between democracy and corporate power will be the defining battle of the twenty-first century. If the corporate interests win, liberal democracy will come to an end. Appeasement cannot be an option. Globalisation must be replaced, and localisation provides a coherent and rigorous alternative.

SOME QUESTIONS ANSWERED: A DEFENSIVE CODA

Some of the most hard-hitting analyses of localisation have come from reformist critics of economic globalisation who have concluded that increased international trade presents the best route out of poverty for developing countries or, in the extreme, the 'only possible means' of 'distributing wealth between nations'.[36] Their argument is that poor countries are currently prevented from deriving the full benefit of international trade because it is conducted on the North's unfair terms. Their main priority is therefore to gain fair market access for exports from the South by dismantling the systems of trade barriers and export subsidies that the North maintains against them. One recent major report on the subject calculated that the poor world receives 32 times as much revenue from exports as it receives in aid, and that a 5 per cent increase in market share for exports from the developing countries would yield an extra $350bn a year, seven times the annual aid budget.[37] Its authors argued: 'World trade has the potential to act as a powerful motor for the reduction of poverty, as well as for economic growth, but that potential is being lost. The problem is not that international trade is inherently opposed to the needs and interests of the poor, but that the rules that govern it are rigged in favour of the rich.'[38]

From this perspective, localisation's suggestion that international trade be minimised would appear to trap poor countries in their destitution by denying market access to their exports. This has provoked some strong criticisms of localisation. George Monbiot has denounced it as 'coercive, destructive and unjust'.[39] His alternative is for all countries, once they have attained a certain level of development behind protective infant industry barriers, to be forced to compete in the global marketplace under a set of fair but free trade rules.

Another prominent critic of localisation claimed:

> ... 'radical' localisers see trade as an automatic route to rising poverty. Their prescription: a retreat into autarchy, with countries closing their markets and shifting from international to local trade ... Making common cause with protectionist lobbies and right-wing populists to exclude poor countries from rich country markets in the interests of 'self-reliance' is a prescription for mass poverty and inequality ... Exports could provide poor countries and producers with access to larger markets, creating opportunities for income, employment and investment. In East Asia, export dynamism has helped lift 400 million people out of poverty since the mid-1970s.[40]

These are superficially persuasive arguments. If international trade promises so much to poor countries, why should anything be allowed to impede it? The question demands a thorough response. However, before we present that response it will help to clarify the scope of the debate. Despite denouncing localisation as a whole, those who hold this reformist line on globalisation actually share much common ground with the localisation agenda. They tend to argue that environmental costs should be internalised wherever possible, thus disadvantaging long-distance trade, and that poor countries be allowed to protect their infant industries. They echo localisation's commitment to fair trade principles. Currently exports from developing countries meet higher barriers than those from the North. Advocates of localisation are therefore at one with the reformist critics of globalisation when they argue that market access between the North and South must, as a matter of principle, be fair, although fairness and liberalisation should not be mistaken as the same objective. The particular points of contention are the existence of alternatives to trade as means of distributing wealth between nations, the likely benefits of export-led growth for poor countries and the suggestion that under localisation rich countries (as well as poor) be permitted to discriminate in favour of local products and investment. We will deal with them in turn.

There is an alternative

First, as we pointed out earlier, trade is not the only means of distributing wealth between nations. Our proposed requirement that rich countries subscribe to the terms of a UN-backed Green Marshall Plan before being allowed to adopt the protective measures of localisation would ensure North-to-South transfers of wealth to dwarf the potential earnings from trade. This fact alone removes much, if not all, of the force of the accusation that localisation is unjust.

Exporting false expectations

Any remaining force evaporates when the 'benefits' of export-led growth are considered more closely. The first thing that can be said is that developing countries' real export earnings are likely to be disappointing when compared with projections that ignore a range of hidden costs. In most developing countries, production for export is more intensive than production for local consumption. It typically benefits big middlemen and TNCs rather than small local producers who are more likely to reinvest profit in the local economy, and diverts resources away from meeting local need. The habitat destruction that accompanies hardwood production is one dramatic example of the hidden costs that can be imposed by export production; another is provided by the leading Indian anti-globalisation researcher and campaigner, Vandana Shiva. She has calculated that for every dollar earned in meat exports, India destroys sustainable ecological functions worth $15, which would otherwise be performed by farm animals. Cattle manure is used in India as organic fertiliser and a source of renewable energy, services that are destroyed when animals are killed for the export meat trade. To replace them, farmers are left to import chemical fertilisers and fossil fuels, thus increasing foreign exchange outflow and climate change.[41]

Moreover, the more dependent a developing country becomes on exports, the more exposed it will be to competition for access to the newly opened Northern markets from other Southern exporters, as happened when the IMF and the World Bank forced developing countries to export the same narrow range of commodities in the past. Understandably, poorly paid workers in the South will welcome increased export opportunities if that is all that is offered to them, but what will happen to those workers if they are undercut by another exporter?

China is predicted to capture between 50 per cent and 100 per cent of world textile exports, undercutting the poorly paid women who work in Bangladesh's garment factories. When Canada removed cotton T-shirts from quota restrictions in 1997, China gained 95 per cent of its market – at the expense of Bangladesh and other developing-country textile manufacturers.[42] China is also threatening to undercut India's software exports and organic tea production in Sri Lanka. This might sound good for workers in China at least, but their meagre livelihoods, typically around $2 a day, are not secured without cost.

China's push for a market economy began in rural areas in the late 1970s, but in the 1990s, rural incomes stagnated and a third of the rural workforce is now unemployed or underemployed. An estimated 100 million rural Chinese have migrated to urban areas to find work; often they must work illegally and suffer appalling conditions. The migrant workers complain of harsh and arbitrary treatment by the authorities and face the continual threat of forced relocation. Their presence in the urban areas has caused tensions as at least 20 million urban Chinese have been laid off from state-owned industries.[43] As the case of China illustrates, the prizes for winning the race to the bargain basement of the global economy will dwindle as more Southern exporters are forced to join it. Even if the level of the basement of the global free trade model were to be raised through the introduction of fair trade rules, production would still concentrate in those places that were prepared to maintain standards that are no higher than that level.

A further danger of relying on export-led growth is that a country must increasingly entrust the well-being of its economy to TNCs, inward investors and volatile markets over which it has little control. In the midst of the Asian crisis, Waldon Bello, a leading Southern commentator on globalisation, summarised these dangers as follows:

> While export markets are important, they are too volatile to serve as reliable engines of growth. Development must be reoriented around the domestic market as the principal locomotive of growth. Together with the pitfalls of excessive reliance on foreign capital, the lessons of the crisis include the tremendous dependence on export markets of the region's economies. This has led to extreme vulnerability to the vagaries of the global market and sparked the current self-defeating race to export one's way out of the crisis through competitive devaluation of the currency. This move is but the latest and most desperate manifestation of the panacea of export-oriented development.[44]

Infant industry protection for grown-ups

George Monbiot deploys a powerful argument in favour of infant industry protection:

> This policy ... reduces the need to attract foreign investment in order to stimulate domestic industry. Foreign companies have been deemed necessary to a nation's development only because, unlike the country's own infant industries, they can compete successfully with other transnational firms, and because intellectual property rights have ensured that the only way to acquire certain technologies is to import the companies which control them. If poor nations are permitted, through protectionism and technology transfer, to develop their own competitive industries, they abandon the need to open their doors to companies which insist on repatriating their profits, importing more than they export and demanding lower labour and environmental standards. If nations do not need to attract foreign corporations, they can close the 'export processing zones' in which unions are banned, pollution controls are abandoned and foreigners need pay no taxes.[45]

However, these benefits are not to be extended to richer countries. As countries prosper, Monbiot proposes that they should 'be obliged to start to liberalize their economies to the same degree as the countries with which they had caught up', thus 'slowly [pushing] the world towards free trade'.[46] In other words, countries that already are or become rich are to be denied the rights enjoyed by poor countries to protect and redirect their own economies to meet local needs. The justification for this one-sided protectionism is based on the false premise that trade is the only means of combating poverty and the misapprehension that export-led growth is a more effective development strategy than localisation. Its results will be that just as soon as a country becomes rich enough to be 'obliged' to liberalise, the cruel wind of free trade is likely to sweep away the many benefits that it had previously been permitted to protect. Chief amongst these will be the jobs of workers whose employers relocate or whose products are undercut by cheaper imports, and on whose support the transformation of the global trade system depends.

Those of us who seek to establish an equitable global trade regime are likely to enjoy far greater success by appealing instead to the enlightened self-interest of people in rich and poor countries alike. The deal is this: in exchange for signing up to the Green Marshall Plan and foregoing some export opportunities, people everywhere would gain the security of being able to protect their local economies and direct them to meet local needs, in line with the aims of localisation. International trade could then return to its original role of facilitating the exchange of 'exotics' or goods that it does not make sense to produce more locally after all regulations and external costs, including the cost of losing economic control, have been taken into account.

Is localisation protectionist?

Protectionism, in the traditional sense, is the erection of trade barriers to provide a particular industry or country a respite from competition, often whilst simultaneously and aggressively attempting to open up rival economies. The fear surrounding protectionism is that it gives an unfair competitive advantage to the protected industries and is likely to lead to retaliatory action from other countries and a vicious circle of increasing barriers and decreasing trade.

The conventional view of the 1930s Depression is that it was caused by just such an outbreak of protectionism. However, a recent study of the relevant archives and diplomatic correspondence challenges this view. The study revealed that the tariffs raised in the run-up to the 1930s – which were not very high – caused little retaliation between countries. It makes the case that the depression was so deep because the *laissez-faire* ideology of the time prevented governments from pumping adequate counter-cyclical public expenditure into their economies to overcome the decline in consumer expenditure. The study concludes that only the Second World War eventually provided sufficient demand to pull the world's economy out of depression.[47]

Nevertheless, there is a very real fear that unconstrained, retaliatory nationalism will dominate trading relationships and generate wider conflict, unless safeguarded against. This danger certainly argues in favour of regulating international trade with a consensually agreed and fairly applied set of rules, but it is not automatically an argument for maximising trade.

Another reason why it is politically incorrect to promote measures that might, to the undiscerning eye, look like old-style protectionism, is that the rich world currently preaches free trade, but practices protectionism. Products from poor countries face tariffs in industrialised countries four times higher than those imposed on products from rich nations, and subsidised agricultural exports from the West are routinely dumped on developing countries, undermining their agricultural sectors. This is clearly unfair and unsustainable – and is far removed from our own proposals.

Kevin Watkins accuses 'localisers' of protectionism, yet in the same (typographical) breath argues: 'Prohibitions on environmentally damaging exports, taxes on aviation fuels and haulage, and incentives for energy-efficient technologies all have a role to play ... [in ensuring that] market prices reflect real environmental costs.'[48]

And that is the point entirely. The range of non-tariff barriers to trade for which he argues, many of which would both localise trade and fall foul of WTO rules, have at their heart the intent to protect the environment. They are, in a new sense, protectionist barriers to damaging trade.

There are many goods worth protecting that are assigned no value in neoliberal thinking: the rich, 'inefficient' way of life in peasant communities; the right to mould the local economy to particular local conditions without having to gain agreement at the WTO; the benefits of 'inflexible' labour markets, such as minimum wages, paid holidays, pensions and union recognition; hard-won environmental and health regulations, and the economic and social resilience of a robust and diverse local economy. Localisation simply aims to restore to people and communities around the world the power, within an internationally agreed framework, to decide for themselves the value they wish to attach to these goods and to regulate trade accordingly. Localisation reclaims the word 'protect'. As Herman Daly writes:

> We would be willing to accept the label of protectionist if it were understood that what we want to protect are efficient national policies of cost internalisation, health insurance and safety standards and a reasonable minimum standard of living for citizens. Historically these benefits have come from national policies, not from global economic integration. Protecting these hard won social gains from blind standards-lowering competition in the global market is what we are interested in – not the protection of some inefficient entrepreneur who wants to grow mangoes in Sweden.[49]

Section 3
Turning the Tide

There is a group of people on the receiving end of every impact of economic globalisation. By spelling out the connection between their immediate problems and the forces that are causing them, demands for radical change can be sparked in surprising places. By helping people to see that that which causes their problem lies also at the root of grievances of other groups with whom they might not normally identify, we can start to build a powerful coalition for change.

If history makes one thing clear it is that the WTO and Bretton Woods institutions, left to their own devices, will not even begin to produce meaningful reform from within. What is required amounts to a revolution from without. Our strategies for revolution must evolve continuously in response to the experience they generate. Of necessity, the path we suggest taking to the post-revolutionary settlement has been charted in advance of most of that experience, but we offer it with a Spanish proverb in mind: 'Traveller, there is no path; paths are made by walking.'

Section 3
Turning the Tide

6
Connecting Hearts and Minds

> The collapse of the global market place would be a traumatic event with unimaginable consequences. Yet I find it easier to imagine than the continuation of the present regime.
>
> George Soros[1]

SHOPPING AROUND FOR A POLITICAL STRATEGY

So strong is the tidal wave propelling globalisation, that standing in its path to argue for localisation can feel a bit like a Canute-style exercise in noble eccentricity. So, how can localisation be brought about? Certainly, others who have surveyed the scene have concluded that globalisation has closed down all other political options. Noreena Hertz concludes her recent acclaimed and oddly shaped book *The Silent Takeover* thus: 'As citizens we must make it clear to governments that unless politics focuses on people as well as business, unless government's love affair with big corporations ends, unless politicians offer us a product worth buying, we will continue to scorn representative democracy, and will choose to shop and protest rather than vote.'[2]

She has a point. People are losing interest in electoral politics – the turnout in the 2001 UK general election hit a record low of just 59 per cent, compared with 71 per cent in 1997. Barely half the electorate voted in the Bush–Gore US election even though the result was predicted to be tight. And protesting has been very much in vogue. An estimated three million people took part in anti-globalisation protests around the world in the two years following Seattle and millions more marched against the war in Iraq. Shopping is even more popular; retail sales stand at a record levels, and shoppers are making increasingly 'political' choices at the check out. Sales of organic food in Europe and the US are expected to grow by 10–20 per cent in the next few years[3] and UK sales of fairly traded products increased nine-fold between 1996 and 2001.[4]

In the face of ever-growing corporate power, consumer pressure will have a growing role to play in persuading companies to adopt fairer and cleaner production practices. However, whilst this can complement a political campaign for stronger regulation of companies, it cannot replace it.

Likewise, the enormous protests in Genoa, and before that Gothenburg, Nice, Prague and Seattle, were hugely successful in putting anti-globalisation issues, which otherwise would have scarcely featured in the media at all, into the sitting rooms of millions of homes around the world. However, on their own, protests are not enough. They are essential, but insufficient. They brilliantly demonstrate opposition, but are much less effective at articulating proposition. That is now the urgent challenge.

It is easy to be carried along with the fashionable view that elections make no difference, and to share in the anger and impatience with a political system that fails to respond to ordinary people's concerns, but as Green politicians, we cannot agree with the implication that shopping and protesting are somehow enough of a response. Power certainly has been handed away from politicians to TNCs on an unprecedented scale, and companies now have extraordinary strength and influence, sometimes far more than governments, but the political crisis of confidence this has generated cannot be allowed to become a self-fulfilling signal of the death of democracy. It must instead be the furnace for a new politics, with a new leadership and a new vision. Indeed, the need for strong local and national government, as well as for democratic regional and global governance is greater now than ever if we are to address the growing social and environmental challenges that we face.

The protesters seem instinctively to agree that the political process must regain control of the critical levers of decision making, however disappointing its record may have been to date. Why else have most of the largest demonstrations been outside meetings of politicians – at the WTO, the World Bank, and the G8? The protesters realise that the 'inevitable' forces of economic globalisation have in fact been painstakingly negotiated and deliberately unleashed by a series of political decisions. There is nothing inevitable about the way power is shifting. It is the logical consequence of deliberate choices, and as such, it can be changed. The current crop of neoliberal consensus politicians is unwilling to admit this; and it is their unwillingness that creates a political vacuum that the Greens are committed to filling.

PAVED WITH GOOD INTENTIONS

It is not as if the political establishment is unaware of the multiple crises of economic globalisation. If it were, its craven adherence to the corporate agenda – which is all the more extraordinary in the light of the Enron and related scandals – would be more understandable. Instead, it is engaging in all sorts of displacement activity, perhaps to ease the cognitive dissonance created by its self-imposed impotence in the face of corporate power. When what is required is economic localisation's fundamental reorientation of the trade, investment and finance rules by which the world is run, we are presented with more summits and declarations, with their unenforceable aspirations and compacts. And when, as in the case of Kyoto, it looks like it might get serious, the US ducks out anyway.

Typically, complaints that attempts at reform are too gradual and too weak raise sympathetic smiles from people who prefer steady boats, and assurances that it is better to work for achievable change from within, than to make unrealistic demands for fundamental reform from without. Of course, this is not a new dilemma; every radical throughout the ages has faced it, but in this debate the grounds for rocking the boat could not be stronger. First, it is not obvious that the reformers within are doing more good than harm. In urging a further WTO round so that some of the more manifest injustices can be addressed, for example, reformers run the risk of subjecting developing countries to more damaging liberalisation in return for nothing more than another round of broken promises. This has certainly been the fate of previous WTO concessions to the poorer nations.[5] Second, there are few if any examples of a few complicit reformers working within the system effecting fundamental change of the seismic proportions that is now required. The Berlin Wall did not fall, apartheid was not lifted, nor National Socialism defeated because everyone agreed to keep his or her head down and work within the system. Active and determined opposition from without was crucial even if, at first, such opposition appeared doomed to fail.

EMPIRES IMPLODING

When it occurs, change can be dramatic. Once-invincible empires have a habit of imploding rapidly when the rulers lose their psychological hold over their subjects. Globalisation's psychological grip is already loosening. In response to the East Asian crisis, many local academics and activists began to argue for a rejection of further trade and investment liberalisation. Instead they proposed a different model of sustainable development within 'regionalised' economies, based primarily on import substitution, and investment of domestic public capital, raised through progressive taxation, rather than growing dependence on volatile export markets.[6]

There are two more trade shocks coming, again, both also Asian in origin, which will help to loosen globalisation's grip yet further.

First, China's recent membership of the WTO will accelerate its expansion into the domestic and foreign markets of its developing world competitors, with disastrous results for those concerned. The American commentator, William Greider, has updated the mid-1990s US presidential candidate Ross Perot's warning of the 'giant sucking sound' of American jobs going to Mexico. He points out today that it is now China sucking away Mexico's jobs as well as those of Taiwan, Thailand and others. With Chinese wages at 20–25 cents an hour compared with $1.50 for Mexico, the big three motor manufacturers are moving car component production to China not just from the US, but also from Mexico.[7]

A second shock to the globalisation process will come from the world's biggest democracy, India. In 2000, a WTO ruling in a case on Quantitative Restrictions brought by the US forced India to remove import barriers. Farm prices and rural incomes are falling dramatically as a result of this imposed import liberalisation. Prices of coconuts have fallen 80 per cent, coffee prices have collapsed by over 60 per cent, pepper prices have fallen 45 per cent. The most dramatic effect is on edible oil. India's domestic production has effectively been wiped out as highly subsidised soya from the US and palm oil from Malaysia flood the market, due to low import duties. Imports now account for 70 per cent of the domestic consumption.[8] Import competition is ruining India's cottage industries, as well as her medium and large-scale industries. Worst of all, agriculture, the last bastion of India's national economy and the livelihood of the majority of its people, is facing unprecedented threats. The response from Indian academics and activists alike has been to call for the reintroduction of import controls, thus challenging the very lynchpin of the globalisation process. In September 2001, two former Indian prime ministers joined with political parties, trade unions, farmers' organisations, and other activists to launch the Indian People's Movement against the WTO. The British Empire could not survive the loss of India; it would raise serious questions over the future of the imperial Washington Consensus should their campaign succeed.

DAMAGE LIMITATION

There is always a danger of chaos and pain at the point of implosion. As Waldon Bello puts it: 'The new economic order is unlikely to be imposed from above in Keynesian technocratic style, but is likely to be forged in social and political struggles. This fire down below is likely to upset the best laid plans of the tiny elite that are trying to salvage an increasingly unstable free-market order by tinkering at the margins of the global financial order and calling it reform.'[9]

Nevertheless, the extent of the fire damage can be limited if there is a well-worked out and widely supported replacement for the old order waiting in the wings, together with a route map for reaching it. Economic localisation is the alternative, but the questions remain, does it enjoy widespread support and do we have the map to get us there? We will answer them in reverse order.

THE ROUTE TO THE LOCAL

The whole of localisation is constituted from many parts. Even though the sum of these parts is less than the whole, they can be introduced individually. This is a great advantage since it means that localisation can be introduced piecemeal, by exploiting openings as and when they arise, a process that is already under way. Indeed, virtually all the central planks of economic localisation can be found in operation or being planned somewhere in the world today.

In a 1996 survey, the New Economics Foundation (NEF) estimated that 1.5 million people in the UK regularly take part in 'community economic action', a variety of initiatives including development trusts, local community enterprises, organic vegetable box-schemes, credit unions, LETS schemes and self-build housing projects.[10] These are the basic building blocks of the sustainable local economy and they are already playing a significant role is some areas. The NEF survey reported that the 170 community enterprises in Scotland had a combined turnover of £18 million and supported 3,300 jobs and training placements. A re-emergence of interest in mutual companies saw the sector grow by 9 per cent in the UK in 2001,[11] and in the same year around the world 112 million people were members of local credit unions with access to assets worth $606bn.[12] In 1999, local employment bonds were issued in Sheffield. The bonds raised £786,000 from local businesses and individuals, which, together with matched funds from the EU, was used to offer low-cost loans to new local businesses and projects. Bonds issued by the New York Metropolitan Transportation Authority have financed extensive upgrading of the New York subway and bus system. These initiatives show that capital can be raised whilst avoiding the 'race to the bottom' for international investment funds.

The need for stricter controls on corporations has been recognised in some quarters. The California state treasurer's office, which controls $45bn of state and local funds, has published a list of 23 companies that it will not do business with because they have relocated their headquarters to a PO Box in off-shore tax havens. It has also called on two massive California public pension funds to withdraw $750m of investments from them.[13] In the wake of the Enron scandal, the US adopted tighter accounting and anti-fraud regulations, and even took some steps to regulate campaign donations to political parties.

Some attempts are being made to internalise environmental costs. The German government has made a start on eco-tax reform and the UK's Climate Change Levy is a small nod in the same direction. In March 2003, following years of negotiation, the EU adopted a comprehensive system of energy taxation, but with rates fixed at derisory levels until at least 2013.

The HIPC initiative, though vastly inadequate, is an admission on the part of the industrialised world that it must do more to help the poorest countries. A similar admission underpinned the US decision in 2001 to drop its complaint against South African legislation that enabled access to cheaper AIDS drugs. The US had argued that the South Africans were infringing the IPRs of US-based pharmaceutical TNCs, and has since reverted to that stance in the continuing negotiations around TRIPs.

Although these exceptions to the prevailing tide of economic globalisation are notable for their rarity, they provide the precedents – the starting points – on the map of the journey to localisation.

Unexpected quarters

We have the beginnings of a map for the reforms that are needed; we also have a growing chorus of voices urging us along the way. It is not too surprising that some of the economic journalists writing for the UK's left-leaning *Guardian* newspaper should have charted part of the route to localisation. Less expected though, are some of their travelling companions: one of the world's leading speculative investors, a former chief economist of the World Bank and a top adviser to the UK Chancellor of the Exchequer. The surprise might be greatest for these last three individuals themselves, since they all support economic globalisation, with varying degrees of qualification. Nevertheless, George Soros, Joe Stiglitz and Ed Balls demonstrate that the central tenets of localisation enjoy considerable support amongst perfectly respectable people who would probably get a little nervous if accused of supporting economic localisation as a whole, if not of being fellow travellers with *Guardian* writers Larry Elliott and Dan Atkinson.

In his latest book, Soros writes: 'Economic theory has shown that – other things being equal – international trade benefits all parties. In practice, other things are rarely equal.'[14] He goes on to propose a wide-ranging package of localisation-style reforms to make 'things' more equal. This approach is echoed by our other champions of economic localisation, witting and unwitting alike. They all support reforms and intervention to reduce the instability of international financial markets, including tighter controls on capital movements. Though Stiglitz is cautious about a Tobin tax on currency speculation,[15] and Balls appears to rule it out,[16] Soros would extend it to cover all forms of international financial transaction. Elliott and Atkinson would go further to tame the flows of private capital by increasing the reserve requirements on commercial banks.[17]

Stiglitz and Soros seek higher levels of international aid, together with bankruptcy procedures and standstills of debt repayment to allow countries to escape unpayable debt. The rules of the WTO come in for particular scrutiny. Soros suggests amendments to the TRIMs agreement to allow for localisation-style protection of domestic small and medium-sized enterprises (SMEs), particularly in developing countries. More widely, he argues that the provisions of other multilateral agencies, such as the ILO, should carry the same weight as those of the WTO, allowing trade sanctions to be imposed on countries that fail to meet their labour or environmental obligations.[18] Stiglitz believes that the balance of TRIPs is tipped too far in the direction of commercial producers, and that developed countries should not wait for the conclusion of the Doha round to strike up a fairer trading relationship with developing countries.

Even if these significant reforms were suggested as props to shore up globalisation, their effect would be to prod the global economy firmly in the direction of localisation.

JOINING THE DOTS

It seems everything is in place: an alternative, a map to reach it, influential voices (unintentionally) urging us on, so why have so few people yet to seize the vision of localisation? It is as if the fragments of the argument do not join up in their minds. No matter how many of globalisation's injustices they list, or reforms they suggest, they cannot step back from the canvas far enough to see that the dots marring their image of globalisation in fact describe the outline of a new picture that must be painted over the old. We must get them to join the dots, or in the famous words of E.M. Forster, 'only connect'.[19]

In today's globalising world, Greens need to help people see their own experiences within the global context, to make the connections between them, and to see how those links might be changed. For example, in the autumn of 2000, we tried to highlight the connections between the devastating floods in Kent and other parts of the UK, and the changing weather patterns caused by global warming, and then connect those to the fuel protests that preceded the floods by little more than a month. The protests were against the price of petrol, which was perceived as too high. Pickets prevented tankers leaving oil refineries and for about a week fuel supplies became scarce. During that week people drove slowly to conserve fuel. They even planned their journeys carefully, using local services more and only used their cars when absolutely necessary. This is precisely the sort of behaviour that would have helped to reduce the risk of flooding in the first place and highlights a set of hugely important connections that most people, as well as the government, simply failed to make. Once made, connections like this act as a powerful driver of change.

People will make the firmest connections when the message starts with what they already know. Perhaps there is no greater example of the impact of globalisation than the global food trade. Many people are aware of the loss of choice, for example, of different apple and pear varieties following the destruction of orchards and the increasing reliance on imports that is associated with the increasing industrialisation of agriculture. It is a short step to link this with the increased levels of food poisoning, of agricultural crises like BSE and the death of traditional food retailers at the hands of a few dominant supermarkets. All these trends point to the increasing industrialisation of our food production systems and the drive for ever-greater international competitiveness in international food markets. This, in turn, is bound up with the decline of rural communities in both developed and developing parts of the world. In short, the problems are all linked by the underlying forces of economic globalisation.

There are many ways in which globalisation impacts on the lives of 'ordinary' people: when competition from multinational out-of-town superstores closes local shops, when jobs disappear to cheaper labour in a poorer country, and when those workers in turn lose their job to an even cheaper location – when Yorkshire's last cloth cap producer moves to China. Globalisation is the death of small farms both in the developed and developing worlds that can no longer compete with global competition. It is the downward spiral of labour, environmental and health and safety standards worldwide. Globalisation is when poor people in developing countries grow food to export to the rich countries, rather than for their own people. And globalisation is when the UK exports 263,000 tonnes of milk and cream, and imports 203,000 tonnes of someone else's milk and cream in the same year (see Chapter 9 for more details of international trade in food).

There is a group of people on the receiving end of every impact of economic globalisation. By spelling out the connection between their immediate problems and the forces that are causing them, demands for radical change can be sparked in surprising places. By helping people to see that that which causes their problem lies also at the root of grievances of other groups with whom they might not normally identify, we can start to build a powerful coalition for change. Once people can see the connections between their concerns and the wider picture, and know that they share the wider picture with millions of others, they can begin to believe that their contribution will make a difference.

Senator Robert Kennedy visited students in South Africa in 1966, at a time when it seemed as though apartheid would never ever be overthrown. He said:

> You can make a difference. Each time a man or a woman stands up for an ideal, acts to improve the lot of others, or strikes out against injustice, he or she sends forth a tiny ripple of hope. And crossing each other from a million different centres of energy and daring, those ripples can create a current, which can sweep down the mightiest walls of oppression and resistance.[20]

History proved Kennedy right and if, by only connecting, people can be inspired to know the power of their own involvement, of their ability to make a difference, and of the necessity of challenging policies, both at the ballot box and on the streets, they will create another historic current: one that will turn the tide towards economic localisation.

7
Learning From History

> Expansion of the free trade mandate and ... the power and jurisdiction of the WTO ... is a mortal threat to development, social justice and equity, and the environment. And it is the goal that we must thwart at all costs, for we might as well kiss goodbye to sustainable development, social justice, equity, and the environment if the big trading powers and their corporate elites have their way and launch another global round for liberalization during the WTO's 5th Ministerial Assembly in Mexico in 2003.
>
> Professor Walden Bello,
> Executive Director of Focus on the Global South[1]

INSTITUTIONAL REFORM: SMOKESCREEN OR REALITY?

The chaos of the Seattle Ministerial prompted a bout of soul-searching in high places. Statements demanding reform became *de rigueur*. Charlene Barshefsky, the US trade representative at Seattle announced: 'the WTO has outgrown the processes appropriate to an earlier time.'[2] The EU trade commissioner's verdict was that the WTO's processes were 'medieval'.[3] Stephen Byers, the then UK secretary of state for trade and industry, went a little further when addressing the Commonwealth trade ministers. His verdict was that the 'WTO will not be able to continue in its present form. There has to be fundamental and radical change in order for it to meet the needs and aspirations of all 134 of its members.'[4] Shortly before Seattle, a similar crisis of confidence hit the IMF and at the annual World Bank-IMF meeting in September 1999, the Fund made an unexpected announcement that, henceforth 'poverty reduction' would be at the centre of its approach toward developing countries.

Talk of reform has prompted some cosmetic changes. The trade round initiated at the first post-Seattle WTO Ministerial in Doha, Qatar was dubbed the 'Development Round', an acknowledgement that the poorer members of the WTO need to be seen to benefit more from its activities. World Bank and IMF rhetoric now encompasses poverty reduction and debt relief; IMF Structural Adjustment Programmes (SAPs) have been replaced by Poverty Reduction and Growth Facilities

(PRGFs). Nevertheless, there are clear signs that the changes are no more than skin deep. The IMF continues to pursue fiscal austerity, even in the midst of crises such as that which has engulfed Argentina, and together with the World Bank is even pressuring developing countries to privatise their pension schemes. Kamal Malhotra of the UNDP has said that it 'stretches both reality and imagination' to claim that the outcome of the Doha Ministerial was a development agenda.[5] The failure of the WTO Ministerial in Cancun in September 2003 demonstrated that the majority of developing countries shared Malhotra's verdict.

There is a yawning chasm between the scale of reform that is required and the business-as-usual reality that the recent reform-minded rhetoric struggles to disguise. This begs the tricky question of whether the existing institutions are actually capable of delivering the necessary changes. We are confronted with the classic 'reform from within or opposition from without' dilemma. We have some answers to this dilemma, but they are best understood within the context of the postwar history of the international regulation of trade and development. It is to this that we now turn.

RE-RIGHTING HISTORY – THE OUTLINE

The gradual emergence of the WTO–IMF–World Bank framework, or the Washington Consensus, is conventionally presented as the triumph of enlightened, rule-based free trade over benighted protectionism. To suggest anything more radical than incremental reform of this version of reality is to advocate anarchy and global 1930s-style depression. However, we subscribe to a different version of reality, which owes much to the work of Waldon Bello.[6] In this version, the emergence of the Washington Consensus was prompted far more by the North's desire to contain the legitimate aspirations of the developing world than its impulse to foster order in an anarchic world.

The postwar history of international trade and development is, in outline, a relatively simple tale. The war enfeebled the colonial masters and accelerated their loss of empire. The many newly independent developing states were for the first time able to band together at the UN where they enjoyed a majority of votes to press their demands for a fairer deal. The North, led by the US, reacted by undermining the UN's role in trade and development, investing it instead in the Bretton Woods institutions over which it had control. Once the Cold War was over, the US was free to pursue without distraction the goal of rigidly enforced liberalisation of markets in the South, and so the WTO emerged from GATT.

It is this interpretation of postwar history that makes best sense of the Bretton Woods institutions' evolution from their original function as guarantors of global liquidity and Keynesian counter-cyclical reflation to their current status as neo-imperialist agents of deflation and debt-slavery. It also explains the gradual emasculation of the UN. However, for anyone who finds this too much to swallow in one go, we fill in some of the detail in the next section.

RE-RIGHTING HISTORY – SOME DETAIL

Rapid decolonisation in the 1950s and 1960s gave birth to many newly independent developing nations that, from across the ideological divide of the Cold War, were drawn towards an agenda of rapid development and redistribution of wealth on a global scale. The most influential and effective version of this agenda was based on the work of the Argentine economist Raul Prebisch in the the late 1950s and early 1960s. Known as 'Structuralism', his theory provided the inspiration for many of the groupings of developing countries that sprang up in the 1960s and 1970s, such as the Non-Aligned Movement, the Organisation of Petroleum Exporting Countries (OPEC), the Group of 77, and the New International Economic Order (NIEO). It also provided critical momentum to the establishment in 1964 of UNCTAD with Prebisch as its first general secretary. For the following decade, UNCTAD was the primary vehicle for the South's relatively successful attempts to restructure the world economy.

The starting point for Structuralism was the prospect of worsening terms of trade between the industrialised and non-industrialised worlds as commodity prices declined. Left unchecked, Prebisch argued, this would lead to more and more raw materials and agricultural products from the South being required to purchase the same quantity of manufactured products from the North, and thus, in the words of one writer, the 'bloodless but inexorable exploitation'[7] of the developing world.

Structuralism gradually became the dominant viewpoint of the various UN agencies, including the General Assembly. Through the UN, and particularly UNCTAD, the developing countries set out a Structuralist programme of global reform aimed at improving the terms of trade they faced. The programme contained three principal elements: first, the stabilisation of commodity prices through negotiated price floors; and second, the encouragement of industrialisation in the South through a system of preferential tariffs for Southern exports of manufactured goods, and a correspondingly reduced dependence on agricultural and commodity markets. Finally, the programme required an expansion of foreign assistance to the South, not as charity but as 'compensation, a rebate to the Third World for the years of declining commodity purchasing power'.[8] UNCTAD also argued that industrialisation in the South should be promoted both by the accelerated transfer of technology from the North, and by allowing Southern countries to use selective protectionist measures against Northern exports.

The imperative of buying the allegiance of developing countries in the Cold War forced the North to make some concessions to the Structuralist agenda. The US tolerated its client states' adoption of protectionist trade policies, investment controls and interventionist government policies, even though it demanded access for its corporations. It was this environment that gave the Asian tiger economies space to undertake rapid industrialisation. The North also committed itself to a limited redistribution of wealth in the form of development aid. Despite this, the North also deliberately set out to undermine the South's growing influence in the UN by adapting the remit of the Bretton Woods institutions so that they came to dominate the arenas of international trade and development.

The Bretton Woods institutions were founded in 1944. Their original purpose had very little to do with relations between the North and South. The IMF was designed to maintain stable exchange rates by providing loans to member states with balance of payment problems. However, once the dollar was taken off the gold standard, this aim become redundant and the IMF increasingly turned its attention to structurally adjusting debtor nations.

The International Bank for Reconstruction and Development (IBRD), one of the two principal agencies of the World Bank, was established chiefly to assist with post-war reconstruction in Western Europe rather than to make loans to the developing world. However, when demands from the South for a UN-based development fund became too insistent to ignore, the World Bank invented a development role for itself by creating the International Development Agency (IDA). Another concession to the same demands was the establishment of the UN Special Fund, later renamed the UN Development Programme (UNDP), which channels advice and small sums of technical aid to developing countries. Through this compromise deal the North succeeded in retaining the lead role in development assistance for the institutions that it controlled, but it did not satisfy growing demands from developing countries for a redistribution of economic power. Thus UNCTAD was established in 1964, and OPEC was emboldened to grab control of oil prices in the early and mid-1970s. The high point for the South was the adoption of the NIEO programme at the UN General Assembly Special Session of 1974.

Though reformist rather than revolutionary, and serving the interests of the Third World elites rather than the masses, the South's agenda achieved enough to worry Washington. The North's search for effective countermeasures was given greater impetus as various revolutionary movements began to make headway in the South.

During the 1970s, the North responded to the newly assertive South by trying to co-opt its ruling elites. World Bank lending grew from $2.7bn in 1968 to $12bn in 1981. However, this apparent outbreak of largesse was a divide-and-rule tactic in which a few 'countries of concentration' received greater than average flows of assistance. The effectiveness of the World Bank's tactics was blunted by OPEC's success in forcing up the price of oil. By the mid-1970s, the commercial banks were awash with deposits from oil-producing countries and were eager lenders to other developing countries who consequently became less reliant on the World Bank. Meanwhile UNCTAD achieved some modest trade concessions, and Southern governments began to tighten up on foreign investment in order to protect their domestically owned industrial sectors.

The failure of liberal-led attempts to contain and co-opt the South was already provoking right-wing opinion in the US when OPEC's second oil shock hit in 1979. For them, this was proof of the South's intent to threaten the industrialised world using its near-monopoly over the supply of oil and possibly many other basic commodities as well.

The UN came to be seen as the main vehicle for the NIEO. Its activities, whether they were aimed at controlling the pharmaceutical industry, regulating TNCs, or subjecting the exploitation of the seabed, space or Antarctica to international treaties, were regarded as part of a Southern agenda to recapture resources from the North. Right-wing proponents of stronger action to curtail the South's ambitions could point to the 1973 Algiers Declaration of the Non-Aligned Movement for conclusive evidence. It stated: 'The Heads of State or Government recommend the establishment of effective solidarity organizations for the defense of the raw materials producing countries such as the

Organization of Petroleum Exporting Countries ... to recover natural resources and ensure increasingly substantial export earnings.'[9]

If, by 1981 when Reagan entered the White House, the ground was well prepared for a more determined assault on the South, the explosion of the debt crisis in the summer of 1982 provided the 'ideal' springboard for its economic recolonisation. By the late 1980s, more than seventy developing countries found themselves unable to manage their debts to the commercial banks and were forced to turn to the IMF and the World Bank, which by then insisted on Structural Adjustment as a condition of assistance. The enforced programmes of Structural Adjustment, ostensibly designed to create the conditions that would enable debtor countries to repay their debts, were a classic neoliberal mix of public spending cuts, privatisation, currency devaluation, and liberalisation of trade, investment and the labour market. Not only did this have predictably disastrous results for the majority of the populations of the affected countries, it also repatriated domestic control of national economies to the Washington-based Bretton Woods institutions, and radically reduced barriers to Northern investment and imports.

A few newly industrialised countries (NICs) in South and South-East Asia evaded the first phase of Structural Adjustment despite the fact that their economic systems mirrored many features of the adjusted countries. However, they tended to have stronger and less corrupt governments that pursued relatively inclusive development agendas. They were characterised by their successful attempts at domestic industrialisation, behind protective trade and investment barriers, and their assertive capture of market share in the North, and particularly in the United States.

The fact that the NICs were on the frontline of the Cold War ensured that Washington took a softer line with them than it did elsewhere. Moreover, Japanese capital provided them with sufficient insulation from the debt crisis to keep the IMF wolves from the door. Despite this, the US adopted an aggressive unilateralist stance aimed at liberalising the NICs. One US official summed up the US approach: 'Although the NICs may be regarded as tigers because they are strong, ferocious traders, the analogy has a darker side. Tigers live in the jungle, and by the law of the jungle. They are a shrinking population.'[10]

By the mid-1990s, US action had cajoled the key NICs into liberalising their capital accounts and, to some extent, their financial sectors. This liberalisation, together with the high interest rate and fixed currency regime that the local financial authorities maintained, attracted large amounts of foreign direct investment (FDI). It also provided the gaping plughole down which $100bn drained in the Asian crisis of 1997. Washington finally gained its opening for full Structural Adjustment of the NICs, an opportunity it exploited to the full by attaching stringent conditions to the IMF assistance that was offered to the crisis-hit economies. These conditions forced the NICs to remove many of their restrictions on FDI and protective barriers surrounding their domestic industries.

The US Trade Representative's verdict on the treatment meted out to Thailand was that its 'commitments to restructure public enterprises and accelerate privatization of certain key sectors – including energy, transportation, utilities, and communications – which will enhance market-driven competition and deregulation – [are expected] to create new business opportunities for US firms'.[11]

Regarding Indonesia, the US Trade Representative celebrated the fact that the IMF's conditions for assistance addressed:

> ... practices that have long been the subject of this [Clinton] Administration's bilateral trade policy ... Most notable in this respect is the commitment by Indonesia to eliminate the tax, tariff, and credit privileges provided to the national car project. Additionally, the IMF program seeks broad reform of Indonesian trade and investment policy, like the aircraft project, monopolies and domestic trade restrictive practices, that stifle competition by limiting access for foreign goods and services.[12]

The US car industry and Boeing had long been agitated by the national car project and Indonesia's plan to set up a passenger jet aircraft industry.

One of the most revealing summaries of Washington's strategy in response to the Asian crisis was provided when Clinton's then undersecretary of commerce, Jeff Garten said, 'Most of these countries are going through a dark and deep tunnel ... But on the other end there is going to be a significantly different Asia in which American firms have achieved a much deeper market penetration, much greater access.'[13]

UNPICKING PROGRESS

Alongside its strategy of deploying the IMF and World Bank to gain economic control of the South, the US has used its power as the UN's major contributor to dismantle the South's hard-won achievements within the institutions of the UN. The key UN institutions dealing with North–South relations, ECOSOC (UN Economic and Social Council), UNDP and the General Assembly, were purged of NIEO rhetoric. The UN Centre on Transnational Corporations, a scourge of TNCs operating in the South, was closed down and, perhaps most damaging of all, UNCTAD was effectively neutered. In 1992, it was denied any role in the ongoing GATT Uruguay Round negotiations that gave birth to the WTO on New Year's Day, 1995. UNCTAD still exists, but its role is limited to providing research and advice. It has been usurped by the WTO.

It would be a simplification too far to suggest that the sole motivation for the creation of the WTO was to complete the North's reassertion of dominance over the South, but it was an important factor. A similar body to the WTO, the International Trade Organisation (ITO), had originally been planned to come into being in 1948 as part of the Bretton Woods settlement, but the proposal was abandoned in favour of the much looser GATT after unilateralist forces in the US Senate threatened not to ratify the ITO proposal. By the mid-1980s, however, the US was facing stiffer competition from its major industrial competitors, Europe and Japan, as well as from the East Asian NICs. Additionally, Southern imports were making greater inroads into US markets than were US exports in the South. Thus, even though international trade was flourishing under GATT's regime, having increased 17-fold between 1948 and 1997,[14] the twin imperatives of regulating the trade rivalry of the industrialised countries, and preventing new competitors from emerging as serious players in the global economy persuaded the US that GATT had served its day. Domestic interests now demanded a body with teeth, and so the US took the lead in the Uruguay Round negotiations that gave birth to the WTO. The WTO's insistence on 'free trade über alles', as Ralph Nader has put it,[15] has since negated almost everything the South had achieved under UNCTAD.

IS DOHA ANY DIFFERENT?

If its name is to be believed, the WTO's 'Development Round' initiated in Doha will mark a turning point in the trade relationships between the North and South, but for many of us who observed the 2001 Ministerial at first hand, Doha was 'déjà vu all over again'.[16] Moreover, the collapse of the Cancun Ministerial in 2003 shows that the consensus reached at Doha was, as many of us said at the time, reluctant, forced and fragile.

Indeed, far from promoting a development agenda, many of the key points of the Doha Declaration directly undermine the interests of developing countries. For example, the declaration contained only a perfunctory acknowledgment of the need to review the 104 outstanding issues raised by the Group of 77 concerning the implementation of existing Uruguay Round agreements. This had been the key issue for many developing countries. Commitments to phase out agricultural subsidies in North were substantially weakened as a result of lobbying by some EU member states. The demand for a 'Development Box' to be attached to the Agreement on Agriculture (AOA), which would exempt countries from some WTO liberalisation rules in the interests of achieving food security, was ignored and other development objectives were simply sidelined. (For more on the 'Development Box', see Box 9.2) Moreover, the EU finally succeeded in including the issues of the liberalisation of competition and investment in the Declaration, which the vast majority of developing countries had wanted to keep off any future negotiating agenda.

But it is not the outcome alone which challenges the idea that Doha established a new 'development agenda'. It was the negotiating process itself. Even before government leaders reached Doha, there were many complaints from the South that issues of interest to them were not sufficiently reflected in the agenda for the Ministerial. As usual, the WTO's theoretical one-member-one-vote constitution notwithstanding, the agenda and outcome were largely fixed in informal gatherings in the corridors, with the EU, the US, Japan and Canada, 'the Quad', running the show. As one of us reported at the time, having witnessed the developed countries' high-handed negotiating tactics at first hand, poorer countries were 'arm-twisted and bullied into the starting blocks', and then subjected to 'immense pressure ... by the powerful trading nations who threatened to withdraw aid, among other things, in order to get their way. It was these backroom bruisings that finally forced developing country delegates into resentful acquiescence.'[17] According to Walden Bello, Doha was a 'defeat' not only for development, but for democracy as well.[18]

Such was the fragility of the agreement reached at Doha that it took relatively little to unravel it in Cancun, where developing countries took an unprecedented stand in together preferring no agreement, to having a bad agreement foisted onto them again.

Although it is still unclear why the Chair of the negotiations, Mexican foreign minister Derbez, closed the meeting at precisely the point he did – when arguably there was still more negotiation time left – it is quite plain that the atmosphere at Cancun was not conducive to finding compromises. The EU had completely overloaded the agenda by insisting on launching negotiations on the so-called 'new issues' – investment, competition, government procurement and trade facilitation – in the face of major opposition from the developing countries. Moreover, the failure of both the EU and the US to make sufficient concessions in agriculture, together with the abrupt dismissal by the US of the case of the cotton farmers from West Africa, generated enormous anger and frustration.

In the subsequent Cancun post-mortems, analysts have been split between those who argue that the collapse was a missed opportunity, and those who regard the emergence of potentialy powerful new groupings of developing countries that were able to defend their own interests as a triumph for democracy. Some are understandably concerned that, if trade talks cease at the WTO, the EU and US will develop even more aggressive bilateral deals, where weak countries have even less leverage. However, this overlooks the fact that they have already been doing this for years, alongside their use of the WTO, with predictably devastating results. We need look no further than the EU-Bangladesh agreement for an example of a wholly inappropriate bilateral trade and cooperation agreement that demands far more of one of the poorest countries in the world than is required by anything in the WTO.

That we need fair multilaterally-agreed rules to oversee and regulate international trade in the interests of poverty eradication and sustainable development is clear – but it is much harder to believe that the WTO can deliver those outcomes. The WTO is not a neutral set of rules and procedures that can be used defensively to protect the interests of the weakest players. The rules themselves have been designed to institutionalise the current system of global economic inequality.

Take the WTO's overriding principle of 'national treatment', for example, which demands that foreign companies must have the same rights and privileges as domestic companies. This rule effectively denies poorer countries the right to promote their own national industries and economies – a right which was indispensable to most industrialised countries, and which they used with impunity in their own development process. More fundamentally, the WTO puts free trade above all other considerations: its role is to get 'barriers' to trade removed, not to contemplate the possibility that, in some circumstances, they may be a very good thing.

The draconian demands made of Cambodia, the first least developed country to join the WTO since it was established in 1995, tell a similar story. In unusually blunt statements during the accession ceremonies in Cancun, Cambodia's trade minister, Cham Prasidh, said his country had to pay a heavy price for the sake of world integration. He had good reason to complain: Cambodia has been forced into immediately halting use of affordable generic versions of new medicines, even though the Doha declaration allows least developed countries to wait until at least 2016 to implement this far-reaching agreement. It has also been asked to provide less protection to its sensitive agricultural sectors than the US, EU and Canada, even though 80 per cent of Cambodia's population is employed in the agricultural sector.

HISTORY LESSONS

A straightforward lesson emerges from this historical diversion: whatever their original intentions, the Bretton Woods institutions and the WTO have become the North's chosen vehicles for the global projection of its corporate-led economic power. The voices of the South have been systematically marginalised within the North's client organisations, as have any other institutions that challenge them from without. The early 1980s marked a significant turning point when the balance of power shifted decisively towards the North and its institutions. Since this time Structural Adjustment and GATT/WTO rules have widened the gap between rich and poor, accelerated the deterioration of the global environment and subjected developing countries to a slower rate of progress than during the two preceding decades during which they made gains through the UN.

If our history lesson makes one thing clear, it is that the WTO and Bretton Woods institutions are systemically antagonistic to the localisation agenda in general and the interests of the South in particular. They have proved themselves intolerant of internal dissent, and the largely cosmetic concessions that have been extracted from them were obtained only after extreme external pressure. Left to their own devices, the institutions will not even begin to produce meaningful reform from within. What is required amounts to a revolution from without.

8
Storming the Citadels: Sacking Bretton Woods and the WTO

> All too often the IMF forged policies which, in addition to exacerbating the very problems they sought to address, allowed these problems to play out over and over again.
> Joe Stiglitz, former chief economist of the World Bank[1]

A STRATEGY FOR INSTITUTIONAL REVOLUTION

How then is revolution to be achieved? Events since Seattle demonstrate that street protest alone is not enough. It provides powerful exclamation marks in the continuing narrative, but it gives voice only to opposition and the institutions are developing antibodies against it. The WTO chose Doha as the venue for its 2001 Ministerial, demonstrating that it had learned to retreat behind higher barriers and carry on regardless. At Cancun, a massive police and security presence kept the many thousands of protesters over ten miles away from the conference centre itself. A revolution needs more than opposition, it requires proposition as well. Unless driven by a clear vision of the very different institutional settlement that would deliver economic localisation, the revolution will lack direction and impetus. Unless that vision is translated into a programme of action that challenges the existing institutions at every turn, by mixing idealism with pragmatism and protest with persuasion, it will not gather the critical mass of support it needs to succeed.

A VISION FOR A NEW WORLD ORDER

Under the new institutional settlement, the international trade and development institutions will encourage national and local economies towards greater self-reliance and environmental sustainability. They will promote equitable economic and trading relationships between rich and poor nations. They will provide global forums where binding minimum safeguards on social and environmental standards can be negotiated and those safeguards will automatically override rules that seek to maximise international trade and investment. Regulatory bodies will oversee the implementation of a Green Marshall Plan including the speedy cancellation of developing countries' debt and the transfer of 'reparations', appropriate technology and know-how to developing countries. They will also regulate the global financial markets, control the activities of TNCs and reduce their power through stronger monopoly and competition laws.

In all cases, there should be an automatic presumption against the current institutions' near-universal practice of rigidly imposing one-size-fits-all policies regardless of local social, environmental or economic conditions. Developing nations should be guaranteed greater assistance and flexibility in meeting the requirements of international agreements and much institutional power must be decentralised to regional economic agreements and institutions, which have greater flexibility to respond to local needs.

International trade that provides for the equitable exchange of goods that should not be produced more locally once *all* externalities have been taken into account is both necessary and desirable, and rules will always be needed to regulate it. However, trade must be regarded as a means to that end and not, as at present, as a goal in itself. It must respect the social and environmental context within which it takes place. UNCTAD, UNEP, the UNDP, the ILO and many other multilateral agencies have developed standards that seek to reduce poverty and to promote basic rights and sustainable development. The status of these standards must be strengthened so that trade rules become subservient to them. Dr Supachai Panitchpakdi's recent pledge to 'continue to work towards finding a solution that would bring [UNCTAD] observer status [within the WTO]'[2] falls far short of this prescription. Individual trading jurisdictions must also regain the right to legislate in order to protect these standards in ways that are appropriate to local conditions, even when doing so introduces tariffs or non-tariff controls on international trade.

Instead of micromanaging the economies of developing countries for the benefit of the developed world, the Bretton Woods institutions must be forced to rediscover roles that lie closer to the vision their founders had for them, or be abolished. The world's poorest countries do not need loans; they need their existing debts to be cancelled, massively increased levels of transitional aid targeted at combating poverty and establishing self-sufficient local and national economies, and the transfer of appropriate know-how and technology to ensure that their future development is environmentally sustainable. This is no more than they deserve from the North as reparation for past exploitation and the rapidly accumulating climate debt. The apparatus and ideology of Structural Adjustment and one-size-fits-all conditionality must be dismantled. Developing countries should be free to develop locally appropriate solutions to their economic, social and environmental problems, with support from the international community where requested. The North should no longer dispatch IMF staff to commandeer the controls of client economies. Instead, the IMF should make way for a new institution that monitors international financial systems and capital markets in an effort to increase their stability and, in a rediscovery of the role Keynes originally envisaged for it, act as an international clearing union to break the cycle of debt by preventing the accumulation of large trade surpluses and deficits.[3]

This vision represents a very different settlement to the one currently pursued by the unholy trinity of the Bretton Woods institutions and the WTO. They must be abolished to make way for new institutions that serve the world's real needs, not the narrow sectional interests of its richest nations.

GETTING THERE: OBSTRUCTION AND DECONSTRUCTION

The revolution must be built on the foundation of a shared vision, and it will only gain a chance of success when, in sufficient numbers, people and organisations from around the world are inspired to claim that vision as their own. For that to happen, today's revolutionaries must be more than dreamers or protesters, they must also be pragmatic doers – engaging in the debate, pushing its boundaries and winning the respect and allegiance of its main players. Protest is essential, but it must be complemented by a clear programme of demands that charts a path across the difficult territory between the pre- and post-revolutionary worlds.

One of the biggest obstacles blocking that path is the lack of clarity amongst critics of economic globalisation on whether their goal is to reform or abolish the existing institutions. In the light of the history lesson in the previous chapter, as well as the existing institutions' appalling track record in delivering reform, we believe there is virtually no chance of achieving revolution by reformist degrees. So, the urgent political task for Greens and our fellow travellers is to build a critical mass of support for the abolition and replacement of the institutions. This can best be achieved by implementing what could be called a 'Programme of Obstruction and Deconstruction' (POD) that frustrates, neuters and marginalises the institutions whenever possible, to the point that their continued existence looks less plausible than the alternative.

Paradoxically, a major element of an effective POD is to supplement calls for revolution and abolition with an apparently reformist agenda of achievable and incremental institutional reforms that would shift the existing institutions step by step in the direction of the new settlement. Most importantly, this will maximise whatever potential exists to limit the damage the institutions inflict during the 'pre-revolutionary' period. But more than this, it will have a 'prodding' effect that will hasten more fundamental change. Through their contact with us as fellow campaigners on particular issues, individual reformists will be prodded away from dismissing our more radical demands too readily as unrealistic and utopian, and might be persuaded to join the revolutionary ranks. And individual reforms that are moderate enough to be achievable under the current regime can nevertheless be used to prod the terms of debate in the right direction.

Take, for example, the proposed 'Development Box' in the WTO negotiations on agriculture. This is the very narrow and therefore potentially achievable demand that developing countries be allowed to protect their domestic agricultural sectors to the point of self-sufficiency for certain key crops. Although it falls short of the ultimate goal of localised food security, it would be an important step in that direction. In campaigning for the Development Box, 'trade revolutionaries' gain a vital opportunity to draw the NGOs and Southern governments who support the proposal towards their position, and, since the Development Box sets a precedent for advocating protection, to widen the terms of the debate to encompass economic localisation.

Of course, history might show our judgement, that revolution from without is more achievable than reform from within, to be incorrect. But this only strengthens the case for advocating an abolitionist POD that contains a reformist package, rather than concentrating solely on reform. The institutions are more likely to deliver reform if they face an uncompromising threat of abolition. If as a result they avert the necessity for abolition through rapid incremental reform, the POD will have succeeded despite the fact that its principal demand will have gone unmet.

Nevertheless, different parts of the wider global justice movement are naturally drawn to different points of view in the reform versus revolution debate and occasionally yield to the temptation to deploy undue antagonism in defending them. Ultimately, 'reform versus revolution' is a matter of tactics, not one of fundamental principle, and it is too early for hindsight – we cannot yet know which tactic will be most effective. It is therefore futile to expend too much energy debating the question. The movement as a whole should simply accept that opinions will vary and work together on the many points of agreement in as vigorous and coordinated a manner as possible.

The POD's primary intent towards the different institutions is the same: revolutionary change, but its detailed implications are different. The following two sections explore those implications first for the WTO and then for the Bretton Woods institutions, outlining both the 'prodding' reforms than must be demanded and the strategies that should be adopted to provoke more fundamental change.

REPLACING THE WTO

Prodding reform

Reform-minded apologists for the WTO advance the beguiling argument that change can only be delivered within the context of a new trade round. WTO policies and rules, they argue, already impinge on issues such as the environment and labour standards, so the WTO's powers should be extended to formally regulate these areas by, for example, including a social clause within the WTO. This might sound positive and plausible, but past experience suggests otherwise. In all likelihood, extending the WTO's mandate in the hope that some of its worst excesses will be curbed in the process will result in further damaging liberalisation, yet leave the excesses untouched. This danger is amply illustrated by the Doha Round's failure to incorporate a development box or make headway in reducing the North's destructive agricultural export subsidies. We must resist the siren calls for reform via expansion of the WTO and work instead to replace it with a new trade organisation to promote economic localisation.

The body that replaces the WTO must work in a radically different way to its predecessor so that it is genuinely democratic, transparent and accountable to civil society. There is no shortage of proposals in this area that have been suggested by NGOs, governments, the European Commission and others, and many useful precedents already exist in the UN treaty bodies and the OECD. These should be used to guide the working practices of the WTO's successor, and in the interim must be used to drive reform of the WTO itself.

There must be greater declassification of documents than currently exists at the WTO, including real-time access to working documents so that parliamentarians and civil society can contribute meaningfully to the development of trade policy. Developing countries should benefit from far greater flexibility, with a stronger voice in the policy process, and a greater role given to 'special and differential treatment' in trade agreements. The processes used to negotiate new trade agreements must be regulated to strictly limit corporate influence and eliminate the WTO custom whereby the Quad fixes agendas and largely decides outcomes in advance and imposes them, by 'consensus', on all other members. This would give reality to the WTO's one-member-one-vote constitution.

There are calls for a Parliamentary Assembly to be established within the WTO, consisting of parliamentarians from the WTO's member states. The Assembly would have the power to present proposals to the WTO's General Council and other bodies, and commission written and oral reports from the WTO. This proposal would promote a more democratic and pluralist approach to the formulation of trade policy and open it to more effective monitoring and scrutiny. It would also help to hold the governments of the WTO member states accountable to their peoples for their actions during trade negotiations. A Parliamentary Assembly would also be an important feature of the successor to the WTO.

The WTO's dispute settlement system ordains the WTO as both judge and jury. It has frequently been used to further liberalisation and narrow the grounds on which exceptions can be based. It should be replaced by a UN-based arbitration mechanism, with strong input from civil society. It is here that trade-related conflict should be resolved. In the meantime, governments that support the POD should exploit the WTO's dispute settlement body by overloading it with complaints based on rules such as the SPS and GATT Article XX which, at face value, place food safety, public morals, health and the conservation of finite natural resources above the imperative of trade liberalisation (see Table 5.1).

If it adopted all of these reforms, the new trade regulating body would be a more democratic organisation, controlled more equally by its members and held more accountable to their peoples. Ultimately answerable to the UN, it would regulate trade within the context established by the standards and regulations of other global and regional multilateral institutions and the domestic measures adopted to support them. However, there is only so much that can be achieved by changing the processes and procedures of the WTO, if its current rules remain intact.

Unsaddling the WTO

Despite appearances, the WTO is a very fragile edifice. Like a bicycle, its stability depends on its forward momentum. If brought to a sudden halt it is likely to collapse in a tangled heap.[4] This is what happened at Seattle, but at Doha the bicycle was righted, its handlebars were straightened and it was sent, a little unsteadily, on its way. The re-righting of the bicycle was only possible because the South was once again forced to capitulate to the North's demands, and because the Doha declaration went no further than committing WTO members to discuss some of the most contentious trade issues. The hard work of resolving them was left until the 2003 Ministerial in Cancun and beyond. The failure of the talks at Cancun demonstrates just how hasty the bicycle repairs were – and how fragile the result. Indeed, the process at Cancun reveals many weak points in the WTO consensus, useful targets for a well-designed POD.

First, the capacity of the WTO's poorest members to influence and, when necessary, block trade negotiations must be increased. Everyone believes capacity building is necessary, even the WTO. It endorsed the concept 18 times in the 42 paragraphs of the Doha Ministerial declaration. Potentially, any individual WTO member has a huge capacity to halt the forward momentum of liberalisation, as the WTO is officially a one-member-one-vote organisation that can only move by consensus. However, the GATT/WTO has resorted to taking a formal vote only twice in its entire history. Normally it only reaches decisions after the Quad has agreed amongst itself and then 'persuaded' (in fact, bullied or bribed) other states to toe the line, a process that disempowers the majority of WTO members.

The WTO might have had a different definition of capacity building in mind, but as a central element of POD, campaigners in the North must reinforce their work with civil society in the South to encourage their governments to adopt a more assertive stance in WTO negotiations. At the very least, the developing countries might secure a better deal at the WTO should they threaten to block all future agreements while the rich nations exclude them from the most important negotiations, override their demands for fairer treatment in WTO agreements, and maintain their hypocritical regimes of export subsidies that undermine the livelihoods of farmers in the South. Indeed, new alliances were formed at Cancun – the G22 led by Brazil, China and India, and the so-called G90 made up of the least developed countries, the African Union, and the countries of the ACP group. These groupings dramatically strengthened the negotiating position of the developing countries, and ensured in particular that they were able to stand up to the demands from the US and the EU.

The need for campaigners in the South and the North to work together cannot be overemphasised. It is happening already: several Southern organisations such as Focus on the Global South and the Third World Network, and individuals like the Indian scientist and campaigner, Vandana Shiva, already have an immense influence within the global justice movement. However, Northern anti-WTO protestors have all too often been misunderstood, intentionally or otherwise, as seeking to impose stringent social and environmental regulations merely as a means to bar imports and save jobs. If this is the view taken by some Southern governments as well as reactionary commentators in the North, it is not one that is shared by the millions of workers and activists in developing countries who have joined anti-WTO protests.

It is not just the relationships between the rich and poor countries that are strained within the WTO; deep cracks also exist in the EU–US alliance. Understandably, the WTO has shunted issues that are contentious within the Quad to the back of the queue. Nevertheless, the Doha Ministerial agreed that three of them should be tackled: agriculture; industrial tariffs and services. The second strand of a well-aimed POD should exploit the friction that exists in many of these areas between the EU and the US in an attempt to stall the negotiations.

Finally, peaceful protest aimed at shaking the resolve of the governments of the WTO's leading members has a big part to play. Even when street protest is prevented by the choice of inaccessible locations for Ministerials and other meetings, virtual protest can take over. In 1998, the OECD finally abandoned its proposed Multilateral Agreement on Investment (MAI) after an unprecedented wave of cyber-protest from individual activists and campaigning organisations unnerved the leading governments, particularly the French who were keen to protect their distinctive film industry. A similar, loosely coordinated and largely Internet-based movement has sprung up to oppose GATS. As a result, numerous UK local authorities have passed anti-GATS motions and the Executive of the Local Government Association (LGA) has expressed concern at the effect GATS will have on the powers of local authorities, 'particularly in the fields of procurement, regulation and environmental protection'.[5] The LGA, not previously a noted anti-globalisation activist, is now raising its concerns with the UK government and more widely through its access to EU and international bodies.

REDISCOVERING BRETTON WOODS

Prodding reform

The Bretton Woods institutions are elitist. They refuse to learn from external criticism or tolerate internal dissent. They suffer systemic failures of accountability and transparency. In practice they answer only to the US Treasury Department and appear to believe in non-transparency as a necessary precondition for effectiveness. It is hard to conceive of any other explanation for the IMF's continued imposition of the same, albeit rebranded, prescription of structural adjustment despite its repeated failure; or of why the World Bank, despite its slightly more convincing reforms, continues to support socially and environmentally damaging projects and impose highly inappropriate one-size-fits-all lending conditions.

The G8 nations hold 49 per cent of the voting power at the IMF and 48 per cent at the World Bank.[6] Decisions within both bodies require an 85 per cent majority. The US alone, with 18 per cent of the IMF vote and 19 per cent at the World Bank, possesses a *de facto* veto over any substantive proposals. Although all member states have a 'basic' vote as a right of membership, additional 'quota' votes are allocated according to each country's economic importance. Additional quotas have been allocated since the founding of the IMF, reducing the share of basic votes from 12.4 per cent of the total to just 2.1 per cent. This sliver of the cake is shared increasingly sparingly. Since the IMF was founded, 135 new member states have joined, leaving the overwhelming majority of states almost totally marginalised.[7]

It is not just the voting arrangements that reinforce the West's grip on the Bretton Woods institutions. They are located in the US and operate in close consultation with the US Treasury Department; the US nominates the head of the World Bank whilst Europe selects the head of the IMF. According to the UNDP's diplomatic understatement, these rules and conventions leave the IMF and the World Bank 'overly accountable to their largest shareholder', the US.[8]

Over time, the focus of the IMF and the World Bank's activities has shifted from mutual aid between their original members to the liberalisation and 'development' of the South. This, together with the systematic and dramatic under-representation of the South in Bretton Woods decision making, has turned the institutions into neocolonialist clubs that lend exclusively to their poor members on terms set exclusively by the rich. This imbalance must be redressed urgently. The Bretton Woods institutions require a radical reorientation both of what they do and how they do it.

There are many interim reforms that must be demanded, if only to highlight the institutions' many failings and build support for revolutionary change. The IMF and the World Bank must become one-member-one-vote organisations. If this cannot be achieved in one step, the value of basic votes relative to quotas should be increased to give poorer member states a growing voice in decision making. There should also be greater representation of poorer states on the Boards of the IMF and the World Bank and genuinely open selection of the heads of the institutions.

All too often, recipient governments have endorsed IMF or World Bank proposals at the expense of the people they are supposed to represent. Accountability must extend beyond governments to the people who are directly affected by the activities of the IMF and the World Bank. The World Bank has taken some steps to adopt judicial-style accountability. In 1993, it set up an Inspection Panel, which deals with complaints from people affected by World Bank loans on the grounds that a loan contravened Bank policy. In 1999, it established the Compliance Advisor/Ombudsman's office, which deals with social and environmental complaints arising from projects supported by the International Finance Corporation and the Multilateral Investment Guarantee Agency (MIGA). Although welcome, the Inspection Panel and Compliance Advisor can only act in an advisory capacity. Their powers should be enhanced so that their judgements are binding in effect, and the concept of judicial-style accountability should be extended to cover all the activities of the World Bank and the IMF. The institutions should be held accountable to a UN body that assesses their performance not just against their own rules, but also against the standards and agreements of the UN bodies and other treaties and MEAs.

Additional reforms are required to make the institutions more transparent. They must increase the range of papers they publish, particularly those from the IMF's semi-independent Office of Internal Audit and Inspection and the World Bank's Operational Evaluation Department. Papers that evaluate a particular project or national economy must be made available in the languages spoken in the area of the study and drawn up in collaberation with all stakeholders in the region concerned. The meetings of their Boards should take place in public; votes should be taken and recorded, and the minutes be made readily available.

Defanging Bretton Woods

The Bretton Woods institutions have already been forced onto the defensive. Public demands for the cancellation of debt prompted the HIPC initiative. Widespread criticisms of structural adjustment led to its replacement by strategies that are officially aimed at poverty reduction, even if their effect remains much the same. The late 1980s' upsurge of concern over the global environment precipitated first the creation of the Global Environment Facility, and subsequently a dilution of control exercised over it by the OECD and the World Bank in favour of the G77 countries, the UNDP and UNEP.[9] Each of these initiatives is incomplete, but equally each represents a partial reversal for the institutions and provides the foundations of a POD directed at them.

The demands of the POD must extend beyond the obvious priority of debt cancellation to include other measures that would extract the fangs of the World Bank and the IMF and liberate developing countries to pursue sustainable development within the framework of economic localisation. Aid must be increased as a transitional measure; conditionality, such as Structural Adjustment, must be ended; and debtor countries must be afforded protection from irresponsible lending and unpayable debt by means of a UN-administered bankruptcy procedure.

In a manner similar to the way in which a currency maintains its value, the Bretton Woods institutions derive their power from the esteem, or fear, with which their creditors and debtors regard them. The World Bank funds its activities and acquires its power by selling bonds; debtor nations obey the strictures of Structural Adjustment for fear that they will be denied credit in the future if they do not. A campaign to defund the World Bank through a boycott of its bonds by potential purchasers must form a central part of the POD.

Similarly, the debtor nations owe so much that by acting together they could reclaim the power which they have, one by one, ceded to the institutions. As part of the POD, a campaign must be mounted to persuade debtors to collectively default on their unpayable debts, reject the terms of Structural Adjustment and support each other, with the backing of sympathetic developed countries, in rejuvenating strong localised economies. By acting together in this way, they could break the grip the IMF maintains over its client states.

Greens, NGOs and civil society in the G8 countries have a particular responsibility to ensure the success of the POD directed at the World Bank and the IMF, as their governments own the controlling shares in both organisations. G8 governments must therefore be held directly to account not just for the cancellation of bilateral debt, but also for the relief of multilateral debt owed to the institutions they control. Responsibility for the IMF's repeated failures rests not only with the faceless bureaucrats who destroy lives and livelihoods by dictating the terms of structural adjustment, but also with the succession of G8 heads of state and ministers who have sanctioned the IMF's actions.

An inspiring example of Western civil society uniting to hold its governments to account for the impact of their client agencies was provided by the Jubilee 2000 campaign. On 16 May 1998, more than 50,000 people joined an entirely peaceful Jubilee 2000 protest in Birmingham, UK, outside a G8 meeting to protest at the impact of 'Third World' debt. Similar protests followed in Cologne and Prague and 24 million people signed the Jubilee 2000 petition. For a moment G8 leaders were forced onto the defensive, and limited concessions were extracted, but that moment passed with the turning of the millennium, the expiry date Jubilee 2000 had set itself.

There are lessons to be learned from the Jubilee 2000 experience. A POD aimed at the remarkably robust Bretton Woods institutions must not set itself an unrealistically short timetable to achieve its objectives, nor let itself be fobbed off with less-than-half-measures. It must have very clear demands in order to rally large numbers of individuals and organisations. The tactics adopted in support of the POD must be tailored to changing events. Big protests are good for G8 summits and IMF/World Bank meetings. Elections in G8 countries present an opportunity for a different sort of campaign, giving Green candidates the opportunity to promote the policies of economic localisation and NGOs the chance to assess the merits of the proposals from each party.

COMMISSIONING CHANGE

The replacement of the existing international institutions will require widespread international debate and agreement. To speed the process, supporters of the POD should work to establish a UN-backed international commission on global governance, with strong representation from G77 countries and the NGO sector. The commission should evaluate the effect to date of Bretton Woods, the WTO and other multilateral agencies using as benchmarks the UNDP's Millennium Development goals and the obligations contained in other international agreements, such as the Kyoto Protocol, ILO standards and the UN Declaration of Human Rights. As well as making recommendations for the future institutional settlement, the commission should have the specific remit of recommending the level and type of reparations that the North should pay to the South under a Green Marshall Plan for its past mismanagement of the global economy, expropriation of natural resources and rapidly accumulating climate debt.

UNCHARTED TERRITORY

As we mentioned earlier, it is too early for hindsight. Our strategies for revolution must evolve continuously in response to the experience they generate. Of necessity, the path we suggest taking to the post-revolutionary settlement has been charted in advance of most of that experience, but we offer it with a Spanish proverb in mind: 'Traveller, there is no path; paths are made by walking.'

Section 4
Applying the Alternative

The principles of economic localisation can be applied to almost any sphere of public policy and in most cases the results would command near-universal support from within the global justice movement. Energy policy is a case in point. A decentralised energy supply has many advantages over large-scale centralised production. It is able to make efficient use of local renewable energy resources that might otherwise be overlooked. It avoids the major environmental and social disturbances that so often result from the construction of large-scale infrastructure such as dams or large power stations. It can help to develop indigenous manufacturing and technical capability. It reduces the risk of indebtedness because it does not require major loans. It creates more jobs per unit of capital invested and is suited to local community control, allowing communities to define and meet their own energy needs. It represents an achievable and sustainable option, particularly for the two billion people, mainly the rural poor in developing countries, who lack access to grid electricity or to other forms of modern commercial energy supply.[1]

Transport is another good example. We have already outlined the environmental costs incurred by transporting more and more goods over ever-increasing distances. Economic localisation would reverse this trend. It would also offer a range of potential economic benefits by reducing the demand for major new transport infrastructure. Advocates for new projects such as airports or major roads always claim that their proposals will create new jobs and growth in the area, but they ignore the possibility that the new road or increased number of flights will make it easier for local demand to be met by suppliers from other areas and that jobs will leave the local area for locations at the other end of the new transport links. This possibility was recognised in a report of a UK government advisory committee that assessed the conventional economic effects of major new roads in the following terms: 'Studies in economic geography confirm that there is no guarantee that transport improvements will benefit the local or regional economy at only one end of the route – roads operate in two directions, and in some circumstances the benefits will accrue to other competing regions.'[2]

If the hidden and opportunity costs of road transport and aviation are added into the equation, then the benefits of a more localised transport system emerge with greater clarity. These would include lower expenditure on defensive health measures as a result of reduced pollution (estimated to be around £20 billion pa in the UK for road transport alone);[3] a reallocation of resources to activities that generate more jobs than long-distance transport, reduced congestion, lower labour and housing market inflation at and near major airports, and the reduction and reallocation of the public subsidy to aviation (estimated at £9.2 billion pa in the UK).[4]

There are, however, issues to which the application of economic localisation will not prove so obvious and uncontroversial within the global justice movement. In an attempt to advance the debate, this final section of the book examines three of these issues that are of pivotal importance to the wider dispute over globalisation. Chapter 9 looks at agriculture, the perennial stumbling block of free trade, Chapter 10 examines monetary union – the EU's principal response to globalisation, and Chapter 11 considers the prospects for effective multilateralism in an ever more ruthlessly competitive world.

9
Local Food – The Global Solution

> If you are looking for a way to get people to lean on you and be dependent on you, in terms of their co-operating with you, it seems to me that food-dependence would be terrific.
>
> US Vice-President Hubert Humphrey[1]

Agriculture is in crisis. In both the developed and developing worlds, farmers are losing their livelihoods and monoculture is suffocating the rich intricacies of the rural economy. In an era when more than enough food is produced to feed the world, millions go hungry. At the time of writing, the World Food Programme estimated that 40 million people in Africa were in urgent need of food aid.[2] Half of India's population is malnourished.[3] Even in a prosperous country like the UK, 7 per cent of the population – 4 million people – live in food poverty.[4] At the same time however, the developed world is suffering an epidemic of obesity. In 1980, 8 per cent of women and 6 per cent of men in England were classified as obese. By 1998, the prevalence of obesity had nearly trebled to 21 per cent of women and 17 per cent of men and there is no sign of this trend changing. Currently, more than half of all women and about two thirds of men in England are either overweight or obese.[5] Likewise, 55.3 per cent of the US population is overweight or obese.[6]

The response of the world's largest economic powers is starkly hypocritical. The US and the EU maintain massive agricultural subsidies at home, yet demand the liberalisation of agriculture abroad. In April 2002, President Bush put his name to a US$248.6bn farm bill that will raise US agricultural subsidies by up to 80 per cent a year for the next ten years.[7] Surpluses, generated in part by EU Common Agricultural Policy (CAP) production subsidies, are dumped at artificially low prices on newly liberalised markets in developing countries, with devastating effects.

As we will show, the liberalisation of agriculture that the North is attempting to foist on the developing world is a very large part of the problem; the solution is to be found in achieving the goal of food security through the localisation of agriculture.

FROM FOOD SECURITY TO INTERNATIONAL COMPETITIVENESS

Ironically, the main motivation for the North's creation of its extensive systems of agricultural subsidies was to achieve domestic food security. The CAP is a typical example. Its objectives were defined in 1957 in response to the widespread food shortages Europe was experiencing at the time. They aimed to increase productivity, boost farmers' incomes, stabilise markets, and crucially, to ensure an adequate supply of reasonably priced food. Understandably, these were popular objectives at the time and a complex range of mechanisms was instituted to implement them. This included production subsidies, direct payments to producers to guarantee minimum prices, levies on imports, export subsidies, and market intervention to purchase surplus production.

It is now widely accepted that the CAP has dramatically overachieved at least some of its objectives, so much so that it is now generating huge surpluses, which are dumped on world markets at prices that undercut local produce. For example, the European dairy giant Arla Foods exports around £43m worth of dairy produce to the Dominican Republic for which it receives £11m in export subsidies from the EU. This makes Arla's milk 25 per cent cheaper than local produce. Over the last twenty years, 10,000 Dominican Republic dairy farmers have lost their jobs.[8]

Rapid intensification of EU agriculture has also led to larger field sizes, increased mechanisation and heavier use of chemical and energy inputs. Hedgerows have been grubbed out, ponds drained, soils eroded and water resources polluted. Populations of birds, mammals and insects have declined dramatically.

Notwithstanding its Pyrrhic 'success' in boosting output, the CAP has failed to provide social and economic security for the majority of farmers and rural communities. The intensification of agriculture has favoured big farms over small ones and those in marginal areas. The percentage of the population involved in agriculture has declined and CAP support is directed to a decreasing number of increasingly large farmers. The richest 20 per cent of EU farmers receive 80 per cent of CAP subsidies. Agricultural infrastructure such as abattoirs and dairies has been centralised, further disadvantaging small producers in more remote areas.

Having more than achieved food security for itself, the North turned its attentions to the South, seeking new markets for its surplus products. But it is not just dumped exports from the North that are distorting markets for agricultural goods in the South. The twin forces of the WTO's Agreement on Agriculture (AOA) and the structural adjustment policies of the IMF are also forcing developing countries, often against their better judgement, to gear production to the export market. Already volatile markets for cash crops have been flooded as more countries are forced to export the same range of basic commodities, and the prices farmers receive for their produce have collapsed as a result. For example, in the mid-1990s, the IMF bulldozed Haiti into liberalising its rice markets. It was flooded with cheap US imports and local production collapsed, destroying tens of thousands of rural livelihoods. A decade ago Haiti was self-sufficient in rice; today it spends half of its export earnings importing rice from the US. In many of the least developed countries, the loss of export earnings attributable to the distorting effects of EU and US subsidies far outweighs the savings made through debt relief.[9]

The shift in emphasis from overcoming postwar food shortages to prising open new markets for subsidised exports amounts to a dramatic change in policy. Countries are now being forced to compete to produce each other's food as cheaply as possible and at the expense of domestic production. Local food security is being swapped for mandatory trade rules that are biased toward agribusiness, industrial production and long-distance transport. Recently, the UK food and farming minister, Larry Whitty, provided a blunt summary of this policy, when he said, 'a [self-sufficiency] target is not what drives policy. Being competitive drives policy.'[10]

THE GREAT FOOD SWAP

Unsurprisingly, this policy shift has produced a dramatic increase in the international food trade. Over the last thirty years for example, exports of a variety of food products from EU member states increased by between 164 per cent and 1340 per cent. However, it is not as if the EU has achieved self-sufficiency and is exporting its surplus – it remains one of the world's largest food importers. Over exactly the same period, food imports into the EU increased, in some cases by as much as 289 per cent. This pattern is repeated at the global level. Between 1968 and 1998, world food production increased by 84 per cent, yet over the same period international trade in food products almost trebled, with trade flows doubling for almost every food category.[11]

Of course, conventional economists would welcome this as evidence of increasing specialisation in food production, such that countries are concentrating on producing those products for which they have a comparative advantage and are importing foods that are produced more efficiently elsewhere. However, closer inspection of the figures reveals that a large part of the growth in international trade in food is accounted for by simultaneous imports and exports of the same products between exactly the same countries. The UK and the EU provide telling case studies. In 1998, Britain imported 61,400 tonnes of poultry meat from the Netherlands and exported 33,100 tonnes of poultry meat to the Netherlands. In the same year, it imported 240,000 tonnes of pork and 125,000 tonnes of lamb, while it exported 195,000 tonnes of pork and 102,000 tonnes of lamb. In 1997, the UK imported 126m litres of milk and exported 270m litres of milk. In the same year, 23,000 tonnes of milk powder were imported into the UK and 153,000 tonnes were exported. In 1999, the EU imported 44,000 tonnes of meat from Argentina, 11,000 tonnes from Botswana, 40,000 tonnes from Poland and over 70,000 tonnes from Brazil. In the same year, the meat exports from the EU to the rest of the world totalled 874,211 tonnes.[12]

Increasingly, agriculture is held in thrall to the overwhelming and hugely mistaken imperative of international competitiveness. Producers are being locked into an absurd and wasteful global food swap, and everyone, save a few agribusiness giants, is paying the price.

PAYING FOR THE GREAT FOOD SWAP

Environmental impact

Intensive food production for export relies heavily on use of artificial fertilisers, pesticides and herbicides, particularly as importers demand high cosmetic standards for high-value products such as fruit, vegetables and flowers. Agricultural chemicals contaminate water, harm wildlife, and, through their widespread residues in food, animal feed and drinking water, pose a risk to human and animal health. The large-scale patterns of monoculture associated with their use cause massive soil erosion, destroy natural habitats and reduce biodiversity.

There is no single measure of the cost of chemical pollution arising from agriculture, but several indicators gives a sense of the scale of the problem in intensive agricultural areas. For example, in the thirty years between the 1960s and the 1990s, the equivalent of more than 1 million football fields of meadows were destroyed in the UK.[13] In 2000, the US Food and Drug Administration found pesticide residues in 43.3 per cent of the US-produced grains and grain products it sampled and in 58.3 per cent of domestic fruit samples.[14] The European Environment Agency reported that in 1997 the levels of surplus nitrogen applied to agricultural land, either as manure or fertiliser, was so great that in 91 of 113 EU regions it surveyed it was certain or 'very likely' to contribute to nitrate contamination of water.[15] Nitrate pollution is the main factor behind eutrophication of marine waters. This causes a massive growth spurt in water plants, robbing the water of its oxygen and making life for other organisms impossible.

Modern methods of intensive cultivation are exacerbating the loss of productive land through soil erosion. The US's drive to export grain from its heartland began in the 1970s and has contributed to a 40 per cent increase in soil erosion in its corn and soya bean growing areas. Currently, about 90 per cent of US cropland is losing topsoil faster than it can be replaced and globally, it is estimated that 12 million hectares of arable land are lost each year, about 1 per cent of the global land area under cultivation.[16] Even ignoring the destruction of habitats that occurs as farmers abandon land and move into previously uncultivated areas, this erosion imposes a wide range of costs. These include the energy and nutrients required to replace the loss of soil fertility, the loss of water through increased run-off from degraded soils, and a large variety of 'off-site' impacts such as the increased sedimentation of waterways, which causes flooding and an increased need for filtration in water treatment systems. One study calculated that these costs amounted to US$400bn a year at 1995 prices, or $70 per US citizen per year.[17]

Another range of environmental costs associated with intensive export-oriented agriculture arises from the packaging of food and its distribution over large distances. These costs include the pollution that is a direct consequence of burning fossil fuels to power lorries, ships and aircraft, as well as the impacts of constructing vehicles and transport infrastructure, and extracting crude oil and other resources required for transport fuel. Again, there is no simple measure of this range of impacts, but for an indication it is revealing to compare the CO_2 emissions arising from the transportation of just one product. Distributing a kilogram of apples from New Zealand to the UK consumer results in 1kg of CO_2 emissions, more than twenty times the level of emissions caused by distributing a kilogram of locally sourced apples through a home-delivery fruit and vegetable box scheme.[18] Indeed, trade-related transportation is one of the fastest growing sources of greenhouse gas emissions.[19] Although most food is distributed by road and ship, the airfreighting of foodstuffs is increasing. For example, UK imports of fish products and fruit and vegetables by plane increased between 1980 and 1990 by 240 per cent and 90 per cent respectively. UK airfreight (imports and exports) grew by about 7 per cent a year in the 1990s and is expected to increase at a rate of 7.5 per cent a year to 2010.[20] Freight transportation by sea is approximately five times more energy-efficient than road freight and 37 times more energy-efficient than international airfreight (see Table 9.1). Apart from its low energy efficiency, airfreight causes very high levels of pollution. A two-minute DC10 take-off produces the same quantity of nitrogen oxides as driving 21,539 cars one mile at 30 miles an hour.[21] Absurdly, aviation fuel is not taxed at all and emissions from aircraft are specifically exempted from the Kyoto protocol for CO_2 reductions.

Table 9.1 Average energy use of different forms of transport[22]

	Energy consumed (kilojoules per T-km)	Emissions of carbon dioxide (g/T-km)	Emissions of hydrocarbons (g/T-km)	Emissions of nitrogen oxides (g/T-km)	Emissions of carbon monoxide (g/T-km)
Rail	677	41	0.06	0.2	0.05
Sea	423	30	0.04	0.4	0.12
Road	2,890	207	0.30	3.6	2.40
Air	15,839	1,206	2.00	5.5	1.40

T-km = tonne-kilometres of goods transported. g/T-km = grams per tonne-kilometre

Small farms under threat

The intensification of agriculture has caused massive job losses in the sector. In the UK, the total agricultural labour force has declined by 20 per cent over the past twenty years; it fell by nearly 20,000 people in 1999 alone.[23] The UK Policy Commission on Food and Farming reported that 51,300 farmers and farm workers left the industry in the two years to June 2000, equivalent to 70 a day. These job losses are often associated with farm amalgamations and UK ministers expect that by 2005 as many as 25 per cent of farms – almost all small ones

– will have closed or merged, with 50,000 people forced to leave the industry.[24]

As workers leave the countryside, so other support services decline. By the end of the 1990s, rural decline in the UK had become acute: 42 per cent of rural parishes had no shop, 43 per cent had no post office, 83 per cent had no doctor, 49 per cent had no school and 75 per cent had no daily bus service.[25]

The loss of agricultural employment is paralleled throughout the developed world. Canada lost three-quarters of its farmers between 1941 and 1996. In the US, there were 6.8 million farmers in 1935; today there are fewer than 1.9 million – less than the US prison population.[26] In the EU, at least 500,000 farm jobs are lost each year. With the prospect of the enlargement of the EU to include countries like Poland where farming still accounts for more than 27 per cent of the workforce, this situation is likely to get worse. The developed world's experience is a foretaste of what is likely to happen in developing countries as their agriculture systems are 'liberalised'. Already, between 1985 and 1995 in Brazil, 5 million farmers left the land.[27] The Indian state of Andhra Pradesh has adopted a development policy 'Vision 2020' that aims to achieve developed-nation status by 2020. Under the plans, small landholdings are to be amalgamated and farmed under contract to major agribusiness companies. Intensive plantation-style production for the commercial seed and export markets, much of it using GM crops, is to replace small-scale family-based farming with the loss of an estimated 20 million rural livelihoods.[28] Similarly in China, rapid urbanisation is placing 400 million rural livelihoods at risk.

The decline in rural employment on smaller farms is no accidental byproduct of the globalisation of agriculture; it is a deliberate feature of governments' policies around the world. The UK government's former rural recovery coordinator, Lord Haskins (former head of the food conglomerate Northern Foods) famously stated, 'Farms will get bigger and that's a good thing. A lot of agricultural reformers, like the Prince of Wales, want farmers to stand around being subsidised and making thatched roofs. Well, that's for the birds. Agriculture has got to strive to be more competitive and more productive.'[29]

A similar line emerged in a UK government statement in the wake of the 2001 foot-and-mouth epidemic, which announced: 'The Government plans a major reduction in the number of farms and farmers as part of a recovery package for British agriculture in the wake of the devastating foot and mouth outbreak.'[30] Following that announcement, the Ministry for Agriculture, Fisheries and Food (MAFF) produced three reports investigating the future of hill farms, the dairy industry and the cost of inputs to farming, such as energy and capital. In each case the reports argued that big farms are more productive and better able to compete with their counterparts in the Pampas and the American Midwest – a conclusion that rests on an extraordinary disregard of the massive external costs of intensive agriculture.

The same employment-destroying policies are being exported around the world. Andhra Pradesh's Vision 2020 policies have received backing from the World Bank and the UK's Department for International Development (DfID). Indeed, the government of Andhra Pradesh receives two-thirds of DfID's entire aid budget to India, despite evidence of unease in the department about the Vision 2020 programme. An internal DfID memo reportedly states that Vision 2020 has 'major failings' and 'says nothing substantial about the implied need to provide alternative agricultural income ... to those who would be displaced from agriculture by [land] consolidation'. The memo concludes, 'The promotion of contract farming ... has many negative implications for the food security and wider livelihood security of the poor.'[31]

Other commentators have highlighted additional benefits of smaller-scale agriculture. For example, in a conspicuous departure from its usual pro-agribusiness stance, the US Department of Agriculture published a study that demonstrated many benefits of small and family farms. Included amongst these were that smaller farms ensure a diversity of ownership and systems of biological organisation. Compared to bigger farms, the 60 per cent of US farms that are smaller than 180 acres were found to provide significantly better management of natural resources. Smaller farms were also found to foster a greater sense of community responsibility, more direct connections between producers and consumers, and a knowledge source for future generations.[32]

Advisers to the UK government have put forward similar arguments. For example, the government-appointed Policy Commission on the Future of Farming and Food explicitly highlighted the potential advantage to rural life and the environment of supporting the family farm sector:

'Small farms are very much the norm in some parts of the country, and local landscapes reflect that. We want to see opportunities for farmers both small and large to thrive into the future.'[33]

Richard North makes a similar point in his book *The Death of British Agriculture*: 'The simple fact is that, although agriculture now accounts for less than one percent of GDP in Britain, it occupies something like 80 percent of the land mass. That land – the landscape – is a vital part of our heritage and is a significant tourist attraction. It has a real value to the economy, which is not found on any agricultural balance sheet.'[34]

In other words, agriculture cannot be regarded as merely another business to be made ever more ruthlessly efficient, albeit with a few environmental 'add-ons.' The small or 'family' farm must be the linchpin of the sustainable rural economy, providing many benefits beyond worthwhile employment and good food.

Food security, hunger and development

The UK provides some telling examples of how the growth of the international food trade is destroying local food security. In 2000, the UK imported 474,000 tonnes of apples, around 70 per cent of its total consumption.[35] Yet more than 60 per cent of the UK's own apple orchards have been grubbed up since 1970, largely as a result of EU subsidies.[36] Even if all the UK's homegrown fruit was consumed domestically, the UK would be only 5 per cent self-sufficient in fruit. Beef is imported to Britain from as far afield as Argentina, Brazil, Namibia, Botswana, Zimbabwe and Australia, and a recent report for MAFF reveals that chicken has been imported from Thailand and Brazil, and exported to Hong Kong, Russia and South Africa.[37]

In the developed world, the erosion of localised patterns of production and consumption has a serious impact on the environment and the health of rural economies, but in much of the developing world, the loss of local food security is also a matter of life or death. Current estimates suggest 40 million people in Africa are in need of food aid, a situation that has been made far worse by the globalisation of agriculture. Malawi would have had sufficient grain supplies to get though the current drought had it not been pressurised into selling its surplus by the World Bank. Farmers in many Southern African states have been forced by their governments to give up cultivating everything apart from maize, which can be exported and is very productive in a good year. Traditional crops such as sorghum and millet are much better at coping with fluctuations in moisture and would have provided some protection from the current drought. In the famine of the 1980s, Ethiopia was a net exporter of grain – nearly 80 per cent of malnourished children in the South live in countries that have food surpluses.[38] In Zimbabwe and Tanzania, farmers are even compelled to buy seed from authorised companies, which only supply maize. Increasingly, these companies are being taken over by predominantly US-based agribusiness TNCs, further undermining local food security.[39]

International action, whether through the WTO, the World Bank or the IMF, is working in the wrong direction. It is enslaving developing countries to volatile international markets for monoculture cash crops, thus destroying their ability to provide for local need. Even bilateral food aid tends to undermine local production. In times of food emergency it would be better if food were bought as locally as possible, thus sustaining any remaining local production.

Increased international trade is not the answer to food poverty. Where hunger exists, what is often lacking is not food, but access either to the money to buy it or the land on which to grow it.[40] In some poorer countries where millions are landless and hungry, this situation is compounded by the large-scale cultivation of cattle feed for export. It is estimated for example that for every acre farmed in the UK, two more are farmed overseas in order to meet the feed requirements of our intensively farmed livestock. Imported feed, such as cassava, soya beans and soya cake, makes up about 30 per cent of all European animal feed. An estimated 5.6 million acres in Brazil and around 1.2 million acres in Argentina are devoted to soya bean production for export – land that would be better used by local people to grow food for local need.

Finally, changes in the agricultural sector disproportionately affect people in developing countries. While only 5 per cent of the population in the EU are farmers, the majority of people in the developing world still depend on this sector for their livelihood: 75 per cent in China, 77 per cent in Kenya, 67 per cent in India, and 82 per cent in Senegal.[41]

Corporate control of the food chain

The great food swap gives large retailers and food manufacturers ever greater freedom to source their supplies from across the world and play producers off against each other with the threat of cheaper imports – a freedom they are exercising to the full in order to increase their control over food production and distribution. In 1960, independent retailers enjoyed a 60 per cent share of the UK retail market; by 2000 their market share had shrunk by nine-tenths. Chain multiple retailers had seen their market share grow from 20 per cent to 88 per cent over the same period and the Co-op's share had reduced from 20 per cent to 6 per cent.[42] Based on historical growth rates in European turnover for the previous five years, the Institute of Grocery Distribution (IGD) predicts that Europe's top ten grocery retailers will increase their market share from 37 per cent to 60 per cent between 2000 and 2005. Their combined turnover is predicted to double from 337.1 billion euros in 2000 to 669.7 billion euros by 2010.[43]

Four huge UK supermarket chains, Tesco, Asda-Walmart, Sainsbury's and Safeway, account for 70 per cent of the market. They make enormous profits. In 2001, the UK's biggest supermarket, Tesco, made a profit in excess of £1bn, more than half of the income of all UK farmers. Put another way, in just one hour, Tesco made ten times more profit than the average British farmer earned in the entire year.

The supermarkets, food manufacturers and processors are using their increasingly dominant market position to beat down farm-gate prices. A National Farmers' Union (NFU) survey comparing the farm-gate and retail prices of 15 food commodities found that farmers received only about 30 per cent of the retail value of their produce. According to UK government figures, 15 per cent of the gross value earned across the UK food chain goes to farmers and primary producers and 85 per cent to processors, manufacturers and retailers.[44]

But it is not just the farmers who are suffering. Wherever supermarket chains expand, small shops close, local jobs are lost, consumers pay more and the environment is damaged (see Box 9.1).

Box 9.1 Supermarkets[45]

- *Supermarkets don't offer the best price to consumers.* Supermarkets only offer low prices on a very limited range of goods. A recent Friends of the Earth survey found they are the most expensive place to buy apples, beaten by market stalls and greengrocers.[46] A survey for Sustain in 2000 found that fruit and vegetables were around 30 per cent cheaper at market stalls than supermarkets.[47]
- *Supermarkets favour imports over domestic produce.* 84 per cent of British shoppers say they want supermarkets to give preference to domestic produce when it is in season.[48] A Friends of the Earth survey found that at the height of the UK apple season under half of the apples on offer in the big four supermarkets were home grown.[49]
- *Supermarkets' bullying tactics can put small farmers out of business.* The Competition Commission found that the big supermarkets inflict unfair

▶

trading practices on their suppliers. For example, supermarkets pay invoices very late, and they pass costs back to suppliers for changes to transport and packaging and even for their own mistakes in ordering.[50]
- *Supermarkets are squeezing prices paid to farmers.* Last year the NFU found that for a basket of food costing the consumer £37 the farmers would only have got £11. The Competition Commission found that Tesco, which has the biggest market share, paid the lowest prices.[51]
- *Supermarkets are forcing small shops out of business.* About eight independent shops close every day.[52] Small independent shops cannot compete with the big multiples.
- *Supermarkets are worse for the local economy than local shops.* The New Economics Foundation has found that local shops keep more money circulating in the local economy.[53]
- *Supermarkets destroy jobs.* The British Retail Planning Forum found that, on average, a net total of 276 jobs are lost every time a large supermarket opens.[54]
- *Supermarkets import food over huge distances, often by air.* For example, 2kg of baby carrots imported to the UK from South Africa will travel 9,622km by plane and result in 11kg of CO_2 emissions.[55]
- *Supermarkets also transport food large distances due to their distribution system.* According to the Institute of Grocery Distribution, Sainsbury's vehicles clocked up 15.7 million km in the UK in 2002 and Asda-Walmart clocked up 147.9 million km.[56]
- *Supermarkets waste food by imposing artificially high cosmetic conditions.* A Friends of the Earth survey of apple growers found that supermarkets frequently reject fruit for being the wrong shape, size or colour even though it is perfectly edible.[57]

Human and animal health

In the developed world, the days have passed when small farms would raise a few animals to be slaughtered at the local abattoir and sold by the local family butcher. Britain has lost one-third of its independent butchers in the past ten years. The number of abattoirs has halved from 850 to just over 400, a trend accelerated by recent EU regulations. In 1979, family butchers sold almost half of Britain's meat; supermarkets sold a quarter. By 1999, butchers were selling just 14 per cent and supermarkets 73 per cent.[58]

Meat is now produced by intensive businesses that process thousands of animals on centralised factory farms, transport them vast distances to abattoirs, and sell their products on the international market. The system could hardly have been better designed to traumatise the animals and spread disease.

Several recent health scares have highlighted the risks inherent in the global trade in food and animal feed. Imported feeds or meat used for pigswill are suspected to have caused the 2001 outbreak of foot-and-mouth disease in the UK. Even producers' representatives acknowledged that globalisation contributed to the problems. Digby Scott of the UK National Pig Association said: 'Supermarket greed and the drive for globalisation at all costs has turned this country into a cesspit for the world's cheapest meat and meat products.'[59] During the outbreak, Ben Gill, the executive director of the NFU, asked: 'Is it a coincidence that we had classical swine fever in East Anglia last year of an Asian origin, and Foot and Mouth now, also of an Asian origin? It raises questions about freer world trade.'[60]

Prompted by its concern to protect exports and regain foot-and-mouth-free status as quickly as possible, the UK government adopted a policy of mass slaughter, rather than vaccinating animals in the area surrounding outbreaks of the infection. Over 10 million animals had to be destroyed. According to the NFU, the UK earns £630m a year from meat and dairy exports. Yet the National Audit Office estimated that the cost of lost tourism and government compensation for animals culled as a result of the foot-and-mouth epidemic was around £9bn.[61] In effect, that would mean it would take more than 14 years of exports to compensate for the damage done in a few weeks of the brutal 'cull to eradicate' approach. Other estimates put the total cost as high as £20bn.[62]

Increased global trade in food is also thought to be responsible for recent foot-and-mouth outbreaks in many other countries. Japan had previously not had an outbreak since 1908, yet was recently affected. An outbreak in South Africa may have been caused by the illegal import of food waste from Asia to make pigswill. It is likely that the export of infected sheep was responsible for the spread of foot-and-mouth from the UK to the European continent during 2001.[63]

Between November 1986 and December 2000, approximately 180,000 cases of bovine spongiform encephalopathy (BSE) were confirmed in cattle in the UK. It is likely that the true number of cases was higher. Since 1989, approximately 1300 native BSE cases have been reported in France, Ireland, Portugal and Switzerland and some were also reported in Belgium, Denmark, Germany, Italy, Liechtenstein, Luxembourg, the Netherlands and Spain. A few cases have also been reported as far away as Canada, the Falkland Islands, and Oman and the number of new variant Creutzfeldt-Jakob disease (CJD) cases recorded in the UK currently stands at 139.[64] The volumes of feeds and feed ingredients traded between countries has undoubtedly contributed to the global spread of the disease, yet the UK government has admitted that it has no idea how much of the 170,000 tonnes of meat and bone meal that were exported to around seventy countries between 1990 and 1996 might have been contaminated with BSE.[65]

It is not only the spread of disease caused by transporting live animals for fattening and slaughter that is of concern: the practice itself is unnecessarily cruel to the animals involved. In one case two lorry loads of lambs were left baking in the sun for 48 hours on their way from Britain to Greece. They had been 'literally cooked alive' according to the inspector who discovered them.[66]

Whilst this is an extreme example, millions of live animals are transported large distances every year. In 1998 for example, 6.8 million pigs, 2.9 million cattle and 2.5 million sheep were transported between EU member states.[67] EU policy actively encourages the export of live animals, just as it does the export of many agricultural 'products'. Producers receive around £400 per live animal exported from the EU in export subsidies to 'compensate' for the higher EU prices. Similarly, EU policies encourage intensive livestock production through 'headage' payments and quotas, which reward those producing at maximum yields with minimum costs.

Since the mid-1980s, the spread of a number of additional food safety crises such as salmonella, E. coli, swine fever and dioxin contamination of animal feeds have been linked with the long-distance transport of live animals and the emergence of complex and widely dispersed food chains. These factors contribute to the problems by swapping diseases between countries, increasing livestock stress and reducing the traceability of food.

The use of antibiotics and hormones in livestock production is another major food safety and animal welfare problem that risks the health both of the animals and the people who eat them. Since 1998, the EU has banned the sale of beef from cattle treated with artificial hormones, and has applied the ban in a non-discriminatory fashion to both domestic and imported beef products. Exposure to the artificial hormones themselves has been linked to cancer and premature pubescence in girls, although the risk to humans of artificial hormone *residues* in the meat they consume is uncertain. On the basis of the known risks and the public's demand for a ban on meat from cattle treated with artificial hormones, the EU adopted a 'zero risk' standard. Rather than 'trying to assess a tolerable amount of an indeterminable risk or waiting for negative human health effects to accrue over time', the EU chose to eliminate public exposure to the risk altogether. As a result, in January 1996, the US challenged the ban at the WTO and, two years later, a WTO panel ruled in its favour. Since the EU has chosen to maintain its ban in the face of the WTO ruling, it is having to pay 'compensation' to the US for the privilege of doing so.[68]

Footing the bill

The system of agriculture that underpins the great food swap stands accused of destroying the environment and countless rural livelihoods; creating larger, more intensive farms at the expense of smaller, more sustainable ones; and inflicting inhumane treatment on animals. The true cost of the apparently cheap food it generates is hidden and paid, if at all, through health and environmental clean-up budgets, and recently through compensation to farmers for BSE and foot-and-mouth. It is virtually impossible to quantify its total overall cost. One study that has attempted to calculate the hidden or 'external' cost that non-organic farming imposes on just the environment and human health in the UK arrived at a total of £2.34bn per year (based on 1996 data). For example, significant costs were associated with the contamination of drinking water by pesticides (£120m per year) and nitrates (£16m); damage to wildlife, habitats, hedgerows and drystone walls (£124m), emissions of polluting gases (£1.113bn), soil erosion and organic carbon losses (£96m), food poisoning (£169m), and BSE (£607m). The total amounts to £208 per hectare in addition to CAP subsidies.[69]

Producers and consumers alike are coming to realise this is a price not worth paying. A global food movement has sprung up, both in the North and South, to demand a radical change. Groups like La Via Campesina, a global alliance of small and family farmers, peasants, the landless and indigenous people are championing the concept of 'food sovereignty', that is, the ability to prioritise local food security above the production of exports and dependence on imports, and free from the control of agribusiness TNCs. They want subsidies shifted away from supporting intensive production, which results in export dumping, towards paying for a transition to more extensive and organic farming, with higher standards of animal welfare, reduced pesticide use and less dependence on expensive and dangerous technologies such as GM production. The redistribution of land is another crucial demand that would help to rebuild rural economies and decrease wealth discrepancies, both within rural areas and between rural and urban dwellers.

To a very limited extent, these demands are being heard and, in some cases, acted on. For example, the EU has ruled that by 2012 European farmers will have to phase out the battery cage for laying hens. Proposals to largely decouple CAP subsidies from farm productivity and integrate support for farming with rural development and environment programmes have been agreed. Demands that the export of live animals be banned are growing. After each successive health scare, food hygiene regulations have been tightened. However, these piecemeal measures only tackle the worst symptoms of a system whose underlying problems are left unaddressed. It is one thing to impose new regulations on abattoirs for example, incidentally forcing many smaller ones out of business, and quite another to reduce the complexity and geographical spread of food chains and stop long-distance transport of live animals that is often responsible for the source and spread of a disease in the first place.

Worse still, as far as many farmers are concerned, most of these measures are double-edged; farmers incur higher costs by meeting higher standards and are therefore left more vulnerable to competition. For example, shifting away from the battery egg system is going to impose extra costs on European producers. However, they will still have to compete with, say, US egg powder that will continue to be produced in a manner that is hugely detrimental to hens, and will be cheaper as a result.

Understandably, farmers feel that they are being asked to perform two mutually exclusive tasks simultaneously. The free trade rules of the WTO are forcing them to become ever more internationally competitive and market-led. At the same time, consumers and some bodies such as the EU are demanding higher standards of animal welfare and environmental sustainability. These demands will be unachievable if farmers are forced to produce at world market prices that are below the cost of production, and compete against imports that are produced to lower environmental, welfare or social standards.

The European Union's Economic and Social Committee clearly acknowledged this clash as a fundamental problem in its recent paper, *The Future of the CAP*: 'Economic pressure on many "traditional" farmers has continued to grow apace. There has been growing tension between the new demands made by society on agricultural production (sustainability, multifunctionality) and the economic exigencies that farmers have to contend with as a result of ever-sharper competition.'[70] Groups such as the Small and Family Farmers Alliance and the Family Farmers' Association have frequently warned that imposing such conflicting priorities on farming threatens the survival of farmers.

It is clear that enforced global competitiveness is a curse that is preventing us from rebuilding thriving and truly sustainable rural economies worldwide to deliver local food security based on safe and nutritious food. We must vigorously reject further globalisation of the food trade, and work instead for the relocalisation of agriculture.

LOCAL FOOD – GLOBAL SOLUTION

Local food security must replace international competitiveness as the central goal of agricultural policy. It may be an unfashionable and undervalued concept, but local food security is the only way to feed the world without incurring the hidden costs of intensive agriculture. Countries (or geographically and economically cohesive regions) should have the right to determine their own policies on food security: in short, they should enjoy 'food sovereignty'.

The US rural sociologist Jack Kloppenberg coined the term 'foodsheds' as a useful way to summarise this approach. According to Kloppenberg's definition, foodsheds are 'self-reliant, locally or regionally based food systems comprised of diversified farms using sustainable practices to supply fresher, more nutritious foodstuffs to small-scale processors and consumers to whom producers are linked by the bonds of community as well as economy'.[71] Foodsheds are a reality in many parts of the world, particularly in developing countries, but where supermarkets are dominant only very faint traces remain. Encouragingly, however, a spontaneous reaction against the globalised marketplace is taking place in some areas and foodsheds are being sketched back onto the agricultural landscape. For example, the UK is experiencing an enormous growth in farmers' markets. In just five years from 1997 to 2002, the number of farmers' markets has multiplied from the first fledgling market in Bath to 450 regular markets. An estimated 7,500 individual markets take place each year. Between them, the markets had an impressive annual turnover of approximately £166.3m in 2002 – more than double the amount just two years previously when it was in the region of £65m.[72] Farmers' markets benefit farmers, who get a fair price for their product, as well as consumers, who get choice, quality and good prices. They are good for the environment, because they involve less transport and packaging and the produce is more likely to be organic or less intensively produced; they are good for the rural economy, since they keep money circulating locally, and they foster stronger community relations.

Impressive though these first signs of relocalisation are, it will take much more than farmers' markets in the UK to deliver local food security on a global scale. Not least, it will require a fundamental shift in the balance of power over agricultural policy away from the agribusiness and supermarket TNCs as well as a fundamental revision of the rules of the WTO and the other free trade treaties. The rest of this section outlines the steps that need to be taken, chiefly in the developed world, to achieve this aim.

Revealing the hidden costs

The introduction of eco-taxation is crucial to the localisation of agriculture. This would ensure that the cost of food reflects the true costs of agriculture in terms of environmental damage, input-intensive production methods and long-distance trade. In particular, fossil fuel taxes should be levied on all transport sectors including airfreight, which at present is tax-free. Fertiliser and pesticide taxes are also needed to reduce pollution and encourage a switch to less energy and chemical intensive farming.

Ending surpluses and protecting the environment

The remedy that is normally suggested to stop the North generating and dumping surpluses and reduce the impact of its overly intensive agricultural methods is to decouple subsidies from production levels and use them instead to support a range of environmental and rural development schemes. On the face of it, these reforms appear to be an obvious means of removing incentives for overproduction and limiting environmentally damaging farming practices. Despite resistance from some EU member states such as Germany and France, the pressure to reform the CAP along these lines has been mounting over many years. A reform package was finally announced in June 2003, which promised some reductions in price support, a partial decoupling of subsidies from production levels and the amalgamation of the CAP's complex system of product specific subsidies into a 'single farm payment'. The payments will be related to farm size and conditional on 'cross-compliance' with a list of 18 environmental, food safety and animal welfare objectives. The reforms are a compromise deal, agreed only after they had been watered down to mollify French objections. As a result, they will not be introduced until the beginning of 2005 at the earliest and completed only in 2007; individual EU member states will also be given freedom to retain strong links between production levels and subsidies if they 'deem it necessary to minimise the risks of land abandonment'.[73]

Reaction to the deal has been mixed. The governments involved in the negotiations were inevitably swift to accentuate the positive. Margaret Beckett, the UK secretary of state, found it 'hard to overstate the importance' of the deal,[74] whilst her French counterpart, Hervé Gaymard, put on enough of a brave face to claim, 'I think very honestly that this compromise can legitimately give us satisfaction',[75] despite the significant concessions that France had been forced to make. Large farmers in many EU states had long since accepted the inevitability of decoupling and were pleased that overall subsidy levels were to remain the same and would still be related to farm size. Thus, the National Farmers' Union of England and Wales was able to welcome the 'historic' agreement on decoupling, which it claimed, 'will enable farmers to focus more clearly on the needs of the market'.[76] Mainstream environmental groups such as the UK's Royal Society for the Protection of Birds and the Campaign for the Protection of Rural England also welcomed the package. It was left to development groups to point to the down-sides of the agreement. The scathing verdict of Barry Coates, the director of the World Development Movement at the time was, 'This deal has more holes in it than a farmer's jumper.'[77] Oxfam echoed this view, scorning both the let-out clauses that will partially retain the link between production and subsidies, and the fact that the overall annual level of support for European agriculture is to remain at 43bn euros (£30bn) until 2013.[78]

Some trade analysts in the South have echoed Oxfam's concern about the overall level of subsidies that European farmers will continue to receive. They argue that decoupling alone simply will not have the desired effect of reducing production if the overall subsidy levels are not cut. Citing the European cereals sector as an example, they point out that production has not decreased even though the EU has been partially decoupling its subsidies since the 1990s. Indeed, EU cereals production *increased* by 25 per cent as overall subsidy levels had in fact increased. Although the EU has intervened at prices much closer to the world price – and 50 per cent lower than the previous intervention price – it has channelled larger direct payments to farmers, which have in effect operated as export subsidies. The analysts conclude that the recent reform will make the price and trade effects of the CAP instruments less, not more, transparent because farmers will continue to gear production to the overall level of subsidy they receive, regardless of the label attached to the payments.[79]

Clearly, in order to bring the crushing inequity of export dumping to an end, developed countries must stop all payments that, by design or accident, subsidise exports. But even this might not achieve cuts in overproduction that are as big as is hoped, since subsidies are not the only factor that generates surpluses and intensification. In some sectors, such as cereals, EU production subsidies certainly do contribute to these problems, but 80 per cent of EU subsidies are directed at just 20 per cent of mainly bigger farms and a large percentage of farmers receive no production subsidies at all. Moreover, some of the most intensive agricultural sectors, such as pigs, poultry and vegetables, are not subsidised by the EU at all. The low farm-gate prices farmers receive for their produce go a long way to explain this apparent paradox. Farmers always do the same thing in the face of a low farm-gate price. They increase production by intensifying their farming: more animals in the same space, more milk from the same number of cows, more tonnes to the hectare, and so on. They are forced to produce more from less simply to survive and provide for their families.

What is needed, then, is a policy that simultaneously removes both of the main incentives that lead to intensification, overproduction and export dumping: namely, export subsidies and cripplingly low farm-gate prices. Working with small farmers' representatives, we recently launched discussions of one such radical proposal that is based on foodshed-specific quotas and guaranteed farm-gate prices.[80] Under localisation, the level of production of any food product within each foodshed can be geared to meet a target that is set to satisfy local need, with allowance made for export in the case of speciality, tropical or exotic crops. Working from the target, individual farms within the foodshed can be allocated a quota contingent on their meeting specific local and national objectives, such as animal welfare, hygiene and nutritional standards, and environmental, biodiversity and rural development goals. Quotas would remove the incentive for intensification and the overall target levels for production would prevent the generation of surpluses.

However, to ensure that farming incomes would be adequate, fair minimum farm-gate prices would need to be guaranteed for all within-quota produce. Minimum prices would be based on the average return needed to provide a reasonable income after production costs that include the highest standards of environmental protection and animal welfare have been met. Additional grants could be made available to fund the development of cooperatives for marketing of local and regional produce, the transition to organic production and the achievement of higher animal welfare and environmental standards. Existing subsidy budgets would fund much, if not all, of any shortfall between market prices and guaranteed farm-gate prices, and paying farmers to produce only for market needs would eliminate the huge costs of storing excess production and the need for the export grants that are currently used to dump surpluses on world markets.

The scheme also has the advantage that the income received by farmers would be linked to their farming effort, something which smaller farmers in particular value. The UK Family Farmers' Association, for example, has argued:

> There is a strong feeling among farmers that their reward should be related to their farming efforts; that if they farm more successfully they should reap a better income. They do not want to receive what would amount to a pension, just for existing as farmers. They really do not want to be dependent on subsidy cheques at all, but would much prefer to be rewarded by fair prices for the food they produce, i.e. the cost of production plus a reasonable profit.[81]

This quota-based system is a radically new approach and many of the details need to be developed more fully. It might not have all the right answers, but we believe it is addressing the right questions, and has the potential to unite consumers and the global justice movement with the overwhelming majority of the world's farmers, whilst creating space, North and South, for local food security.

Protecting domestic markets through import controls

Cheap imports could easily undermine a quota system or any other programme that is designed to engender local food security. Import tariffs and quotas are therefore essential to protect domestic markets and allow a transition to production for self-reliance. Potentially, they have several additional benefits, which include avoiding imports that do not conform to domestic welfare and environmental standards, reducing the distances travelled by food products and controlling the spread of disease. The next two sections deal with their possible drawbacks.

Clearly, the current rules of the WTO and other regional trade treaties make it impossible to limit trade in order to protect food security. A crucial goal for trade reformers must therefore be to establish food security as an objective that overrides the free trade objectives of the agreements, effectively excluding trade in food from the agreements altogether.

Protecting consumers

One consequence of sourcing more food domestically rather than importing cheaper produce, internalising external costs of agriculture, and paying fairer prices for imported exotic crops, is that the cost of food might rise. Several steps would be taken under localisation to ensure that this does not increase food poverty and that poorer consumers in particular are protected from any price increases.

Extra costs for the consumer would be avoided by measures designed to curb the power of the supermarkets and processors, and force them to pay higher farm-gate prices at the expense of their profit levels. A report from the UK Competition Commission in the year 2000 highlighted a range of anti-competitive measures the major supermarkets impose on their suppliers and this report prompted the introduction of a Code of Practice in March 2002.[82] However, the Code was watered down after consultation with the industry and is severely limited. It is voluntary and only covers farmers who sell direct to the supermarkets, rather than to food processors. Furthermore, a survey of farmers conducted by Friends of the Earth found that less than half of respondents (44 per cent) were aware that a Code of Practice had been introduced, and out of those that were aware, most had not seen a copy. More than half of the farmers who responded (58 per cent) did not think that the Code of Practice had made any difference to the way in which supermarkets did business with them. All the supermarkets bound by the Code of Practice (Asda-Walmart, Safeway, Sainsbury and Tesco) were named by farmers as engaging in practices recognised as unfair by the Competition Commission.[83] New legislation is needed to prohibit the unfair trading practices of the supermarkets and to establish a regulatory watchdog for supermarkets, OfShop, which would have the same powers as any other watchdog, such as Oftel or Ofsted. The Code of Practice should be toughened, extended to cover food processors as well as retailers, and made legally binding.

Even if supermarkets are forced to lower prices by cutting their profits, there might still be a danger of increases in food prices. Social welfare mechanisms such as the minimum wage, citizens' income or benefits should be adjusted to compensate for any increase in the cost of a 'basket' of basic food products to ensure that this does not harm the poor.[84]

Supporting farmers in the developing world

A rather predictable objection to the proposal to allow import controls is that they would be unfair to poor producers in the South whose livelihoods depend upon access to Northern markets. This would be a fair criticism if the only element of our proposals were the erection of import barriers in the North. However, they also include measures that would end the dumping of the North's subsidised exports in the South, and uphold the right of developing countries to impose barriers against imports that would otherwise undermine their own food security – the so-called 'Development Box' proposal (see Box 9.2). For this reason, farmers and activists in the South are already advocating proposals similar to ours.

As we saw in Chapter 6, Indian academics and activists are calling for the reintroduction of import controls as a response to the collapse in rural incomes following a WTO ruling that enforced import liberalisation. A recent report by the prestigious Delhi-based Centre for the Study of Global Trade Systems and Development identified the importing of foreign goods and services without quantitative or tariff restrictions as instrumental in destroying India's agriculture and industry, and in causing further unemployment. It called for more emphasis on domestic investment, and the protection of domestic employment through the curbing of foreign investment, selective capital controls and higher tariffs.[85] The Indian People's Movement Against the WTO, made up of trade unions, farmers' organisations, and other activists, echoes these demands.[86]

Indeed, many prominent commentators in the developing world are also highly critical of the emphasis on agricultural exports as a strategy for poverty reduction. The Indian academic and activist Vandana Shiva has said:

> The ecological and democratic model of food security is based as far as possible on ecological production and local consumption.

> **Box 9.2 The 'Development Box'**[87]
>
> A number of NGOs have recently suggested introducing a 'Development Box' into the WTO's Agreement on Agriculture. This would be a package of exemptions from WTO rules designed specifically to allow developing-country governments to protect their poorest farmers and to support national food security.
>
> The Development Box would be targeted at small farmers in developing countries, rather than the South's own agribusiness lobby. Governments would be able to raise tariffs to protect small farmers from being swamped by imports, and would be exempt from WTO commitments to reduce support to small farmers (such as funding transport to get their crops to market).
>
> This will give the governments flexibility to protect key 'food security crops', which mainly consist of staple foods grown by small farmers and are vital to the way a country feeds itself.
>
> This particular proposal is designed to apply only to developing countries, since, in the views of its NGO proponents, 'once you allow Northern governments to get in on the act, battalions of lawyers will start twisting the rules to benefit big business.'[88] However, we believe similar principles could and should apply to both North and South, and that adequate safeguards could be introduced to prevent big business from being the chief beneficiary.

Trade liberalisation ignores this truth ... Diverting food from rural households and communities to global markets or diverting land from food crops for local consumption to luxury crops for export to the rich North might show growth in dollars in international trade figures but it translates into increased hunger and deprivation in the rural areas of the Third World.[89]

By the same argument, hunger and deprivation will be reduced in Southern countries once they are freed to divert food and land back from the global export markets to their rural households and communities.

Crucially, these trade-related measures are part of the wider localisation agenda that involves many other initiatives to complement the global shift towards local food security. One such initiative is the cancellation of debts and the other elements of the Green Marshall Plan outlined in Chapter 6. This would remove the chief factors that are forcing developing countries into dependence on export markets in the first place. Nevertheless, to give time for producers, both Northern and Southern, to adapt, the proposals should be introduced gradually and with, if necessary, as much effort expended to achieve international consensus as is currently to achieve further trade liberalisation.

Another objection, readily advanced by the agribusiness TNCs, is that even if not producing for export, Southern farmers can best alleviate hunger by adopting GM and other intensive technologies. However, a recent study led by Professor Jules Pretty at Essex University has shown that small farmers can dramatically increase production, not through intensive monoculture, but by using simple, low-cost techniques with local inputs. The research studied the effect of 'sustainable agriculture' projects involving 4.42 million small farmers in developing countries farming 3.58 million hectares of land. Projects were categorised as sustainable if the farming practices they used aimed to reduce water use, regenerate soils by using manure, prevent erosion though shallow ploughing and minimise the use of agrochemicals. The study found that average food production in these projects increased by about 73 per cent per household. For those that were growing important staple crops such as potatoes and cassava, the increase was about 150 per cent, far greater than anything promised by GM technology[90] (see Box 9.3).

Box 9.3 GM Crops – Myths and Reality

What are GM crops?

GM (genetically modified) crops have their genetic make-up modified by adding genes from other species, in order to make them resistant to insects or disease, or tolerant to pesticides, among other things. Genetic engineering is imprecise and unpredictable. By inserting foreign genes into the DNA of a host, new life forms are created that have never occurred in nature. The long-term impacts of this are unknown.

Will they solve hunger?

The advocates of GM technology, desperate to find new arguments to persuade a sceptical public of the benefits of GM foods (and GMOs – genetically modified organisms), are increasingly presenting GM crops as a panacea for world hunger. Yet the reality is that the root cause of hunger is not absence of food *per se*, but lack of *access to* food – often for complex political, social and economic reasons. Famines frequently occur, after all, in countries that have a food surplus.

Indeed, developing countries have good reason to be wary of GM crops. In many of them, staple food crops such as rice, maize and potatoes have wild relatives growing close by which are prone to cross-pollination, and thus GM

▶

contamination is likely to be worse. In Mexico, for example, imported GM maize has already contaminated native varieties.[91]

According to evidence gathered by Action Aid in countries like Mozambique, Brazil and Pakistan, GM crops will not solve hunger in these countries.[92] On the contrary, the main beneficiaries are likely to be the biotechnology giants as they increase their control over markets.

Similarly, although GM vitamin A-enhanced rice (so-called Golden Rice) is being advocated by GM companies as a solution to Vitamin A deficiency, in reality it is unlikely to be successful. A GM fix cannot address the fact that micronutrient deficiencies are symptoms of poverty, poor hygiene, environmental degradation and social inequality. Moreover, in order to satisfy the required daily intake of vitamin A, an adult would need to consume huge quantities of cooked rice a day – around 9kg, compared to the current daily average of 300g a day.

Halting the spread of GM crops and GMOs

GM crops pose unpredictable and irreversible long-term risks to environmental and human health; only the biotech companies stand to benefit. We therefore oppose the release of GM crops into the environment. Countries that do not allow GM crops to be grown should be able to prevent all imports of GM food and animal feed. Among our concerns are that:

- GM crops are living organisms and, once released, can spread in the environment via insect-borne and airborne pollen and seeds, contaminating other crops and wild plants.
- New 'super-weeds' may evolve which will be difficult or even impossible to eradicate. This has already happened in Canada where farmers are having to use several applications of more toxic herbicides to eliminate volunteer (that is, self-sown) crops that are the product of cross-breeding between different GM varieties and have developed resistance to several common herbicides.[93]
- Wildlife may be harmed by toxins in the environment or changes in agricultural practices.[94]
- The new GM characteristics may cause allergies.
- If antibiotic-resistant 'marker' genes are used, they may be passed from food to bacteria in people's digestive tracts, thus reducing the effectiveness of antibiotics in protecting human health.
- The GM process might have unintended biochemical effects on the plant, which might affect food safety.

In the South, as in the North, food security is best delivered through simple, locally based solutions. Radical land reform policies that give landless peasants access to small areas of land will do far more to alleviate hunger than forcing small farmers off the land or into dependence on agribusiness companies and export monoculture. Even in situations of acute hunger, simple improvements to the local food distribution and storage systems are often all that is required to ensure that everyone has adequate access to food. In Zambia, there are large surpluses of cassava in the north of the country, but it cannot be moved to the hungry south. A similar situation prevails in Ethiopia.

The 'best' efforts of the international institutions have done little to solve the problem of hunger over the last few decades. In fact, their export-oriented solutions have proved to be an integral part of the problem. They should adopt instead the global solution of local food security.

WHAT, NO BANANAS?

Achieving local food security would not put an end to all trade in agricultural products. Rather, countries would attempt to become self-sufficient in the foodstuffs best suited to their own climate, soils and farming methods, whilst relying on residual long-distance trade to supply products that cannot be produced in every region. In this way achieving local food security would limit the needless transport of food by trying to meet as many of our basic needs as possible from closer to home. It would bring diversity back to the land, enabling us to provide for ourselves in a sustainable and equitable way. It would rebuild communities and their connection to the land. And, it would not mean having to go without coffee, oranges or bananas in temperate climates.

However, if the remaining international food trade is not to undermine the goal of food security in the exporting regions, it must be conducted equitably and in a way that minimises its ecological impact. Some commentators have summarised this as the 'Fair Trade Miles' approach, which combines the requirements of fair trade with food miles.[95] Under this approach, export crops would be produced predominantly by small farmers using sustainable farming methods and sourced as close to the market as possible in order to minimise transportation. As an extension of the domestic quota and fair farm-gate price regime, Fair Trade Miles would require importing countries to guarantee to buy a certain quantity of goods within a guaranteed range of prices. As far as is feasible, this would deliver exporting nations a secure level of earnings, which they could use to achieve the overriding goal of rediversifying local production. Another major advantage of Fair Trade Miles for consumers and producers is that it would deny the TNCs that dominate global trade in cash crops the power to play one producing country off against another.

OPENINGS FOR CHANGE

For the sake of food safety, animal welfare and environmental protection; to rebuild rural economies and communities; and to properly address the threat of global climate change, it is vital that we relocalise food production. Yet, this will not be easy to achieve. A collective 'mindshift' is needed for the logic of this new direction for agriculture to prevail, and significant political will is required to overcome the momentum that is propelling us in the opposite direction. International agreements will have to be changed, in particular the rules of the WTO, which do not allow countries to make choices between imports on the basis of the way they have been produced or erect barriers to protect local food security.

These are undoubtedly huge challenges. Yet several influential voices have spoken in support of the localisation of agriculture. The former president of the European Parliament's Committee on Agriculture and Rural Development, Friedrich Wilhelm Graefe zu Baringdorf has welcomed this approach and called for it to be debated not just in Brussels, but also in the WTO and in agriculture and environment ministries everywhere. Germany's agricultural minister Renate Kunast has also demanded that changes in Europe's agriculture should result in 'a great leap forward for local economies'.[96]

The crisis in agriculture is so acute that pressure for radical change is mounting from all directions. In ever-greater numbers, Southern producers are rejecting the 'solution' of market dependence. Northern consumers are increasingly aware that they pay, in effect, three times over for food: through shop prices, through taxes to fund subsidies, and through the external costs intensive agriculture imposes on farm animals, rural communities, human health and the environment.

Budgetary pressures are also concentrating minds in the North. For example, the CAP costs over 40 billion euros, around half of the total EU budget and one hundred times more than the EU's youth, culture and education budget; 300 times more than the EU's environment budget; and 2000 times more than the its consumer protection budget. The prospect of extending this level of expenditure to ten new members to a large extent propelled CAP reform; in the event, farmers in the applicant countries will initially receive subsidies at just one-quarter of the level of their counterparts in the existing member states.

Nowhere is the pressure for change more acute than at the WTO where agriculture is easily the most contentious issue on the agenda. The developing world is demanding greater freedom to protect its food sovereignty, whilst the developed world demands ever greater access to its markets. The EU and the US are at loggerheads and cannot agree a package of 'concessions', and the member states of the EU can barely agree on the extent and pace of CAP reform. The deadlock threatens to stall the WTO's Doha round. Just three months before a March 2003 deadline for resolving differences on its Agreement on Agriculture, the WTO issued a 90-page negotiating text that, in the words of the US-based Institute for Agriculture and Trade Policy (IATP), revealed 'vast differences between proposals from developed and developing countries'.[97] The IATP's trade director, Sophia Murphy, commented: 'It stretches reality to think that the WTO can take 90 pages of major differences and turn it into 10 pages of agreement in three months.'[98] In the event, reality was not stretched and the deadline was missed. Something in this deadlock has to give; it must be the developed world's hypocritical insistence on liberalisation in the developing world, not the livelihoods and food security of millions of the poorest people around the world.

The international community is confronting a dilemma. It can see already the cost of handing mainstream food production over to international agribusiness, with its disregard for the particularity of place, its people and environment, yet it seems powerless to resist the forces that are inflicting those costs. Localisation provides the missing focus for resistance and the global solution of local food security.

10
Localising Money

> The euro is centralising the economy of Western Europe. Interest rates are imposed by an undemocratic central bank, regardless of local economic and environmental conditions. The tight monetarist framework of EMU is destroying jobs and public services. Britain should not join the euro.
> Green Party Manifesto, 2001[1]

Throughout much of continental Europe the historic project of European integration, culminating in the adoption of a single currency, has been a touchstone of progressive internationalism ever since the Second World War. It is not hard to see why countries that have been invaded by their neighbours within living memory should seek to lock those neighbours into common structures, nor why progressives in the defeated aggressor should shy away from asserting the primacy of national institutions over their shared international counterparts. Perhaps for this reason, Greens in continental Europe have largely accepted the euro and the single market that was its necessary precondition, and settled for attempting to reform from within their excesses of economic centralisation. It is left to their irascible cousins who inhabit the north-western fringes of the continent to point out that in the euro, the EU's internationalist ideals have been captured by the corporate agenda.

We believe that the real internationalist agenda does not extend to the creation of an ever more ruthlessly competitive supranational trade bloc, but our position has not always been helped by the strange and often questionable bedfellows opposition to the euro brings. It is all too easy for anyone who is opposed to the single currency to be characterised as an antediluvian 'little Englander'. After all, the argument goes, anyone who is on the same side of the debate as Rupert Murdoch and Margaret Thatcher must be reactionary, xenophobic, and for some, even worse, 'anti-European'. Nevertheless, the climate of political correctness, which at times threatens to stifle the European debate, is one of the reasons why progressive, internationalist critics of the EU project have been at pains to find their voice, and not make the mistake of leaving the pitch clear for the xenophobic and nationalistic Right to lose the argument.

Opposing the single currency does not make us nationalistic or anti-European, far from it. It is precisely because we have a wider vision about the role of Europe that we are so critical of the narrowly defined economic objectives of the EU, of which European Monetary Union (EMU) and the euro form such a key part.

We believe that the EU must put social and environmental justice at the heart of its domestic and international policies by pursuing the economics of localisation. By contrast, one of the overriding aims of the single currency is to turn Europe into a giant economic superpower, able to compete more 'efficiently' with the US and Japan. To this end it is increasing economic centralisation and accelerating economic globalisation.

We therefore oppose EMU and the single currency, not for narrow nationalistic reasons, but because we believe that the economic logic of this dubious experiment is flawed and rides roughshod over our key social and environmental concerns.

This chapter sets out a Green critique of EMU, demonstrates how the euro damages the economics of sustainability and outlines how, by applying the logic of localisation to monetary policy, currencies can be transformed from their current status as totems of assertive national self-interest to become the servants of a new equitable, sustainable and internationalist economics.

THE ECONOMICS OF SUSTAINABILITY

Green politics aims to create a truly sustainable society; one that will allow the natural systems of the planet to continue to meet basic human needs indefinitely. This requires a genuinely equitable distribution of resources, not only amongst the current human population, but also between our own and future generations. It also depends on a truly democratic system of governance where the needs of all, including the most marginalised, are recognised and met. Only when a full commitment to equity has been established will people be prepared to work together across cultural and political divides to overcome the many challenging obstacles to sustainability.

A commitment to sustainability translates into a clear set of socioeconomic priorities and constraints. These differ markedly from the consumption-and-growth-at-all-costs assumptions of free market economics. Decent housing and healthy food must be available to all. High standards of environmental protection must guarantee unpolluted air and water and the opportunity to enjoy access to an unspoilt natural environment. Everyone should be able to find a useful and fulfilling occupation without facing exploitation at work or having to sacrifice contact with family and friends. Redistributive measures should be employed to reduce divisive inequalities, provide a safety net against poverty and ensure a good standard of education and health care. Fiscal and regulatory frameworks should systematically favour environmentally benign forms of production and consumption.

Britain should only join the single currency if membership would make it easier to meet these priorities and constraints. Our view is that it would not. Britain will be better able to establish a truly sustainable economy outside the euro. This conclusion stems from three main features of EMU: the first is the undemocratic nature of the EMU project; the second is the size and diversity of the euro-zone, and the third is the monetary policy of the European Central Bank (ECB). Each of these factors reflects the fact that the entire project has been moulded to fit the corporate agenda. We will examine them later in the chapter.

EMU: ACCELERATING GLOBALISATION

It suits multinational corporations to have a uniform market with a single currency over as large an area as possible, regardless of the natural diversity of that area. They like nothing better than a rigid monetarist environment with maximum price stability, enforced by a central bank that is beyond all democratic control. In EMU we are witnessing nothing other than the creation of the European branch of the globalised economy.

Over the past ten years, EU liberalisation, deregulation and privatisation policies have facilitated waves of mergers and acquisitions that have resulted in ever greater corporate concentration. EMU is likely to encourage this trend yet further. The banking and insurance sectors have been particularly hard hit as companies search for larger markets, advantages of scale, cuts in costs and higher profit margins. The takeover of the Belgian bank BBL by the Dutch-based ING Group, and the merger of Zurich and BAT, two large insurance companies, are among recent examples. Tens of thousands of jobs were lost and many thousands of bank branches were closed throughout the EU.

The introduction of more competition in the postal services of EU member states is having a similar effect.

At the same time, companies that previously organised their operations at the level of individual countries are now increasingly operating on a European level. The single currency promotes this process by removing the final barriers of the single market, such as currency fluctuations. As a result, pan-European companies have huge advantages over smaller companies that produce primarily for local markets, since EMU reduces the expenses these large businesses face and offers them economies of scale. In 1995, for example, the US-based sportswear producer Reebok International had 14 distribution warehouses for its European market; three years later, only ten were left. By 1 January 1999, when the euro was introduced, a single distribution centre remained. This trend is causing both massive job cuts and a significant increase in the environmentally damaging long-distance transport of goods.

Monetary union is also likely to result in ever fiercer cross-border competition. The euro makes the instant comparison of prices and productivity within the whole euro-zone possible, increasing the trend of relocations to the most competitive areas, and exacerbating the competition between countries and regions to attract investments. As one Morgan Stanley economist remarked, 'If you remove currency as a safety valve, governments will be forced to focus on real changes to become more competitive: lower taxes, labour market flexibility, and a more favourable regulatory backdrop for business.'[2] Under this scenario, the future for progressive policies such as ecological tax reform and other measures to protect people and the environment looks bleak indeed.

THE ERT: AN EARLY ADVOCATE OF THE SINGLE CURRENCY

Unsurprisingly, the European Roundtable of Industrialists (ERT) was an early and vocal advocate of European monetary union. 'Japan has one currency. The US has one currency. How can the Community live with twelve?', it asked in 1991.[3] A few years earlier it set up a separate body, the Paris-based Association for the Monetary Union of Europe (AMUE), to take forward its agenda on EMU. Its influence has been significant, as former Commission President Jacques Santer has gratefully acknowledged. Addressing an AMUE board of directors meeting in 1998, he said:, 'The members of the Association have been a major driving force behind the EMU project. Many of your companies have played a leadership role by clearly advocating the advantages of the single currency for the private sector and society as a whole.'[4]

The AMUE claims to have organised over a thousand conferences and seminars involving officials from the Commission and from national states to promote the single currency. It also held three seats on a twelve-seat 'independent' expert committee on the introduction of the euro that was set up by the Commission, on AMUE advice. The committee's work was instrumental in securing the European Council decision to launch a speedy introduction of EMU at the December 1995 EU Summit in Madrid. Both the Commission and the European Parliament also often choose the AMUE for public tenders requiring expertise in monetary matters; indeed, the Commission frequently consults the group on monetary questions, both formally and informally. 'It's a very confident way of working', explains AMUE Secretary-General Bertrand de Maigret. 'They call us, we call them, they see us, we discuss matters. They are quite flexible.'

For the AMUE, EMU is a logical step towards the completion of the single market, which is still not as 'efficient' as industry would like. According to de Maigret, EMU will bring 'monetary stability and long-term certainty, which will increase productive investment, generate economies of scale and eliminate production costs, which in turn will increase competitiveness, sales, economic growth and employment'.[5] Significantly, he says nothing about the widespread social and economic upheaval across Europe, which EMU has already caused.

The AMUE, of course, is not alone. Alongside it, the Union of Industrial and Employers' Confederations of Europe (UNICE) and the EU Committee of the American Chamber of Commerce (AmCham) share a similar approach. As AmCham's former manager for European affairs, John Russell explains, 'We exchange a lot of information, have joint meetings and even publish joint papers.'[6] These three corporate groups use what Russell calls the 'choir approach', echoing and reinforcing each other's positions: 'It is normally more effective not to say everything together, but to have different people telling the institutions more or less the same thing.'[7] Since the single currency was introduced, UNICE has been calling for structural reforms and flexible markets so that the 'benefits' of EMU can be reaped more efficiently. The reforms are meant to achieve a permanent reduction in public spending, 'particularly in the areas of public consumption, pension provision and health care, welfare benefits and state subsidies'.[8] UNICE's views on the single currency are uncompromising: 'Try to favour business, that's the point. This is a clear follow-up of the EMU.'[9]

Favouring business and favouring employment is not always the same thing however, and while EMU certainly favours the former, its interest in the latter is small.

IN WHOSE INTEREST?

Given its parentage, it is not surprising that supporters of EMU argue that the euro reduces costs and uncertainty for industry, and therefore boosts international trade. Before the introduction of the single currency, businesses trading between euro-zone countries had to allow for foreign exchange transactions and fluctuations in exchange rates. Even though these currency exchange costs amounted to only about 0.1 per cent of GDP immediately prior to the introduction of the euro, they have been eliminated. Similarly, though of marginal benefit in the scale of things, individual euro-zone citizens have been relieved of the inconvenience and expense of changing currency when travelling between member states. A related claim is that the euro has made governments' economic planning simpler because of the greater stability of currency markets and removal of the threat of competitive devaluation by fellow member states. Greater price and wage transparency across borders will, they claim, also help to ensure the efficient allocation of goods, labour and resources and control inflation.

Economists are divided on whether or not these benefits outweigh the economic costs of joining the single currency. For the reasons outlined below, we believe they do not, even in conventional economic terms. But further still, the basic flaws in the structure of EMU mean that by joining the euro Britain would be prevented from establishing a sustainable economy.

EMU ATTACKS DEMOCRACY

The most obvious of EMU's many flaws is its lack of democracy. A precondition of achieving a sustainable economy is that it can be democratically regulated to meet a wide range of social and environmental objectives. Yet, with the introduction of the euro, member states handed control of their interest rates to the ECB. Inflation targets are pursued by the ECB and the exchange rate strategy for the single currency is determined by the EMU finance ministers in consultation with the ECB. Domestic fiscal and public spending policy is constrained by the terms of the Stability and Growth Pact. In short, much of the economic sovereignty of member states of the euro-zone has been pooled and handed over to European institutions, primarily the ECB.

In a true democracy the various electorates of the EU would of course be free to pool their sovereignty as they wish and to hand it to the institutions of their choice. However, two major questions hang over the democratic credentials of the EMU project.

The first relates to the ECB itself. It is guaranteed far greater freedom from political intervention than was previously enjoyed by any of the central banks of the euro-zone. The Treaty of Rome, as amended at Maastricht, states, 'Neither the ECB, nor any member of their decision making bodies shall seek or take instructions from community institutions or bodies, from any government of a member state or any other body ... The governments of the member states undertake ... not to seek to influence the members of the decision-making bodies of the ECB.'[10]

This contrasts with the situation in Britain for example, where even the 'independent' Bank of England works to the government's inflation targets. Allowing for differences in the way the inflation index is calculated in Britain and the euro-zone, the Bank of England's inflation targets are currently as tight as the ECB's. However, they can be varied to suit wider economic conditions and the Bank of England could even see its independence removed by a future government. Nothing short of a revision of the Treaty of Rome or the new European Constitution, when it is introduced, would be necessary to change the relationship between the ECB and political institutions of the EU.

The powerful and independent position enjoyed by the ECB does not rest on a democratic mandate. It is controlled by a committee of six, including the president and vice-president. They are unelected and unaccountable to the voters. In effect, it is these people who have their hands on the principal economic levers of the euro-zone. They position those levers to meet the tight monetarist criteria of the Stability and Growth Pact, leaving domestic governments to answer for the level of unemployment or cost of mortgages that result. This situation falls a long way short of our definition of true democracy.

EMU's second area of democratic deficit stems from the process that gave birth to the euro. EMU has always been as much if not more a political rather than an economic project and rarely, if ever, has it been debated as an economic proposition without the political imperative of European integration overshadowing the proceedings. Rarely have the people of the EU member states had the opportunity to decide whether to accept EMU without the wider issues of political integration coming into play. The Maastricht Treaty sealed the conditions of EMU, but was negotiated in such extreme secrecy that it has become a parable of a political elite losing touch with the people. The treaty places the ECB beyond any democratic control and, incredibly, contains no provision for a country to leave the single currency. The draft European Constitution is little better. It only permits a state to leave the euro by leaving the EU.

Several member states held a referendum on the Maastricht Treaty, but aside from EMU, the treaty dealt with several other important issues. It is therefore impossible to interpret the half-hearted backing that it received in those referenda as a firm endorsement of EMU itself.

DEFLATIONARY MONETARISM WRIT LARGE

EMU's democratic deficit is compounded by the doctrinaire and narrow form of monetarism it incorporates. EMU has imposed a raft of financial and budgetary rules on participating countries. Their aim is to maintain a tight grip on inflation by restricting the supply of money. The ideology on which EMU is based pays little or no attention to the wider economic consequences of its monetarist obsessions, despite the fact that deflation has replaced inflation as the main threat to economic stability in the euro-zone.

The preconditions for membership of the euro were established in the Maastricht Treaty. In order to qualify, member states had to meet four economic convergence criteria. These were:

- a rate of inflation no more than 1.5 per cent above the average of the three member states with the most stable prices;
- a budget deficit not greater than 3 per cent of GDP and public debt not more than 60 per cent of GDP;
- long-term interest rates not more than 2 per cent above the average of the three best performing member states in terms of price stability, and
- two years' participation in the ERM.

The years leading up to the introduction of the euro on 1 January 1999 were characterised by governments' attempts to cut their budget deficits in order to qualify for membership. During these years, unemployment in the EU began to approach 20 million. Nevertheless, when the time came, Italy and Belgium were permitted to join the euro, despite the fact that their debts exceeded the limit of 60 per cent of GDP.

The final piece in EMU's monetarist jigsaw is the Stability and Growth Pact, agreed at the Dublin Summit of 1996. This commits members of the euro to set budget deficits no greater than 3 per cent of GDP in any one year, with the medium-term aim of balancing their budgets. A government that exceeds this limit will be subject to financial penalties if it does not take corrective action and is not specifically exempted by a two-thirds voting majority of the EMU members of the Council for Economic and Financial Affairs (ECOFIN). The penalties take the form of a fine of 0.2 per cent of GDP plus 0.1 per cent of GDP for every 1 per cent of GDP the budget deficit exceeds the 3 per cent limit, up to a maximum of 0.5 per cent of GDP.

The combined effect of these measures has significantly coloured the economic environment of Western Europe. The ECB's priority is to set interest rates at levels that ensure inflation stays below its target of 2 per cent. Unlike the inflation target the UK government sets for the Bank of England, the ECB's target is not symmetrical. In other words, anything under 2 per cent, including 0 per cent, is good; anything over 2 per cent is bad. This institutes a deflationary bias that even extends to EU member states outside the euro-zone, which are nevertheless assessed against the rules of EMU. EMU's monetarist zeal has been felt throughout the EU in the form of deep cuts to public spending.

The German government reduced its spending by £10bn in 2002, including cuts of around £2bn to its health budget. This brought 15,000 health workers on to the streets of Berlin in protest. Cuts of £35.8bn are planned in the period up to 2006. In September 2002, the Dutch government unveiled spending cuts of 3.5bn euros and the Italian government's budget for 2002 included spending cuts of 8bn euros.

Despite the cuts, many governments are failing to keep within the regulations of the Stability and Growth Pact. As the euro-zone economies stagnate, government revenues fall and welfare costs rise. By mid-2003, Germany, Portugal and France had all breached the 3 per cent rule for government deficits. Germany is potentially liable for fines amounting to as much as much as 10bn euros, or £77 for every German citizen, which would only lessen its ability to provide decent public services and stick to the rules of the Stability and Growth Pact.

Not surprisingly, resentment towards EMU is growing. It has even reached the president of the European Commission, Romano Prodi, who denounced the Stability and Growth Pact as 'stupid',[11] and opinion polls have begun to show majorities in the Netherlands, Germany and France in favour of returning to their national currencies.[12] Concern is also mounting in the UK over the effects euro membership would have on public spending. Bill Morris, general secretary of the Transport and General Workers' Union, commented, 'you cannot have improved public services at this particular point and have the EU Stability and Growth Pact. You have to choose.'[13] Bob Crow, general secretary of the Rail, Maritime and Transport Union, wrote in a letter to *The Times* that 'millions of trade unionists' were concerned about the way economic policy was being conducted in the eurozone and opposed 'this country being reduced to a rate-capped county council run from Brussels'.[14]

As if to bolster the trade unionists' arguments, the European Commission warned Britain that its public spending plans for both 2001 and 2002 would fall foul of its Economic Guidelines if Britain were inside the euro. In 2002, Britain was told that it would have to cut public spending or increase taxes by £41bn over the three years up to and including 2005–06, the likely time of a general election, if it were in the euro. In the event, the Chancellor, Gordon Brown, simply accused the Commission of 'interference' and went on to announce even larger rises in public spending.[15]

Anyone looking for signs of a softening of the European institutions' rigid monetarist stance in the face of a mounting clamour for reform will be disappointed. Domingo Solans, a member of the ECB executive council, said in a speech, 'Let me emphasize the world "strict". No reinterpretation, no second readings, no flexibility should be allowed in this domain',[16] and in response to indications that France intends to flout the Pact, Ernst Welteke, president of the Bundesbank, said: 'If you start thinking about reinterpreting the pact, as the French have done, then you bury all credibility in EMU.'[17] Similarly, in 14 appearances before the European Parliament up until February 2002, ECB officials have advocated public spending cuts on twelve occasions and the deregulation of labour markets on all but one.[18]

PFI-DDLING THE BOOKS

One way in which governments are able to curtail their budget deficits is to keep public spending 'off balance-sheet' by transferring the borrowing risk to the private sector. In the UK, this is achieved by means of private finance initiatives (PFIs) and public private partnerships (PPPs) and an increasing range of projects, such as new hospitals, schools and transport infrastructure, are being financed in this way. Under a PFI or PPP, private sector companies design and build public sector facilities, which are then leased back to the relevant public sector body. Public expenditure is limited in the short term because the capital advanced by the private sector does not appear as an immediate lump sum in the public borrowing requirement. However, the public body that commissions the facility has to pay off a high-cost mortgage for the lifetime of the lease, typically thirty years. In addition, the involvement of the private sector curtails the public accountability of the services that are provided.

PFI/PPPs have encountered widespread criticism as a more costly, less effective and less democratic way of delivering services than direct public funding. Whilst the invective against PFIs varies, the theme is consistent. An editorial in the *British Medical Journal* branded them 'perfidious financial idiocy'[19] whilst the general secretary of Britain's largest trade union has called on government to abandon the 'discredited PFI gamble'.[20] A more measured analysis was recently presented in an academic study of the costs of PFI hospital schemes. This concluded that the NHS has paid nearly twice as much for new PFI hospitals than it would if they had been built using taxpayers' money. This was partly due to the fact that private borrowing is more expensive than public borrowing, and partly because under PFI even apparently basic tasks such as raising capital and carrying out negotiations incurred substantial additional costs. As a result, the amount of money NHS trusts had to spend annually to finance the capital costs of new hospitals was more than three times greater than had the project been built using public money. Despite this, government figures suggest that PFI schemes represent better value for money than publicly financed projects. The study's authors conclude that this is only because the government's formula for assessing economic value of PFIs is flawed and has not been properly evaluated. Overall they conclude:

The high cost of PFI schemes has presented NHS trusts with an affordability gap. This has been closed by external subsidies, the diversion of funds from clinical budgets, sales of assets, appeals for charitable donations, and, crucially, by 30 per cent cuts in bed capacity and 20 per cent reductions in staff in hospitals financed through PFI. Though NHS funds have increased since 1999, there is no evidence that much has flowed through to baseline services.[21]

In our view, this is an unacceptable price to pay to keep the ECB happy.

DOES THE EURO FIT THE EURO-ZONE?

One of the requirements of localisation is that 'external' costs are internalised. Fiscal policy backed up by regulation can go some way to achieve this. For example, a strong carbon/energy tax combined with road pricing and city-centre restrictions on the use of private vehicles would go some way towards internalising the costs of congestion and air pollution in urban areas. However, the effect will be reinforced if economic policy decisions are as sensitive as possible to social, environmental and economic conditions at a local level. In Britain, for example, congestion and the cost of housing are more of a problem in the buoyant South-East than in some other relatively depressed areas and ideally, economic policy would be adjusted on a regional basis to reflect this. Since certain key instruments of economic control, such as interest rates, cannot be varied between different parts of a single currency area, it will be hard to gear economic policy to local conditions in a very diverse currency area. Decisions will necessarily be inappropriate for some of its regions.

For example, if a central bank were to set base interest rates at a relatively high level in order to dampen inflationary pressures in the prosperous regions of its currency area, this would worsen recession in the more deprived regions. Conversely, if the central bank were to lower interest rates to meet the needs of these poorer regions, the economy in the prosperous regions might overheat, with undesirable local effects such as the increased traffic congestion, environmental pressures and rapidly rising house prices that currently characterise the South East of England. It might also feed inflationary pressures throughout the currency area. This would, in turn, undermine the effectiveness of the original attempts to help the poorer regions.

Clearly, the larger and more diverse a currency area is, the harder it will be for its central bank to set interest rates at a level to suit the entire area.

All the evidence suggests that the euro-zone is too big for a one-size-fits-all interest rate. Using a methodology known as the Taylor rule to determine the optimal interest rates for the seven leading euro-zone economies, Maurice Fitzpatrick, chief economist for the City of London firm Tenon, found that Germany's interest rate in the summer of 2002 should have been 0.8 per cent rather than the ECB rate at that time of 3.25 per cent. Meanwhile, the higher levels of inflation that were prevailing at the time in the neighbouring Netherlands suggested an optimal rate of 6.5 per cent.[22]

Proponents of the euro counter that EMU will produce sufficient benefits in terms of economies of scale, exchange rate stability, and increased international trade and inward investment to outweigh any negative effects of a one-size-fits-all interest rate. The evidence so far does not support their case: euro-zone unemployment is rising and economic growth is falling, and the euro-zone economies have not outperformed the other EU states in terms of international trade and investment.[23]

German unemployment, which remained stubbornly high after the economic shock of reunification took full effect in the early 1990s, has risen sharply under the ECB's one-size-fits-all interest rate. In the first year after euro notes and coins were introduced in Germany, 41,500 businesses folded, causing the loss of 650,000 jobs, or 1,800 jobs every day. During the same period, French unemployment rose in every month except one, whilst it fell in the UK.[24] In 2003, economic growth in the euro-zone stagnated. Manufacturing output declined and its leading economies feared a Japanese-style deflationary crisis. Their governments could only appeal to the ECB to cut interest rates.[25] At the same time, other euro-zone economies were struggling with record levels of inflation that would hardly be helped by a cut in interest rates. Between December 1999 and December 2002, prices in Ireland increased by 14.2 per cent, compared with the EU average of 6.6 per cent. Despite a slowdown in the Irish economy since then, its inflation rate continued to outstrip that experienced by the rest of the EU. In the year up to February 2003, average EU consumer price inflation was subdued at 2.3 per cent, whereas in Ireland it accelerated to 5.1 per cent. Ireland became the second most expensive place to live in Europe, close behind Finland.[26]

From the launch of the euro to the third quarter of 2002, the value of the UK's international trade has grown by 36.8 per cent, more than France at 16.3 per cent, Germany at 29.5 per cent and Italy at 27.5 per cent.[27] Furthermore, a recent report by Ernst & Young showed that Britain's share of inward investment coming into the EU increased from 26 percent in 2001 to 28 percent in 2002 and that Britain overtook France as the top destination for manufacturing projects. The report concluded:

> The issue of euro membership appears to be a bit of a damp squib as far as inward investors into Europe are concerned. Whilst there are undoubted financial benefits for the countries within the single currency, these appear to be counterbalanced in inward investment terms by concerns over reductions in growth rates in major markets, probably in part due to the loss of some independent national economic levers such as interest rates and exchange rates.[28]

Whatever the theoretical benefits of a single currency they appear to be more than outweighed by the fact that the euro does not fit the euro-zone.

WHAT IS AN OPTIMAL CURRENCY AREA?

The question of what constitutes an optimal currency area has been much debated since the Nobel Prize winner, Robert Mundell, published his seminal work on the subject in 1961.[29] Economists agree that an optimal currency area is one where the impact of any economic shock is symmetrical, or at least not so asymmetrical that any part of the area requires additional demand management to help it absorb the shock. This definition does not require the regions of an optimal currency area to be completely homogenous as there are, according to orthodox economic theory, a number of mechanisms that increase their cohesion and help them to react similarly to economic shocks.

Chief amongst such mechanisms are labour and capital mobility. In other words, unemployed workers in depressed regions are expected to relocate to any prosperous regions that are experiencing labour shortages – the Tebbitt school of 'get on yer bike' economics.[30] According to Otmar Issing, chief economist at the ECB, the lack of 'flexibility' in the European labour market is 'an almost lethal threat to monetary union'. His solution is to deregulate the labour market and attack the 'misguided incentives provided by the social security and welfare systems' that entice unemployed workers to stay where they are.[31]

Investors too are supposed to move around at will. Theoretically, they will find greater returns in depressed regions where there is a pool of readily available and cheap labour, and lesser returns in prosperous regions where the factors of production are more scarce and expensive. If the point is reached where enough new investment has occurred in the depressed areas to allow the remaining workers to stay put and get a new job locally, then equilibrium will have been re-established within the currency area. Failing that, the different regions should specialise, the poorer ones in labour-intensive activities, the richer ones in capital-intensive production, and trade with each other to even out the imbalances. If equilibrium is still not achieved, then the government of the currency area can always bolster flagging regions with some regional aid and fiscal transfers from wealthier regions.

There are problems with the theory. For instance, left to their own devices, investors tend to favour centres of market buoyancy within a currency area, rather than its depressed areas. Similarly, the migration of workers away from a depressed area tends to accelerate the downward spiral of market contraction and recession, rather than opening new opportunities for the people who are left behind. Together, these factors will exacerbate rather than reduce regional disparities, thus increasing the need for redistribution between regions before the currency area can be considered optimal.

IS THE EURO-ZONE AN OPTIMAL CURRENCY AREA?

In the decades running up to EMU, the EU devoted much energy to increasing the mobility of capital and labour and to removing barriers to trade within the single market. It has also established a programme of regional assistance aimed at reducing the economic disparities between different areas. Together with the convergence criteria, these measures were aimed at reducing the economic disparities between the different regions of the EU, but have they succeeded? Is the euro-zone an optimal currency area?

Notwithstanding the EU's strenuous efforts, the countries of the EU and the euro-zone are economically, culturally, environmentally and socially very diverse. For example, in 2000, per capita GDP in the EU's richest cities was five times that in the poorest rural regions.[32]

In 2001, unemployment levels in the worst hit regions of Spain and Italy were 15–20 times higher than in the more prosperous areas of the Netherlands and the UK.[33] The cultural and environmental capacity for further economic growth in traditional agrarian areas is very different from that in more industrialised regions.

Additionally, there are ties, such as language and family, which quite naturally make people reluctant to relocate between different regions of the EU. According to the European Commission, for every person that relocates from one EU member state to another, 27 people move between states in the US. At just 1.27 per cent of EU GDP, the EU's regional aid policies and fiscal transfers between regions, which are deliberately intended to reduce regional disparities, are far smaller in proportion to the extent of these EU-wide regional disparities than are the equivalent domestic measures within most member states. They are also far smaller than the counterpart measures in the US dollar currency area, which account for around 20 per cent of US GDP.

Tony Thirwall has reviewed the evidence of regional disparities in the EU. He finds little clear evidence of economic convergence over time. Per capita incomes in the poorer regions and countries have caught up with those of the richer areas at an annual average rate of 2 per cent between 1950 and 2000, but that rate was faster in the 1950s, 1960s and 1970s than in the 1980s and 1990s. The productivity gap between rich and poor regions has converged at a slightly faster rate, but this has been at the expense of growing levels of unemployment in the poorer regions. Disparities in unemployment levels appear to be remarkably stubborn. From the early 1980s they have shown a pro-cyclical pattern, increasing during recessions and narrowing during booms. However, they also show a slight but noticeable underlying upward trend.

Overall, research shows that regional disparities in living standards and unemployment across Europe depend largely on the relative performance of individual countries. In other words, the relative fate of regions is predominantly tied to the performance of their national economy rather than to EU-wide economic trends.

Thirwall concludes, 'I know no one who believes the current eleven countries of Euroland constitute an optimum currency area.'[34] We do not seek to step outside that consensus, which if true of the eurozone will hold even more firmly in relation to all member states of the EU following its enlargement to include ten more states in 2004, and a further two by 2007.

REGIONAL DISPARITIES UNDER THE EURO

Because the euro-zone is not an optimal currency area, economic shocks impact asymmetrically on its constituent countries and regions. This was illustrated most graphically in 1992 by the impact of German reunification on the forerunner of the euro, the exchange rate mechanism (ERM). The ERM tried to keep participating currencies within a narrow band of exchange rate fluctuations, as a first step towards merging them into a single currency. The British government's ultimately unsuccessful attempts to keep the pound's value within the correct band after German reunification severely distorted domestic economic planning. The government lost £18bn of currency reserves, 1 million jobs disappeared and 1.75 million homeowners were pushed into negative equity. Since Britain's unceremonious ejection from the ERM, inflation has fallen and whilst unemployment on the continent has continued to rise, in Britain it has halved.

Where the ERM limited government control over interest rates, inflation targets and hence exchange rates, membership of the euro abolishes it completely. Policy becomes 'one size fits all' and is driven centrally by the ECB. Yet as the ERM fiasco demonstrated, economically divergent countries react differently to economic shocks, and revaluing their currencies against each other is a vitally important safety valve for avoiding the balance of payments problems that this would otherwise generate. Furthermore, the imposition of an inappropriate interest rate itself can operate like an external economic shock and increase disparities. Returning to the example of Germany, Fitzpatrick concludes that once saddled with the wrong interest rate, divergence tends to accelerate. Germany's optimal interest rate halved from 1.6 per cent to 0.8 per cent in just nine months.[35]

Under EMU, regions are forced to compete with each other across larger areas and so the basis of their competition will move increasingly away from local comparative advantages, more towards absolute advantage. In this brave new world many regions will find that they have no absolute advantages and therefore no basis on which to compete. They will in effect be consigned to dependence on regional aid handouts. They will become pockets of deprivation and unemployment. Their economic difficulties are likely to be matched by a sense of alienation and despair as more people are forced to live on benefits, opt out of the formal economy, or move away to find work.

The converse will also be true. Successful regions will tend to become more successful. The danger is that their economies will overheat, with all the attendant social and environmental problems that brings: pressure on schools and hospitals, more pollution and congestion, spiralling house prices, pressure for more built development and new roads. The so-called North–South divide in the sterling currency area (in reality a divide between the South-East and the rest) already provides both an illustration of this problem and an argument for stronger regional policy or even regional currencies in Britain. By 2001, GDP per head in London and the ring of counties surrounding it had reached 139 per cent of the average for the rest of the UK,[36] and the gap in competitiveness between these two areas of the country grew by 30 per cent between 1997 and 2003.[37] Neither the North nor the South provides a good model of the economics of sustainability; still less would they under the euro.

Diane Perrons offers a convincing demonstration that the Maastricht convergence criteria have in fact exacerbated regional disparities within the EU. Between 1983 and 1995, regional disparities increased in all EU states apart from the Netherlands.[38] More recent evidence, cited in the UK Treasury's *EMU and Labour Market Flexibility* assessment, shows that the unemployment in some EU regions is about ten times greater than in the 'best performing regions'. This is particularly notable in the four largest euro-zone states, and the gap has been increasing in recent years.[39]

Arguably, regional disparities within the euro-zone could be limited by far-reaching reforms to the EU including the democratisation of the ECB, and the adoption of much more active regional industrial and employment policies. The European budget could allow for automatic fiscal transfers, such that if one area were in recession, it would pay less tax to Brussels and receive a greater proportion of benefits. However, these policies would have to be ingeniously crafted to be effective and would require a far greater appetite for political and fiscal integration than currently exists even in the most ardent integrationist breast – an appetite that would work directly against the logic of localisation.

EMU: A PACT FOR INSTABILITY

After, and partly because of, the centuries of European conflict that culminated in the Second World War, very few people do not now profess the ideals of European internationalism and common progress. Supporters of a single currency claim that the euro will further those ideals, but the very opposite is likely to be the case. EMU is moulding the European economy to the corporate agenda of globalisation, regardless of the fact that this agenda has never worked for the majority of the world's poor and is increasingly eroding the job security, environment and sense of community many people previously enjoyed in developed countries. Its one-size-fits-all straitjacket is exacerbating regional disparities within the euro-zone and leaving elected national governments powerless to respond. In EMU we are witnessing the spread of free-market fundamentalism, promoted by an EU that continues to place a corporate-led, neoliberal agenda above social justice and sustainable development.

At the same time, monetary union is straining the EU's commitment to enlargement and has made it much harder to achieve. For many analysts, the aims of further deepening the EU and of widening its membership are becoming mutually exclusive. Eastern European countries preparing to join the EU are already coming under intense pressure to prepare for the euro as well, in spite of the fact that convergence will be extremely costly and difficult, and will offer them few, if any, genuine benefits. If enlargement is ill thought out, inadequately resourced and wrongly focused, this will stoke up resentment against the EU institutions and breed resentment between member states, as some are seen to prosper at the expense of others.

The price of ignoring these issues will be high. The growing social inequalities between and within EU member states could force more people into economic migration and generate fertile conditions for the rise of an ugly nationalist Right. This would unpick many of the hard-won benefits of international cooperation and nurture dangerous forces of European disintegration and nationalism.

LOCALISING MONEY: A MOVEMENT FOR ECONOMIC SOLIDARITY

EMU is threatening the future of European cooperation and shared progress because it is driven by political imperatives, regardless of economic realities. It is precisely when currencies are regarded as symbols of control, or tokens of identity that stupid economic decisions are likely to be made. A currency should be regarded instead as no more than a mechanism to facilitate exchange. The monetary levers that surround a currency, such as interest and exchange rates, are simply the channels of regulatory feedback to the economy within the currency area. As we have already discovered, that feedback will be most sensitive when it relates directly to a relatively uniform area, an argument made in reverse by the radical economist Jane Jacobs in 1986:

> Imagine a group of people who are all properly equipped with diaphragms and lungs, but share only one single brainstem breathing centre. In this goofy arrangement, through breathing they would receive consolidated feedback on the carbon dioxide level of the whole group, without discriminating among the individuals producing it ... But suppose some of these people were sleeping, while others were playing tennis ... Worse yet, suppose some were swimming and diving, and for some reason, such as the breaking of the surf, had no control over the timing of these submersions ... In such an arrangement, feedback control would be working perfectly on its own terms, but the results would be devastating'[40]

This is an excellent analogy for the euro, and the different consequences of that particular 'goofy arrangement', whether drowning, hyperventilation or suffocation, are beginning to be seen in the various regions of the euro-zone.

By contrast, localisation aims to give each local economy its own brain stem – a feedback system tailor-made to the local level of economic activity. That way, each local economy can be regulated in accordance with its own activities and goals. This sounds straightforward in principle, but in practice it raises once again the question of what is local. As we have seen, the answer to that question varies from one place to another.

As long ago as 1923, the small country of Luxembourg decided that local was bigger than national and gave up the advantages of maintaining its own national currency in favour of facilitating exchange through a currency union with neighbouring Belgium. In 2003, the officially pro-euro government in the UK reached a different decision, for the time being at least. It found that the economies of the sterling and euro currency areas had not converged sufficiently for Britain to adopt the euro. In other words, supranational is too big to be considered local – a conclusion illustrated by the economic woes suffered by Germany at the time. By the same argument, the persistent and growing regional disparities in the UK suggest that the south-eastern corner of the UK has different economic habits from the rest of the country and perhaps needs to breathe at a different rate, something it could only fully achieve if it had its own regional currency.

At some point in this logical progression towards ever more localised currency areas, the inconvenience and instability caused by the need to trade across currency boundaries will outweigh the advantages of highly specific regulatory feedback, as Luxembourg discovered. Just where this point of equilibrium lies will depend on the relative importance of exchange within a currency area compared with its trade with other currency areas. Thus, under localisation, the point of equilibrium will shift towards the local and optimal currency areas will tend to shrink.

However, different sectors of an economy will always tend to reach different views as to where the point of equilibrium should lie. Imagine a typically characterless industrial estate on the edge of a fictional town in a run-down region of an otherwise reasonably prosperous and averagely sized currency area. The town could be in Canada or the UK, for example, but it is starved of currency because interest rates are too high to suit the local economic climate. Occupying one of the units is a high-tech manufacturer of specialist equipment. The company sources components from around the world and has to export to many different countries to generate sufficient sales volumes. Business is good, particularly in Asia and the company has been pricing its products in euros and US dollars for three years. Next door is a small dairy that buys its milk from a local farmers' co-op and sells its products in local shops and farmers' markets. The local recession has hit the dairy's business.

If asked for their views on the optimal size for the local currency area, the economically literate bosses of the dairy and the manufacturing company would give very different answers. The dairy would do much better under a more localised currency with lower interest rates, the manufacturers would be more concerned about the ease of exchange and would probably favour joining the much bigger currency area next door. There is no single answer to suit them both.

The political dangers inherent in EMU, as outlined above, stem in part from the fact that it forces local dairies and high-tech manufacturers to make the same stark and politically charged binary choice, even though their best interests diverge. The situation that would suit them best is the one where they could trade in any of the different parallel currencies operating in their area to suit their needs. This is already happening to a certain extent in the UK, where some companies, like our fictional manufacturers, are pricing their output in euros and some large retailers accept euro notes and coins from customers. This situation could be formalised if the euro were recognised as legal tender, but the pound retained as the official currency. This would facilitate international exchange, when that is appropriate under the principle of trade subsidiarity, without incurring a loss of control over interest rate policy. What is generally lacking is the opportunity for local regions to create their own means of exchange to operate alongside the national and international currencies and stimulate the local economy.

There are some exceptions to this general rule. Local exchange trading schemes (LETS) provide a very small-scale and informal example. The Swiss Wir system operates along similar lines to LETS schemes to provide low-cost finance to local business. It started in 1934 and by 1993 had 65,000 corporate members and a turnover valued at £12bn. Regional currencies have occasionally emerged, usually in the form of notes issued by regional governments needing to inject liquidity into their local economy. Regional currencies became an important part of Argentina's efforts to recover from its economic crisis of 2001.[41] The New Economics Foundation recently put forward an intriguing proposal for a London-based currency (see Box 10.1).

Local exchange schemes usually encounter official hostility. Central banks are not keen on competition and the schemes are frequently suspected as a means of tax evasion, despite the fact that one-third of global tax revenues are estimated to be lost, not through LETS schemes, but to off-shore tax havens. If a local currency is based on a unit of exchange that is of practical value to the tax-raising authority, as would be the case in the London example, there is no reason why it should not accept taxes in that currency.

Local currencies and exchange schemes, running in parallel with national and international currencies, could have a vital role to play in boosting the resilience of local economies. They would allow local communities to assign value according to local conditions, retain wealth within the local area, supply low-cost finance to local businesses and provide an alternative source of liquidity when it is denied by the one-size-fits-all prescriptions of the wider economy. In short, they provide the means to weave economic solidarity into the heart of the local economy.

> **Box 10.1 An Underground Currency for London**[42]
>
> Tickets for the London Underground will shortly be electronic digits on a smartcard, thanks to a £1.8bn project. But imagine if you could buy these journey units in small shops all over the capital and could exchange them easily, along the lines of a Mondex or Visacash card, from card to card. Imagine, like Mondex, that you could download them onto a card in a mobile phone. Mondex and Visacash are experimental electronic versions of pounds that can be held on cards, downloaded over the phone or via computer direct from your bank. The technology has advanced so much that you can now pay parking meters or drinks dispensers in Finland simply by phoning them up.
>
> Now imagine that these units also circulated around London's local economy, swapped from card to card by card readers in shops and pubs or kept in a handbag or pocket. Imagine that, as well as paying the price of an underground journey, you could also use them to buy what you need in the local economy. Let's call this new electronic currency 'tubes'. London Underground may then find they have created a *de facto* regional currency, which can be redeemed in journeys – and is therefore not subject to the same inflation as pounds or euros – but which we can also use to buy a range of other things in the informal and maybe formal economy too. Tubes could be bought in the normal way, of course. But they could also be issued into the economy in no-interest loans to small business – in return for a fee – and then earned by people providing a range of services in the local economy, ranging from building work to informal baby-sitting. The Underground would get the fees and some benefit from 'float' – because it may be months before the tubes are redeemed by journeys.
>
> Why shouldn't bars have a particularly happy hour when they accept part payment in tubes? Why shouldn't we launch a range of new babysitting circles and 'favours' groups that exchange tubes? The currency would be trustworthy and able to underpin a range of semi-economic activities that are simply not viable in an international currency like euros or pounds. The Underground would be a bank for the local London economy, underpinning a network of smaller business as Wir does in Switzerland, and the big brand names probably wouldn't accept them. The big utilities would find this kind of currency – one that can only be redeemed in London – hard to deal with. The chances are it would probably stay within the capital.

ENDING THE DOLLAR EMPIRE

The idea that different currencies should operate in parallel to facilitate exchange at different geographic levels is consistent with the principle of trade subsidiarity. It is not widely discussed,[43] but it is by no means a revolutionary concept. Almost 70 per cent of the currency reserves that countries hold to finance international trade and insure themselves against speculators are already held, not in their various national currencies, but in a global currency that is otherwise known as the US dollar. The dollar is used as the main global currency partly because it is regarded as a strong and stable currency, partly because major commodities such as oil are priced in dollars and partly because the World Bank and the IMF insist on it. The US does particularly well out of the arrangement because other nations must sell it goods and services in order to earn the dollar reserves they need. These reserves are then invested in US-issued bonds, which, in turn boosts the US capital account. Additionally, as the authority that issues dollars, the US gains at least $400bn every year in *seignorage* – the difference between the value of the currency it issues and the cost of producing it.[44] If the US needs more oil, it can, in effect, print the money to pay for it.

The net result is that the US is able to overconsume to the extent that it currently sustains a huge deficit with the rest of the world totalling some $2.2 trillion, without fear of being structurally adjusted by the IMF. This explains why, as the world's sole superpower with a population of 290 million people, the US can afford to spend more on armaments than the next 20 biggest military spenders put together, with a combined population of 3.5bn. It also explains why the US can impose its unilateral will on the multilateral institutions with impunity.

There is an urgent need to weaken the US's hyper-dominant position and this could be achieved by replacing the dollar as the global means of exchange. For a start, oil producers could insist on taking payment in a different currency. They could choose the euro, but equally, they could pick the yuan, or even the Venezuelan bolivare. The African Union's proposal to create a new currency for inter-African trade is another example of a step that could be taken to reduce the domination of the dollar. With each of these initiatives, demand for the dollar would reduce and, with it, so would the size of the deficit the US is able to sustain.

Some commentators have run with this argument all the way to the conclusion that Britain's adoption of the euro is the straw waiting to break the camel's back.[45] This, they contest, would strengthen the credibility of the single currency to the point where it can finally challenge US hegemony. Even if we leave on one side the fact that the euro appears destined to weaken the European economy rather than promote it to superpower status, this argument misses the point. There is little to suggest a 'Pax Europeaica' would be fundamentally different from a Pax Americana or the Pax Romana of history. If we are to prevent a re-run of the obscene accumulation of economic, military and political power the US currently 'enjoys', we must rekindle Keynes's original vision of an international clearing union that prioritises balanced trade accounts and uses a global currency that is not controlled by any one nation.

EXCHANGING EMISSIONS

One radical idea for a new neutral global currency is the Emissions-backed Currency Unit (Ebcu), proposed by Richard Douthwaite as a development of the Contraction and Convergence (C&C) method of cutting greenhouse gas emissions.[46] Under C&C, each country would receive an annual allocation of emissions permits on a per capita basis. Over an agreed period of time, the total annual allocation would be reduced until it no longer exceeds the planet's ability safely to absorb the emissions it permits. Countries would be able to trade in emissions permits using Ebcus, which would also be allocated on a per capita basis. Until they became more energy efficient, rich countries that emit more than their fair share of greenhouse gas emissions would need to buy emission permits from poorer countries. Poor countries would have an incentive to invest the Ebcus they receive in the development of energy-efficient economies so that they retained a surplus of tradable permits. Ebcus could also be used as a global reserve currency, as the dollar is now. Thus, the Ebcu would operate within an environmentally sustainable economic framework as a neutral and redistributive means of international exchange, deriving its value from a universally useful commodity, the right to emit greenhouse gases.

The Ebcu proposal is still at an early stage of development and, in common with any other proposals to replace the dollar, US opposition would hamper its implementation. Nevertheless, the economic implications of that opposition would become less powerful as self-reliance increased under economic localisation.

LOCAL MONEY: GLOBAL JUSTICE

The right to create and control currencies has been jealously guarded by sovereigns and governments for centuries because, as we have seen, it confers enormous political and economic advantages. We can then, infer a great deal about the seat of economic power from the dollar's status as the main international currency and the fact that only 5 per cent of the UK's money supply is created as notes and coins by the Bank of England and Royal Mint. The rest is willed into existence by the commercial banks in the form of interest-bearing loans to their customers.

In stark contrast to EMU, and just as the previous chapter demonstrated for agriculture and food, a localist monetary policy would restore economic security at the local and national levels, and, by creating an equitably distributed and ecologically based means of international exchange, embed sustainability and economic justice into the global economy.

11
A New Context for Multilateralism

> While the very existence of the UN attests to a general unity of acceptance of an international society with certain agreed institutions, it is division, not unity, which has been the more conspicuous feature of the world since 1945, as indeed it was ... before that date.
>
> Adam Roberts and Benedict Kingsbury[1]

As we write, the international community is reeling from the US and UK's decision to sideline the UN and invade Iraq. The UNDP has just announced that the Millennium Development Goals will not be fully met until 2165 at the current rate of progress, fully 150 years after the target date.[2] Despite the raging heat of a record-breaking European summer, the painstakingly negotiated Kyoto protocol hangs by a thread as a sceptical Russian government considers whether to ratify. And the world is recoiling from the acrimonious deadlock at the WTO Ministerial in Cancun. On every front, multilateralism, our only means of addressing global problems equitably, is in crisis.

We believe that multilateralism is failing because economic self-interest undermines internationalist cooperation at every turn. By contrast, the pursuit by the dominant powers of economic localisation, rather than economic globalisation, would provide a new context for multilateral negotiations that would help to ensure their success.

SHEDDING THE CLOAKS

The calamity of the Second World War sparked an unprecedented round of international cooperation. Propelled by the war as an example of what happens when cooperation breaks down, the victorious Allies set about the task of creating new global institutions that they hoped would maintain future order with remarkable speed. Before the war came to an end in 1945, fifty countries had signed the Charter of the UN. The deal that led to the establishment of the Bretton Woods institutions had been sealed in the previous year and by 1948 GATT had entered into force.

Many of those who worked to establish the new institutions were inspired by the best ideals of internationalism, which amply cloaked the Allies' naked self-interest. Yet over time, those ideals were diluted by the Allies' determination that the institutions should reinforce their dominant position in the world. As we have seen, the WTO, the IMF, the World Bank and, through the five permanent members of its Security Council, the UN, are all effectively controlled by the same handful of powerful nations. Sixty years on, the cloaks have become insubstantial and easy to discard whenever they impede the dominant powers – and equally easy to slip on again for a quick trip down the catwalk at major international summits. Everyone cooperates and the common good prevails – as almost happened in Kyoto – at moments when the consequences of non-cooperation are demonstrably perilous. For the rest of the time, the weak cling desperately to unequal agreements with the powerful in the hope of restraining the latter's exhibitionist tendencies, and the powerful pursue their own agenda – as ably demonstrated by successive rounds of WTO negotiations.

Multilateral agreements are thus driven by mixed and often conflicting motives. Very occasionally, nothing but the common good is pursued; somewhat less rarely any agreement is prevented by the pursuit of unadulterated self-interest. Most of the time, agreement is spurred by a pragmatic realisation on the part of the powerful that self-interest is best served through limited cooperation and a regretful acceptance on the part of the weak that no better deal is on offer from the strong.

PARADOX FOUND

If there is one international institution that encapsulates the tensions between the different motives for engaging in multilateral negotiations, it is the EU. A stark contradiction exists between the EU's founding ideals and its long-established ambition to muster and project European power onto the world stage. The UK Green Party's manifesto for the European parliamentary elections of 1999 summarised this contradiction in the following terms:

> The EU started more than 40 years ago with the ideals of peace and internationalism. Over time these have been swamped by a relentless drive for power and profits. The Single Market, the Maastricht Treaty and Monetary Union have followed one another.

Each puts profit before people and the environment. With every step economic control has been centralised, giving ordinary people less and less say in the decisions that affect their daily lives.[3]

However, Romano Prodi (President of the EU Commission) appears not to have noticed the contradiction at all. According to him, the EU's ultimate goal is 'to consolidate a European Union that can guarantee our citizens' prosperity and peaceful co-existence on the basis of democracy, competition, solidarity and unconditional respect for human rights'.[4] Competition, it seems, has been elevated to a value as fundamental as democracy and human rights.

This goes some way towards explaining the mixed messages that emerge from the EU. It is widely acknowledged, for example, as a role model for environmental policy making, possessing some of the toughest regulations in the world for air quality, water pollution and vehicle emissions. The reality of Europe's environment is somewhat different. According to the European Environmental Agency, in its second assessment of the European environment in 1998, there had been little or no progress in Europe since 1991 on twelve key environmental problems. 'Positive development in the state of the environment' was found with respect to just one of the twelve problems – the ability to address technological and natural hazards. 'Little or no change' was detected for four problems, while 'unfavourable development' was found for the remaining seven problem areas such as soil degradation, loss of biodiversity and climate change. Even in areas of environmental policy where the EU has been particularly active, such as ground-level ozone pollution, the situation had deteriorated since 1991. Successive assessments from 1999 and 2001 only report a continuation of these disappointing trends.[5]

A similar confusion found expression in the EU's Sustainable Development Strategy, which was launched by Romano Prodi, at the 2001 Gothenburg summit. The Strategy states:

> Just over one year ago at Lisbon, the European Council set a new strategic goal for the Union: 'to become the most competitive and dynamic knowledge-based economy in the world'. The Stockholm European Council then decided that the EU sustainable development strategy should complete and build on this political commitment by including an environmental dimension.[6]

The wording is revealing. It talks of 'an environmental dimension' – a perspective, a cloak – to be draped over the existing economic strategy. If the wording of the Sustainable Development Strategy is revealing, so too was the process it was subjected to at Gothenburg. The Council of Ministers stripped the cloak away: ever obedient to industry demands back home, they gutted the Strategy of all of its specific targets, timetables and vision.

What remains is a severely limited document. It was written with inadequate time for consultation; it fails to consider fully the impact of EU activity on developing countries; it has been deprived of its specific, measurable targets and indicators. Yet, for all that, many of its aspirations are welcome enough. But the question remains: how will the Gothenburg 'dimension' of becoming the most sustainable society in the world fare when it comes into contact, or more accurately, collision, with the Lisbon objective of becoming 'the most competitive ... economy in the world'?

For instance, the Strategy includes the objectives of introducing energy taxation and fully internalising external costs. But unless the WTO permits border tax adjustments and other amendments to its rules, EU producers would very soon be complaining that the additional energy taxes and internalised costs put them at a competitive disadvantage in international markets.

Another of the Sustainable Development Strategy's objectives is to reduce transport congestion and pollution. This is undermined by the EU's commitment to an ever-increasing flow of goods and services within the internal market and beyond. The EU's planned 400bn-euro Trans-European Networks (TEN) programme of new transport infrastructure projects will put this objective beyond reach. The TEN programme alone is predicted to increase CO_2 emissions from the transport sector by 15–18 per cent.

Gothenburg's environmental dimension was tacked on to the objective of international competitiveness as no more than a watered-down afterthought. This is entirely symptomatic of the routine subjugation of the common good to self-interest in international negotiations; it also bears testament to the enormous influence TNCs wield over the development of the EU. Brussels teems with more than 10,000 professional lobbyists who are free to roam the halls and corridors of the Commission, Council and Parliament buildings. The vast majority of them are from PR firms, industry lobby groups, and individual companies. Some of the companies have turnovers greater than many countries and employ whole teams of lobbyists.

The European Parliament's recent report on aviation's environmental impact argued that the huge tax advantages enjoyed by the industry should be ended in order to reduce its greenhouse gas emissions. As one of us, the original author of the report, wrote at the time:

> ... my office became like a waiting room for the corporate lobbyists. Every sector of the aviation industry came to see me: representatives from airports, airlines, aircraft manufacturers, courier companies, you name it, they came in. And their message was at least consistent: 'we care about the environment, we've put a nature reserve in the corner of our airport, don't pick on us, pick on another industry like ...'. Here the consistency broke down as they picked different industries: railways for putting weed killer on their tracks, or motorists because of congestion, or whatever.[7]

The corporate lobbying of EU institutions has been extremely successful. The single market, Maastricht and the single currency have all been moulded to its agenda of international competitiveness and the EU has been effectively restrained from imposing anything other than voluntary codes of corporate social responsibility.[8] Narrow economic self-interest has prevailed.

The same pressures have been replicated at the global level. After six months of negotiations and the assembly of one of the world's largest gatherings of world leaders, the 2002 Johannesburg World Summit on Sustainable Development (WSSD) achieved almost nothing. Most of the negotiating effort had to be directed at preventing a reversal of previous agreements. For instance, a proposal to give formal and explicit precedence to the WTO agreements over international environment and development agreements was only defeated after strong lobbying from NGOs. A few slight glimmers of hope were kindled. The summit agreed on the need for international agreements on corporate accountability. Of the 218 partnership projects announced between governments and the private sector, a few will have a positive effect – although many will force the privatisation of public utilities such as water supply in developing countries. And one tangible target was agreed as an addition to the Millennium Development Goals: to halve the number of people in the world without basic sanitation by 2015. However, the Action Plan issued at the end of the summit contained no mechanism for achieving this or any other target.

It is not difficult to trace the failure of the WSSD to the stance taken by the main developed countries. The US president chose not to attend the event and his country had in any case already renounced any potential it had to provide positive leadership before the summit had even started when it declined, at the behest of the oil lobby, to ratify the Kyoto protocol. The EU could have filled the vacuum by providing the necessary political leadership to promote the sustainable development its leaders called for in their plenary addresses, but it failed. This was partly because it could not agree beforehand to reduce its agricultural export subsidies, and partly because of the strength of its corporate lobby. For example, representatives of the water multinational Vivendi were included on the EU delegation, while Thames Water was given a place in the UK delegation.[9]

EXPORTING SELF-INTEREST?

Addressing a plenary session of the WSSD, President Museveni of Uganda condemned the rich nations for promoting 'parasitic globalisation' rather than 'mutually beneficial multilateralism'.[10] Indeed, the failure to advance 'mutually beneficial multilateralism' at Johannesburg stands in stark contrast to the success with which the rich nations are subverting multilateralism to export 'parasitic globalisation'. Whether by extending existing international agreements or creating new ones, the rich nations are drawing an increasing number of poorer nations into trade and investment deals that are stacked against them. The EU is exporting its offensive and narrowly defined free trade agenda by prioritising the commercial aspects of its enlargement to the East above the wider social, environmental and human rights interests. A similar pattern emerges in its bilateral trade deals with poorer countries. The EU used its recent bilateral agreement with Mexico, a country in which well over half the population lives in poverty, to force open trade in services, investment and intellectual property to a depth and at a speed not even dreamt of in the WTO. The recent EU-Bangladesh Agreement pursued a similarly single-minded and aggressive approach on intellectual property rights. NAFTA extended the original bilateral trade deal between the US and Canada to Mexico, and the same agenda looks set to expand yet further under the Free Trade Area of the Americas (FTAA). Meanwhile, the rich countries are currently trying to use the WTO to increase the depth to which they are able to penetrate the economies of developing countries by pursuing the so-called 'new' issues of liberalising investment, procurement and competition.

NAFTA LEADS THE WAY

Mexico's experience under NAFTA provides a telling illustration of what can happen to poorer countries when 'parasitic globalisation' is foisted on them by unequal trade deals with richer partners. Mexico was promised that it would prosper under NAFTA and there were some signs that the promise might be kept. In NAFTA's first six years, FDI in Mexico grew by nearly 270 per cent, creating nearly 700,000 new jobs in Mexican factories (*maquiladoras*) that assemble imported components into products for export, typically toys and electrical goods. Exports to the US surged from $49.4bn in 1994 to $135.9bn in 2000, and manufacturing productivity had increased by 47.7 per cent from pre-NAFTA levels by May 2001.[11]

Despite this, there has been little enduring benefit for the average Mexican. Attempts to unionise the new industrial sectors have been systematically repressed. Between 1993 and 1999, the real value of the minimum wage fell by 17.9 per cent and average manufacturing wages fell by 20.6 per cent. Air pollution nearly doubled in the first four years of NAFTA and Mexico's forests, the largest remaining intact in North America, are under threat from US-owned timber companies. NAFTA forced Mexico to liberalise its capital markets. This opened the way for the large inflows of FDI, but has also generated a high degree of volatility on the portfolio investment market. A flight of capital in 1994–95 triggered a currency crisis. As the government struggled to steady the economy, soaring interest rates sent many Mexican-owned businesses into bankruptcy and a devaluation of the peso decreased people's purchasing power by 39 per cent. By 1998, 58.4 per cent of Mexicans were living in poverty, up from 50.97 per cent when NAFTA started in 1994.[12]

NAFTA's most devastating impact has been on Mexican agriculture. Despite promises of increased prosperity, the reality has been that the livelihoods of Mexican small farmers have been ruined by cheap agricultural imports from the US's large-scale, subsidised grain producers. At the same time, well-paid jobs were relocated from the US to the environmental disaster-zone of the border region and, although this provided some Mexican jobs, it also led to huge swathes of Mexico's existing 'inefficient' SMEs going to the wall.

ENLARGING THE PROBLEM?

By bringing political unity to a continent that stood divided for half a century, EU enlargement presents an historic opportunity for mutually beneficial multilateralism. Yet, just as with NAFTA, the pursuit of trade-dominated and pro-rich priorities means that the EU is likely to allow economic self-interest to squander much of the opportunity that lies before it. The European Council and Commission envisage an enlargement based on the same free trade approach that is already driving a wedge between the current members of the EU and that will accelerate the rapid market-driven liberalisation that is already increasing unemployment, inequality, environmental degradation and regional economic disparities in Eastern Europe.[13] The Greens in the European Parliament are making the case that the current EU enlargement strategy leaves the major burden of structural adjustment and the impact of economic liberalisation on the accession countries themselves. If enlargement is to be successful, it must be undertaken on more equitable terms, with sustainable development, rather than free trade, at its heart.

Inequality and unemployment

The rail sector in Slovakia is a case in point. With approximately 50,000 staff, the Slovak Railway Company (ZSR) is the biggest employer in the country. In 1998, the Slovak Government announced preparations to lay off around 25,000 ZSR employees, and in 1999 signed a loan agreement with the European Investment Bank (EIB). The predicted results were a 30 per cent rise in fares, a cut of two-thirds in both state subsidies and in staff payroll over eight years, a reduction in rail freight, and a drop in the overall number of lines on the rail network.

There was no discussion about the conditions imposed by the bank. Indeed, the media reported that the Slovak government and ZSR were given just two weeks to reply to the conditions: if they agreed to meet them, the EIB was ready to provide the loan immediately. The Slovakian Centre for Environmental Policy Advocacy sent a protest letter to the president of the EIB, Brian Unwin, who replied, 'The proposed restructuring measures in this case mirror those agreed over recent years between the Bank and virtually all railway companies in the 10 Central and Eastern Europe Countries which have applied for EU membership.'[14]

Proponents of enlargement concede that unemployment has increased significantly in most candidate countries. Their answer is for all countries to increase labour flexibility and mobility in the run-up to and during enlargement. This is free market speak for lower wages, poorer employment conditions and getting 'on your bike' to escape unemployment or low wages. Once the painful reforms and restructuring, together with the large job losses, have been completed, the candidate countries are assured that there will be more jobs. The East Germans were told to expect exactly the same following reunification. Instead, despite the enormous amount of money transferred and the financial advantage of equalising the value of both currencies, they have experienced rising inequality and substantial job losses. All sectors of the East German economy are still experiencing a long-term structural crisis that has produced increased competition for jobs in which people with few qualifications have a high risk of being displaced by those holding higher formal qualification.[15] This is in spite of the fact that in the 1990s, West Germany transferred some 600bn euros to East Germany. The net amount the EU proposes to transfer to its ten new members over the three years between 2004 and 2006 is around just 25bn euros. This paltry sum is put further into context by comparing it to the Marshall Plan, under which the US transferred the equivalent of 97bn euros to Western Europe over the four years from 1948 to 1951.[16]

CAP and Eastern Europe

Slovakia has already seen severe problems in its rural areas. Cheap imports, in particular dairy products, from the EU, have flooded local markets. Prices of agricultural inputs have risen dramatically while at the same time those for agricultural products have stagnated or decreased. Many domestic producers have been taken over by large multinational companies, become bankrupt or switched to export production.

It is clear to most analysts that if the CAP were extended in its current form to the accession countries, not only would the EU be bankrupted, but millions of agricultural workers in Central and Eastern European (CEE) countries would lose their jobs. The CAP's emphasis on so-called 'efficient' farming, and the inevitable intensification of agriculture that this implies, would mean that Poland, for example, could lose up to two million agricultural livelihoods. The majority of its farms are tiny, and simply could not compete with those of its Western European neighbours.

Relocation from West to East

Enlargement may also promote further industrial relocation from the West to cheaper labour sources in the East.[17] However, the precariousness of some of the investment that is coming into the CEE countries is epitomised by General Electric (GE). Founded by famous American inventor Thomas Edison, GE is now headed by Jack Welch, who has candidly remarked: 'Ideally you'd have every plant you own on a barge' – meaning, ready to move if any national government tries to impose restraints on the factories' operations, or if workers demand better wages and working conditions.

GE has slashed its US workforce by almost half since 1986 through automation, downsizing, outsourcing, and plant closures. It has globalised its operations by shifting production to low-wage countries, including Eastern European countries. But even in such countries, the jobs remain precarious. GE recently closed a factory in Turkey to move it to lower-wage Hungary. It has since threatened to close a factory in Hungary and move it to India.[18]

Corporate winners

As with NAFTA, TNCs will be prominent amongst those who gain from enlargement. Unsurprisingly, their lobbying organisations in Europe, UNICE and the ERT, are hard at work promoting the speedy expansion of the EU towards the East. For Western corporations, the CEE countries offer an enormous market waiting to be conquered, as well as a reservoir of skilled and lower-waged labour, as the former director general of UNICE enthusiastically and unapologetically explained: 'In the West we have mature markets. We are already consuming everything that we are able to consume. You cannot drive two cars at the same time. So we have a slow growth economy ...To the East of us, we have around a hundred million people with sophisticated tastes who lack all the items we are already consuming. They need those items.'[19]

It can be made to sound almost altruistic, but the TNCs' desire to furnish Eastern Europeans with every latest consumer good comes at a price far greater than the one printed on the label attached to those goods. It will be paid in terms of structural adjustment, the harmonisation of economic policies and the opening of markets to cheap Western goods, services and short-term investment. And inevitably, just as in Mexico, it will be the people of accession countries who pay and the corporations that benefit. Governments of the current EU member states have wasted no time in setting out the forthcoming opportunities for their national companies. The former UK minister for competitiveness in Europe wrote of enlargement in the following terms: 'I want to be sure that British businesses are ready to seize the benefits. Competition from other member states for the commercial and other economic gains of enlargement will be intense. To be certain that your business secures the most from EU enlargement, you need to be aware of the opportunities offered, and how to exploit them.'[20] Thus, the popular desire for political cooperation across Europe and the pursuit of mutually beneficial multilateralism looks set to be undermined once again by parasitic self-interest.

If it is to find the capacity to undertake a genuinely equitable enlargement, the EU must fundamentally rethink the direction that the process will take and replace the free market priorities of globalisation with a different approach. This approach must value cultural, social and political relationships between the peoples of Europe more than trading links. It must be based on sustainable development and the protection and rebuilding of local and regional economies, and it must provide a framework of internationally agreed minimum standards to support a Europe of strong regions, with decision making brought closer to the people. Not only would this benefit the people of Europe, East and West, it would also equip the EU with sufficient political integrity for it to act as an effective counterweight to the US-led, militaristic expansion of parasitic globalisation. Unfortunately, this approach is not quite what Tony Blair had in mind when he proclaimed to a Polish audience: 'Europe's citizens need Europe to be strong and united. Europe today is no longer just about peace. It is about projecting collective power.'[21]

FEELING DISCONNECTED

The protests that now feature regularly at major international meetings graphically illustrate the popular rejection of the subversion of the internationalist agenda. Additional illustrations were presented to the EU in the form of the Danish and Swedish rejections of the single currency, the 'no' vote in Ireland's first referendum on the Nice Treaty,[22] and the low turnout in the 1999 European elections. The European Commission's regular Eurobarometer opinion polls show that barely half of the 377 million people in the EU consider membership of the EU to be 'a good thing' (the figure fluctuated between 48 per cent and 55 per cent during 1998–2003), and in the latest poll less than half of those asked said that they trust the EU.[23]

Ever since the unprecedented protest by some 25,000 people at the 2001 EU summit in Gothenburg, the official talk is of the EU's 'disconnection' from its people. The protests shook the EU establishment to its core and by the time of the next summit, six months later in Laeken, Belgium, EU heads of state and government had concluded that although the public undoubtedly supported the Union's broad aims:

> ... they do not always see a connection between those goals and the Union's everyday action. They want the European institutions to be less unwieldy and rigid and, above all, more efficient and open. Many also feel that the Union should involve itself more with their particular concerns, instead of intervening, in every detail, in matters by their nature better left to Member States' and regions' elected representatives. This is even perceived by some as a threat to their identity. More importantly, however, they feel that deals are all too often cut out of their sight and they want better democratic scrutiny.[24]

In an attempt to reconnect the EU with its people, the Laeken summit set up the Convention on the Future of Europe, a 15-month consultation exercise presided over by Valéry Giscard d'Estaing, the former French president. This was the widest consultation exercise ever undertaken by the EU and marked a departure from its normal routine of member state governments negotiating treaty changes in secret. This time government representatives were joined by the Commissioner responsible for institutional reform, European and national parliamentarians, and officials and NGOs from member states and accession countries. The Convention tackled many of the most controversial institutional issues surrounding the EU: should it evolve into a German-style federation or a looser grouping of nation states; should it elect a president, and in what areas should the national veto be abolished.

Although the EU has responded to the crisis of confidence in multilateral institutions with greater openness and resolve than the other main international trade and financial bodies, no amount of institutional reform, aimed simply at oiling the wheels of EU decision making, will address the root cause of its disconnection from the people. 'Reconnection' will only occur when the pro-globalisation instincts that have been allowed to drive the EU's development are firmly recloaked in its founding ideals of internationalism.

A NEW CONTEXT FOR MULTILATERALISM

Public opinion in the UK is deeply sceptical of economic globalisation. A MORI survey in 2001 found that only 13 per cent of people believed that globalisation enhances everyone's quality of life. As many as 92 per cent believed that multinational companies should meet the highest human health, animal welfare and environment standards wherever they are operating and 58 per cent (rising to 71 per cent of broadsheet readers) thought that 'what's good for business is not good for most people in developing, poorer countries.' Between 87 per cent and 92 per cent of people thought that the government should protect the environment, employment conditions and health – even when this conflicts with the interests of multinationals.[25] As we have seen, such scepticism is well justified. The multilateral agenda has been captured by the narrow self-interests of the powerful. Hence, the poor are falling further behind the rich and the people of 54 countries became poorer in absolute terms during the 1990s.[26] The global environmental crisis is deepening; new investment in emerging economies has proved fickle and destabilising. As the disparity widens between the official rhetoric and reality, so disillusionment and resentment will grow.

As the current upsurge in international terrorism demonstrates, resentment breeds conflict. This in turn provides the powerful with the pretext they need to stop trying to understand others and to impose their will on them instead. This vicious cycle will only be broken if the multilateral process can be refocused on genuine internationalism, so that the common good prevails over the self-interest of the powerful.

Several attempts have been made to achieve just such a new focus, notably the 2002 Johannesburg WSSD. Rarely, however, have these attempts significantly addressed the root causes of the prevailing failure of multilateralism: the overriding imperative of international competitiveness within a global economy. This encourages the powerful nations to regard international cooperation as a zero-sum game in which any obligation it might entail is seen not as a valuable contribution towards the attainment of a shared goal, but as a threat to their immediate economic self-interest. The US opted out of the Kyoto protocol, for example, precisely because it feared the protocol would decrease the competitiveness of US industry. The challenge then is to create a new context within which mutually beneficial multilateralism can succeed because economic self-interest is contained and no longer stands in its way.

Our contention is that economic localisation provides just such a context. It delivers a regulatory framework that is at once both robust enough to counter the powerful vested interests that operate at the global level, thus removing the imperative of international competitiveness, and yet flexible enough to respond to local needs, recognising that one size does not fit all. It can also be introduced in any individual economic unit that is politically and economically powerful enough to face down the TNCs and international capital markets without first waiting for the outbreak of a global consensus or the dawning of a new and perfect age of global democracy. This would be difficult for an individual nation, but is more likely to succeed initially at the level of a regional bloc such as the EU or perhaps ASEAN in South-East Asia or Mercosur in South America.

Crucially, countries that choose to pursue economic localisation will gain the security to innovate in order to promote the highest standards of social, environmental and economic well-being at home and abroad without automatically trampling on the rights of others to achieve the same objectives or, equally automatically, suffering from a loss of international competitiveness. The most successful innovations will provide examples of best practice for others to emulate; international relations will thus be transformed from 'beggar-your-neighbour competition', where the self-interest of different nations necessarily collides, to 'better-your-neighbour cooperation' where the self-interests of different nations are contained more locally and can therefore coexist without conflict.

More than one billion people live in grinding poverty on less than a dollar a day, where 20 per cent of the world's population consumes 80 per cent of the world's resources and where environmental destruction is accelerating. The need for alternatives to the current damaging patterns of economic globalisation to be implemented is now more urgent than ever. Multilateralism must triumph if global society is to reverse these trends and build a more peaceful and secure world. By removing the obstacle of competitive economic self-interest, economic localisation will provide a new context for multilateralism that offers it the best chance of success.

Conclusion

Our original explanation of the essence of Green politics – whilst standing on one leg – was 'equity, ecology, democracy'. Our metaphorical Rabbi Hillel would have long since toppled over, but he would at least be content that we have not deviated from his teachings.[1] The proposal for a Green Marshall Plan ensures that economic localisation is underpinned by equity. Ecological tax reform and the creation of the Ebcu would enmesh ecology into the heart of our proposals. Meaningful democratic control of markets and companies would be secured under economic localisation by 'site here to sell here' policies, the reinvigoration of democratic governance and the taming of speculative finance. Whenever possible, democratic control would be rooted at a level that is directly accessible to individuals and the communities in which they live. When this is inappropriate, the democratisation of the global institutions would serve to retain democratic oversight. Economic localisation embodies the principles of Green politics. We believe it offers solutions to some of the most contentious disputes that currently mar the trading and economic relationships between nations, and the best prospects for a more cooperative world.

We have argued consistently, on the basis of the overwhelming evidence of the damage being done by economic globalisation, that revolutionary change is required. Revolutions are not instigated by the advocacy of incremental reforms to the status quo, no matter how welcome those reforms might be in the interim. Calling for a revolution might strike some as over-ambitious or unachievable. But, the same could easily have been said in the 1960s had someone published the plan for the major companies, governments and financial institutions of a few rich nations to saddle the majority of the world's population with unpayable debts, commandeer the running of their economies and force them into dependence on markets over which they have no control. Yet, this, of course, is precisely what they have done.

Since its inception, it has been the role of Green politics to stand aside from the mainstream, analyse problems afresh and call for radical change. Sometimes Greens have got the details wrong (contrary to initial predictions, pollution, not resource depletion, has proved to be the most important 'limit to growth', for example),[2] but far more often than not our basic analysis has been proved correct. Reactions to our proposals follow a predictable pattern. At first they are ignored, then ridiculed, and finally accepted and sometimes even acted upon. We offer this manifesto in the belief that its basic analysis is correct, the acceptance that some of its details might be wrong, and the hope that effective action will swiftly follow.

Notes

INTRODUCTION

1. The official policies of the Green Party of England and Wales can be found at <www.greenparty.org.uk>. The ideas in this book draw heavily on the party's policies and we are grateful to everyone who has toiled through plenary debates at party conferences over the last thirty years in order to create them. In several places, we have extrapolated beyond the party's agreed policies and the views we express, as well as any errors, should therefore be regarded as our own.
2. We use the terms 'anti-globalisation movement' and 'global justice movement' interchangeably. We prefer the latter since it defines the movement positively in terms of what it supports, rather than negatively in terms of what it opposes. However, we recognise that the former is used more widely.
3. The Green Party of England and Wales <http://www.greenparty.org.uk/> is run by a national executive committee and does not have an official leader. It elects two Principal Speakers, one woman and one man.
4. Further information about Caroline's work in the European Parliament can be found at <http://carolinelucasmep.org.uk/>.

CHAPTER I

1. Zoellick, R.B. (2001), 'Countering terror with trade', *Washington Post*, 20 September, p. A35.
2. Harding, J. (2001), 'The anti-globalisation movement', *Financial Times*, 15 October.
3. Zoellick, R.B., 'Countering terror with trade'.
4. Quoted in Lozada, C. (2001), 'Trading in terror', *Christian Science Monitor*, 6 November.
5. Karliner, J. (2001), *Where Do We Go From Here? Challenging Corporate-Globalization After September 11*, San Francisco: CorpWatch.
6. Dale, R. (2001), 'Terrorists exploit anti-globalization', *International Herald Tribune*, 22 September.
7. Perkins, A. (2003), 'Hewitt links world poverty with terror', *Guardian*, 31 January.
8. National Intelligence Council (2000), *Global Trends 2015: A Dialogue About the Future with Nongovernment Experts*, Washington, DC: CIA. <http://www.cia.gov/nic/pubs/index.htm>.
9. UN Environment Programme (2002), *Global Environment Outlook 3*, London: UNEP/Earthscan.
10. Speaking at the launch of *Global Environment Outlook 3*.
11. Department for International Development (2000), *White Paper on International Development*, London: HMSO.

12. Internationalism is itself a troublesome term as some interpret it only as relating to dealings between nation states. We use the term in a wider sense than this, to refer a philosophy that seeks the best interest at an international or global level, whether or not the actors are nation states.
13. Quoted in Gray, J. (1988), *False Dawn: The Delusions of Global Capitalism*, London: Granta Books.
14. Smith, A. (1994 [1776]), *The Wealth of Nations*, New York: Modern Library, imprint of Random House Inc.
15. Friends of the Earth (2000), *The Citizen's Guide to Trade, Environment and Sustainability*, London: FoE.
16. Gray, *False Dawn*.
17. World Trade Organization (undated), *Trade and the Environment in the WTO*, Geneva: WTO.
18. New Internationalist (2000), *Restructuring the Global Economy*, No. 320.
19. Hertz, H. (2001), *The Silent Takeover: Global Capitalism and the Death of Democracy*, London: William Heinemann.
20. Clarke, T. (2001), 'Mechanisms of corporate rule', in E. Goldsmith and J. Mander (eds), *The Case Against the Global Economy*, London: Earthscan.
21. Cited in Keet, D. (1999), *Globalisation and Regionalism – Contradictory Tendencies? Counteractive Tactics? Or Strategic Possibilities?*, Cape Town: Alternative Information and Development Centre.
22. *Johannesburg Business Day*, 20 February 1997.
23. Keet, D., *Globalisation and Regionalism*.
24. The Babylonian Talmud, Shabbat 31, relates that when asked to summarise all of the law while standing on one leg, Rabbi Hillel picked up one leg and replied: 'What is hateful to you, do not do to others; the rest is commentary.'
25. Meadows, D.H., Meadows, D.L., Randers, J. and Behrens, W.W. III (1974), *The Limits to Growth: A Report for the Club of Rome's Project on the Predicament of Mankind*, 2nd edn, New York: Universe Books.
26. Daly, H.E. (1973), *Toward a Steady State Economy*, San Francisco: W.H. Freeman.
27. Selden, T.M. and Song, D. (1994), 'Environmental quality and development: Is there a Kuznets curve for air pollution emissions?', *Journal of Environmental Economics and Management*, 27, pp. 147–62.
28. Bhattarai, M. and Hammig, M. (2001), 'Institutions and the environmental Kuznets curve for deforestation: a cross-country analysis for Latin America, Africa and Asia', *World Development*, 29, pp. 995–1010.
29. Stern, D.I. and Common, M.S. (2001), 'Is there an environmental Kuznets curve for sulphur?', *Journal of Environmental Economics and Management*, 41, pp. 162–78.
30. Lópes, R. (1994), 'The environment as a factor of production: The effects of economic growth and trade liberalization', *Journal of Environmental Economics and Management*, 27, pp. 163–84.
31. Address at the University of Kansas, Lawrence, Kansas, 18 March 1968.
32. Kuznets, S. (1934), First report to Congress, quoted in C. Cobb, T. Halstead and J. Rowe (1995), *The Genuine Progress Indicator: Summary of Data and Methodology*, San Francisco: Redefining Progress.

33. For more information on ISEW see <http://www.foe.co.uk/campaigns/sustainable_development/progress/>.
34. For more information on GPI see <http://www.rprogress.org/projects/gpi/>.
35. For more information on HDI see <http://hdr.undp.org/>.
36. Scott Cato, M. (2004), 'The watermelon myth exploded: Greens and anti-capitalism', in J. Carter and D. Morland (eds), *Anti-Capitalist Britain*, London: New Clarion Press.
37. A range of Green Party policies including the Citizens' Income Scheme, the Land Value Tax, shifting the burden of tax from income to ownership, and making inheritance tax dependent on the wealth of the inheritor, would all contribute to the goal of equity. For more information on these and other Green Party policies, see the *Manifesto for a Sustainable Society* at <http://www.greenparty.org.uk>.
38. Korten, D. (1999), *The Post-Corporate World: Life After Capitalism*, Bloomfield, CT: Kumarian Press.
39. Korten, D. (1999), 'The post-corporate world', *YES! A Journal of Positive Futures*, Spring, pp. 17–18.

CHAPTER 2

1. In a speech in New York, advocating US approval of the establishment of the WTO, 3 March 1994.
2. Elliott, L. and Atkinson, D. (1998), *The Age of Insecurity*, London: Verso, p. 26.
3. IMF (2000), *Debt Relief, Globalization, and IMF Reform: Some Questions and Answers*, IMF Issues Brief <http://www.imf.org/external/np/exr/ib/2000/041200b.htm>.
4. International Society for Ecology and Culture (1999), *From Global to Local: Resisting Monoculture, Rebuilding Community*, Dartington, Devon: ISEC.
5. Mander, J. (2001), 'Facing the rising tide', in E. Goldsmith and J. Mander (eds), *The Case Against the Global Economy*, London: Earthscan.
6. Quoted in Hertz, N. (2001), *The Silent Takeover: Global Capitalism and the Death of Democracy*, London: William Heinemann.
7. MORI (2001), 'Labour supporters and public services: "But don't give money to private sector", says survey' <http://www.mori.com/polls/2001/gmb-011129.shtml>.
8. MORI (2001), 'Britain turning against globalisation' <http://www.mori.com/polls/2001/globalisation.shtml>.
9. Wallach, L. and Sforza, M. (1999), *Whose Trade Organization? Corporate Globalization and the Erosion of Democracy*, Washington, DC: Public Citizen <http://www.citizen.org>.
10. Elliott, L. (2003), 'Third-way addicts need a fix', *Guardian*, 14 July.
11. Monbiot, G. (2000), *Captive State: The Corporate Takeover of Britain*, London: Macmillan.
12. The section on NAFTA draws heavily on Bottari, M., Wallach, L. and Waskow, D. (2001), *NAFTA Chapter 11 Investor-to-State Cases: Bankrupting*

Democracy. Lessons for Fast Track and the Free Trade Area of the Americas, Washington, DC: Public Citizen and Friends of the Earth.
13. Palast, G. (2001), 'The fast track trade Jihad', *Observer*, 14 October.
14. For more information on Loewen's case, see <www.nafta.claims.com/disputes_us/disputes_us_5.htm>.
15. Magnusson, P. (2002), 'The highest court you've never heard of: Do NAFTA judges have too much authority?', *Business Week*, 1 April.
16. For a useful briefing on the GATS agreement see Spencer Chapman, K. (2002), *The General Agreement on Trade in Services (GATS): Democracy, Public Services and Government Regulation*, published by Jean Lambert MEP/The Greens & European Free Alliance in the European Parliament <http://www.jeanlambertmep.org.uk>.
17. Watkins, K. (2002), 'Money talks', *Guardian*, 24 April.
18. Bhagirath Lal Das, India's former ambassador to GATT, quoted in Sexton, S. (undated), *Trading Health Care Away?*, CornerHouse Briefing 23: Trade and Health Care. Available at <http://www.gatswatch.org/docs/CornerHouse23.pdf> on 24 November 2003.
19. Local Government Association (2002), *WTO General Agreement on Trade in Services (GATS) – Decisions and Actions Required*, Report to the European and International Affairs Executive, London: LGA.
20. WTO (2001), *Communication from Cuba, Senegal, Tanzania, Uganda, Zimbabwe and Zambia – Assessment of Trade in Services*, 6 December, WTO reference S/CSS/W/132; accessible through European Services Forum website <http://www.esf.be/f_e_negotiations.htm>.
21. Save the Children UK Press Release, 5 November 2001 <http://www.savethechildren.org.uk/pressrels/051101.html>.
22. European Commission (2000), *Opening World Markets for Services, Towards GATS 2000*, Brussels: EC, p. 17.
23. David Hartridge, former Director of the Services Division at the WTO in his speech 'What the General Agreement on Trade in Services can do' at the conference 'Opening Markets for Banking Worldwide: The WTO General Agreement on Trade in Services', London, 8 January 1997.
24. Lang, J. and Lake, C.D. II (2000), 'The first five years of the WTO: General Agreement on Trade in Services', *Law & Policy in International Business*, 31.
25. There are no entirely satisfactory terms that can be used to refer to groups of rich and poor countries. Rich countries are in some ways poor and many people living in them have very little money. Some 'developing' countries are in fact not developing at all and there are certain developments that we would like to see take place in countries that are already said to have developed. Not all poor countries are in the South, though most rich ones are in the North. We nevertheless use all these terms, whilst trying to avoid 'third world' and 'first world'.
26. Chandrika, B. (2001), *TRIPS, HIV/AIDS and Access to Drugs*, New York: UNDP.
27. Speaking at the World Development Movement's Annual Conference, London, 8 June 2002.
28. IMF (2000), *Globalization: Threat or Opportunity?*, IMF Issues Brief <http://www.imf.org/external/np/exr/ib/2000/041200.htm#X>.

29. Chossudovsky, M. (1997), *The Globalisation of Poverty: Impacts of IMF and World Bank Reforms*, London and Atlantic Highlands, NJ: Zed Books and Penang, Malaysia: Third World Network.
30. Stiglitz, J.E. (2002), *Globalization and its Discontents*, London: Allen Lane/Penguin, p. 89.

CHAPTER 3

1. Advert in *Fortune* magazine, quoted in Korten, D. (1995), *When Corporations Rule the World*, London: Earthscan.
2. UNEP (2002), *Global Environment Outlook 3*, London and Geneva: UNEP/Earthscan.
3. Rainforest Foundation <http://www.rainforestfoundationuk.org/rainhome.html>.
4. Bruges, J. (2001), *The Little Earth Book*, Barrow Gurney: Alastair Sawday Publishing Co. Ltd.
5. UNEP, *Global Environment Outlook 3*.
6. UNEP (2000), *Report of the Twelfth Meeting of the Parties to the Montreal Protocol*, Nairobi: UNEP Ozone Secretariat.
7. European Environment Agency (2002), *Environmental Signals 2002 – Benchmarking the Millennium: Environmental Assessment Report No 9*, Copenhagen: EEA.
8. UNEP, *Global Environment Outlook 3*.
9. World Wide Fund for Nature (2002), *The Living Planet Report 2002*, Gland, Switzerland: WWF International.
10. Wackernagel, M. et al. (2002), 'Tracking the ecological overshoot of the human economy', *Proceedings of the National Academy of Science*, 99, pp. 9266–71.
11. Khor, M. (2001), *Globalisation and the Crisis of Sustainable Development*, Penang, Malaysia: Third World Network.
12. Ibid., p. 18.
13. Hines, C. (2000), *Localization: A Global Manifesto*, London: Earthscan.
14. Testimony to the USTR prior to WTO Summit, Sierra Club, Washington, DC, 20 May 1999.
15. Friends of the Earth International (2001), *Citizen's Guide to Trade, Environment and Sustainability*, Amsterdam: FoEI <http://www.foei.org/trade/activistguide/>.
16. European Commission (2001), *White Paper. European Transport Policy for 2010: Time to Decide*, Brussels: EC <http://europa.eu.int/comm/energy_transport/en/lb_en.html>.
17. DETR (2000), *The Future of Aviation: The Government's Consultation Document on Air Transport Policy*, London: Department of Environment, Transport and the Regions.
18. Simms, A. (2000), *Collision Course: Free Trade's Free Ride on the Global Climate*, London: New Economics Foundation.
19. Korten, D. (1995), *When Corporations Rule the World*, London: Earthscan.

20. OECD (1997), *Freight and Environment: Effects of Trade Liberalisation and Transport Sector Reforms*, Paris: OECD.
21. Food and Agriculture Organisation (1999), *The State of the World's Fisheries and Aquaculture 1998*, Rome: FAO.
22. Matthews, E. et al. (2000), *Pilot Analysis of Global Ecosystems: Forest Ecosystems*, Washington, DC: World Resources Institute.
23. The following WTO examples are drawn from Wallach, L. and Sforza, M. (1999), *Whose Trade Organization? Corporate Globalization and the Erosion of Democracy*, Washington, DC: Public Citizen <http://www.citizen.org>.
24. WTO (1988), *United States – Import Prohibition of Certain Shrimps and Shrimp Products (WT/DS58/R), Final Report*, Geneva: WTO.
25. For fuller details see Hines, C., *Localization* pp. 221–4, and Lucas, C. (1999), *The Greens' 'Beef' with the WTO*, London: Green Party.
26. European Commission (1999), *Report from the European Union's Scientific Committee on Veterinary Measures Relating to Public Health*, Brussels: EC.
27. Weisbrot, M. (2001), 'Tricks of free trade', *Sierra Magazine*, September/October.
28. WTO (2001), *WTO Policy Issues for Parliamentarians*, Geneva: WTO.
29. Ibid.
30. WTO (1996), *United States – Standards for Reformulated and Conventional Gasoline (WT/DS2/R), Report of the Panel*, Geneva: WTO.
31. WTO (2001), *WTO Policy Issues for Parliamentarians*, Geneva: WTO.
32. GATT (1947),*General Agreement on Tariffs and Trade*, Article XX <http://www.wto.org/wto/english/docs_e/legal_e/final_e.htm>.

CHAPTER 4

1. Bello, W. (1999), 'Why reform of the WTO is the wrong agenda', *Focus on Trade*, 43, December.
2. There is considerable debate over the best way to measure income distribution and the relevant importance of inequality and absolute poverty. An introduction to these issues can be found in Wade, R. and Wolfe, M. (2002), 'Are global poverty and inequality getting worse?', *Prospect Magazine*, 72, March <http://www.prospect-magazine.co.uk/ArticleViewT2.asp?accessible=yes&P_Article=10242>, and Wade, R. (2001), *Is Globalization Making World Income Distribution More Equal?*, LSE-DESTIN Working Paper, No.01–01 <http://www.lse.ac.uk/Depts/destin/workpapers/wadeincome.pdf>.
3. IMF (2000) *Globalization: Threat or Opportunity?*, IMF Issues Brief <http://www.imf.org/external/np/exr/ib/2000/041200.htm#X>.
4. Milanovic, B. (2002), 'True world income distribution, 1988 and 1993: First calculation based on household surveys alone', *The Economic Journal*, 112, pp. 51–92.
5. UNDP (2003), *Human Development Report 2003 Millennium Development Goals: A Compact Among Nations to End Human Poverty*, New York: Oxford University Press.
6. UNDP (1999), *Human Development Report: Globalization with a Human Face*, New York: Oxford University Press.

7. IMF, *Globalization: Threat or Opportunity*.
8. Quoted in Hilary, J. (1999), *Globalisation and Employment, New Opportunities, Real Threat*, Panos Briefing, No. 33, May, p. 5.
9. International Labour Office (2003), *Global Employment Trends*, Geneva: ILO.
10. UNCTAD (1997), *Trade and Development Report: Globalization, Distribution and Growth*, Geneva: UNCTAD.
11. UNCTAD (2002), *Trade and Development Report: Developing Countries in World Trade*, Geneva: UNCTAD.
12. World Bank (2000), *World Development Report: Attacking Poverty*, Washington, DC: World Bank.
13. UNDP (2003), *Human Development Report 2003 Millennium Development Goals: A Compact Among Nations to End Human Poverty*, New York, Oxford University Press.
14. Speaking at the launch of the World Bank's 1999/2000 World Development Report, 15 September 1999.
15. <http://www.worldbank.org/>.
16. See UNDP website, 'Women/Gender' at <http://www.undp.org/teams/english/gender.htm>.
17. See, for example, the work of the International Trade and Gender Network at <http://www.genderandtrade.net/index.html> and Development Alternatives with Women for a New Era at <http://www.dawn.org.fj/>.
18. World Bank (2001), *Annual Report*, Washington, DC: World Bank.
19. From the foreword to DfID (2000), *Eliminating World Poverty: Making Globalisation Work for the Poor. White Paper on International Development*, London: HMSO.
20. Dollar, D. and Kraay, A. (2000), *Growth Is Good for the Poor*, Washington, DC: World Bank Development Research Group <http://www.worldbank.org/research/growth/absddolakray.htm>.
21. *Economist*, 27 May 2000.
22. *Financial Times*, 12 April 2000, p. 23.
23. *Guardian*, 14 June 2000.
24. Wade, R. and Wolfe, M. (2002), 'Are global poverty and inequality getting worse?', *Prospect Magazine*, 72, March <http://www.prospect-magazine.co.uk/ArticleViewT2.asp?accessible=yes&P_Article=10242>.
25. Ibid.
26. Eatwell, J. (2000), 'Unemployment: National policies in a global economy', *International Journal of Manpower*, 21, pp. 343–73.
27. Weisbrot, M., Baker, D., Kraev, E. and Chen, J. (2001), *The Scorecard on Globalization 1980–2000: Twenty Years of Diminished Progress*, Washington, DC: Centre for Economic Policy Research.
28. UNDP (2003), *Human Development Report 2003 Millennium Development Goals: A Compact Among Nations to End Human Poverty*, New York: Oxford University Press, p. 2.
29. Quoted in Palast, G. (2000), 'An internal IMF study reveals the price "rescued" nations pay: dearer essentials, worse poverty, and shorter lives', *Observer*, 8 October.
30. Dollar, D. and Kraay, A (2001), *Trade, Growth, and Poverty*, Washington, DC: Development Research Group, The World Bank.

31. Rodrik, D. (2000), Comments on *Trade, Growth, and Poverty* by D. Dollar and A. Kraay, Harvard University <http://ksghome.harvard.edu/per cent7E.drodrik.academic.ksg/Rodrik per cent20on per cent20Dollar-Kraay.PDF>.
32. Ibid.
33. Weisbrot, et al., *Scorecard on Globalization*.
34. Alesina, A., Grilli, V. and Milesi-Ferretti, G.M. (1993), 'The political economy of capital controls', in L. Leiderman and A. Razin (eds), *Capital Mobility: New Perspectives*, Cambridge: Cambridge University Press; Vittorio, V. and Milesi-Ferretti, G.M. (1995), 'Economic effects and structural determinants of capital controls', *IMF Staff Papers*, 42 (3), pp. 517–51.
35. Bello, W. (2000), 'WTO: Serving the wealthy, not the poor', in S. Retallack (ed.), *Globalising Poverty: The World Bank, IMF and WTO – Their Policies Exposed*, London: The Ecologist Report, pp. 36–9.
36. Rodrik, D (2001), 'Trading in illusions', *Foreign Policy*, March/April.
37. Ibid.
38. Cited in Retallack, *Globalising Poverty*, p. 6.
39. Lundberg, M. and Squire, L. (1999), *The Simultaneous Evolution of Growth and Inequality*, Washington, DC: World Bank.
40. Cavanagh, J., Welch, C. and Retallack, S. (2000), 'The IMF formula: Generating poverty', in S. Retallack, *Globalising Poverty*, pp. 23–5.
41. Blackwell, B. (2002), 'Argentina and the IMF – the art of falling apart', *Ecologist*, July.
42. For a discussion of the effect of EMU on unemployment in the EU see Lombard, M. (2000), 'Restrictive macroeconomic policies and unemployment in the European Union', *Review of Political Economy*, 12, pp. 317–32.
43. Ingram, P. and Davis, I. (2001), *The Subsidy Trap: British Government Financial Support for Arms Exports and the Defence Industry*, Oxford: Oxford Research Group/Safer World.
44. Hines, C. (2000). *Localization: A Global Manifesto*. London: Earthscan.
45. Wiltshire, V., Jones, E., King, C., Jenkins, T. and Barry, R. (1998), *Green Job Creation in the UK*, London: FoE, ACE, GMB and UNISON <http://www.foe.co.uk/resource/reports/green_job_creation.pdf>.
46. Quoted in *Guardian*, 6 February 2002.
47. Greider, W. (2000), *One World Ready or Not: The Manic Logic of Global Capitalism*, New York: Simon and Schuster.
48. Mokhiber, R. and Weissman, R. (2000), 'General Electric's global assault', *Mother Jones*, 26 May.
49. <http://www.tuc.org.uk/globalisation/>.
50. Greider, W. (2001), 'A new giant sucking sound', *Nation*, 31 December.
51. *Migration News* (2002), 'Trends: Population, migration, food', *Migration News*, 9 (11).
52. Ibid.

CHAPTER 5

1. Norberg-Hodge, H. (2001), 'Ladakh – development as destruction', in A. Roddick (ed.), *Globalization: Take it Personally*, London: Thorsons, pp. 112–15.

2. Pomeroy, R. (2002), 'Earth summit failure could imperil trade talks – EU', Reuters, 23 July.
3. Department for International Development (2000), *Eliminating World Poverty: Making Globalisation Work for the Poor. White Paper on International Development*, London: HMSO.
4. International Society for Ecology and Culture (1999), *From Global to Local: Resisting Monoculture, Building Community*, Dartington: ISEC; *Ecologist* (1999), 'Beyond the monoculture: Shifting from global to local', *Ecologist*, 29 (3); Shuman, M. (1998), *Going Local: Creating Self-Reliant Communities in a Global Age*, New York: Free Press; Mander, J. and Goldsmith, E. (1996), *The Case Against the Global Economy and For a Turn Towards the Local*, San Francisco: Sierra Club Books; Douthwaite, R. (1996), *Short Circuit: Strengthening Local Economies for Security in an Unstable World*, Totnes: Green Books; Hines, C. (2000), *Localization: A Global Manifesto*, London: Earthscan; International Forum on Globalization (2002), *Alternatives to Economic Globalization*, San Francisco: Berrett-Kohler.
5. John Maynard Keynes, speaking in Dublin, April 1933.
6. <http://www.neweconomics.org>.
7. Trade subsidiarity is explained in the section 'Site here to sell here: Controlling the TNCs'.
8. Shuman, M.H. (2000), *Going Local: Creating Self-Reliant Communities in the Global Age*, New York: Routledge.
9. Blecker, R. (1999), *Taming Global Finance: A Better Architecture for Growth and Equity*, Washington, DC: Economic Policy Institute.
10. The Nobel Prize-winning economist, James Tobin, first proposed the idea of a tax on foreign exchange transactions in 1978. He suggested that all major countries should levy the tax at a rate (less than 0.5 per cent) that is low enough not to hamper longer-term investment, but high enough to dampen the impact of large-scale, speculative currency movements aimed at exploiting minute differentials in currency fluctuations.
11. Following the October 1987 Black Monday stock-market crash, a US presidential task force recommended that circuit breakers should be introduced to automatically trigger a pause in trading following a large fall to give buyers and sellers time to assimilate incoming information and arrange transactions calmly rather than in a panic. As a result, the NYSE adopted a circuit breaker rule in 1999 that automatically stops trading for 30 minutes whenever the Dow Jones industrial average falls 350 points from its previous day's close. Another circuit breaker halts trading for an hour if the market drops a further 200 points.
12. Collin, S., Fisher, T., Mayo, E., Mullineux, A. and Sattar, D. (2001), *The State of Community Development Finance 2001*, London: New Economics Foundation.
13. Murphy, R., Hines, C. and Simpson, A. (2003), *People's Pensions: New Thinking for the 21st Century*, London: New Economics Foundation <http://www.neweconomics.org/gen/z_sys_PublicationDetail.aspx?PID=131>.
14. Anderson, A. and Cavanagh, J. (1998), 'The rise of global corporate power', *Third World Resurgence*, 97.

15. Balanyá, B., Doherty, A., Hoedeman, O., Ma'anit, A. and Wesselius, E. (2000), *Europe Inc., Regional and Global Restructuring and the Rise of Corporate Power*, London: Pluto Press.
16. Khor, M. (2001), *Globalisation and the Crisis of Sustainable Development*, Penang, Malaysia: Third World Network.
17. Willmore, I. (2002), 'How to make corporations accountable', *Global economy: Observer Special*, 14 July.
18. von Weizsäcker, E., Lovins, A.B., and Lovins, L.H. (1997), *Factor Four: Doubling Wealth, Halving Resource Use*, London: Earthscan.
19. Cambridge Econometrics, cited in C. Hines, *Localization*.
20. Hines, C., *Localization*; also Lucas, C. and Hines, C. (2001), *Time to Replace Globalisation: A Green Localist Manifesto for the World Trade Organisation Ministerial*, Brussels: The Greens/European Free Alliance in the European Parliament <http://www.carolinelucasmep.org.uk>.
21. Monbiot, G. (2003), *The Age of Consent: A Manifesto for a New World Order*, London: Flamingo.
22. For example, George Monbiot has written: 'Trade, at present, is an improbable means of distributing wealth between nations ... But it is the only possible means', Monbiot, G. (2003), 'I was wrong about trade', *Guardian*, 24 June.
23. Khor, *Globalisation and the Crisis of Sustainable Development*.
24. International Federation of Red Cross and Red Crescent Societies (2002). *World Disasters Report 2002*. Geneva. IFRCRCS.
25. Based on briefing papers at <http://www.jubileeresearch.org/>.
26. International Federation of Red Cross and Red Crescent Societies (2001), *World Disasters Report 2001: Focus on Recovery*, Geneva: IFRCRCS.
27. Simms, A. (2001), 'Climate change: The real debtors', *Ecologist*, October.
28. Robins, N., Meyer, A. and Simms, A. (1999), *Who Owes Who? Climate Change, Debt, Equity and Survival*, London: Christian Aid.
29. Pettifor, A. (2002), *Resolving International Debt Crises – The Jubilee Framework for International Insolvency*, London: New Economics Foundation.
30. Monbiot, *The Age of Consent*, p. 186.
31. Meyer, A. (2000), *Contraction & Convergence: The Global Solution to Climate Change*, Schumacher Briefing 5, Totnes: Green Books.
32. Monbiot, *The Age of Consent*, pp. 12–13.
33. Ibid., p. 99.
34. Desai, M. (1998), 'A basic income proposal', Paper 4 in *The State of the Future*, London: Social Market Foundation.
35. Gwartney, J.T. and Tideman, N.S.O. (1996), 'The Jerome Levy economic institute conference: Land, wealth, and property', *American Journal of Economics and Sociology*, 55 (3), pp. 349–56.
36. Monbiot, 'I was wrong about trade'.
37. Oxfam (2002), *Rigged Rules and Double Standards: Trade Globalisation and the Fight Against Poverty*, Oxford: Oxfam.
38. Ibid.
39. Monbiot, 'I was wrong about trade'.
40. Watkins, K. (2002), 'The Oxfam debate', *Ecologist*, July.

41. Shiva, V. (2002), 'Export at any cost: Oxfam's free trade recipe for the third world' <http://www.maketradefair.com/>.
42. Hines, C. (2000), 'Globalisation's cruel smokescreen', in S. Retallack (ed.), *Globalising Poverty: The World Bank, IMF and WTO – Their Policies Exposed*, London: Ecologist Report.
43. *Migration News* (2002), 'China: Migrants, North Korea, economy', *Migration News*, 9 (8).
44. Bello, W. (1999), 'Architectural Blueprints, Development Models and Political Strategy', paper presented at Conference on Economic Sovereignty in a Globalised World, Bangkok, 23–26 March.
45. Monbiot, *The Age of Consent*, p. 220.
46. Ibid, p. 219. Monbiot regards free trade as a 'desirable outcome' because, 'when nations achieve a roughly similar economic status, free trade is likely to be the most equitable means of governing their relationship with each other'. To which Colin Hines has replied: 'What on earth leads George Monbiot to this conclusion is not explained or justified. What is known is that free trade even amongst "equals" increases ruthless competition between countries, reduces local control of the future of national economies and concentrates production in ever fewer sites, thus increasing transport and hence carbon emissions. The trade within the European Union is a classic example of this', Hines, C. (2003), *Misrepresenting Localization – A Critique Of George Monbiot's 'The Age Of Consent'* <http://www.sovereignty.org.uk/features/footnmouth/local11.html>.
47. Eckes, A.E. Jr (1995), *Opening America's Market: US Foreign Trade Policy Since 1776*, Chapel Hill: University of North Carolina Press.
48. Watkins, 'The Oxfam debate'.
49. Daly, H. and Goodland, R. (1992), 'An ecological-economic assessment of deregulation of international commerce under GATT', unpublished report for the World Bank Environment Department, Washington, DC.

CHAPTER 6

1. Soros, G. (1995), *Soros on Soros*, New York: John Wiley.
2. Hertz, N. (2001), *The Silent Takeover: Global Capitalism and the Death of Democracy*, London: William Heinemann.
3. International Trade Centre (2002), *Overview of World Markets for Organic Food & Beverages*, Geneva: International Trade Centre, UNCTAD/WTO <http://www.intracen.org/mds/sectors/organic/overview.pdf>.
4. Fairtrade Foundation (2002), *Annual Review 2000/2001*, London: Fairtrade Foundation.
5. Bello, W. (2000), 'WTO: Serving the wealthy, not the poor', in S. Retallack (ed.), *Globalising Poverty: The World Bank, IMF and WTO – Their Policies Exposed*, London: The Ecologist Report, pp. 36–9.
6. Bello, W. (1999), 'Why reform of the WTO is the wrong agenda', *Focus on Trade*, 43, Amsterdam: Transnational Institute.
7. Greider, W. (2001), 'A new giant sucking sound', *The Nation*, 18 December.

8. Shiva, V. (2001), *Yoked to Death: Globalisation and Corporate Control of Agriculture*, New Delhi: Research Foundation for Science, Technology and Ecology.
9. Bello, 'WTO; Serving the wealthy, not the poor'.
10. Harker, D. et al. (1996), *Community Works! A Guide to Community Economic Action*, London: New Economics Foundation.
11. Mayo, E. and Moore, H. (2001), *The Mutual State: How Local Communities Can Run Public Services*, London: New Economics Foundation.
12. World Council of Credit Unions (2001), *2001 Statistical Report* <http://www.woccu.org/pubs/publist.htm#stats>.
13. McGurn, P. (2002), 'California bans tax dodgers', *BBC News Online*, 26 July http://news.bbc.co.uk/1/hi/business/2152923.stm>.
14. Soros, G. (2002), *George Soros on Globalization*, Oxford: Public Affairs Ltd.
15. Stiglitz, J. (2002), *Globalization and its Discontent*, London: Allen Lane.
16. Stewart, H. (2002), 'Brown dismisses Tobin tax plan', *Guardian*, 23 July.
17. Elliott, L. and Atkinson, D. (1998), *The Age of Insecurity*, London: Verso.
18. Soros, *George Soros on Globalization*.
19. Forster, E.M. (1910), *Howard's End*.
20. Speaking in Cape Town, South Africa, 1966.

CHAPTER 7

1. Bello, W. (2002), *The Oxfam Debate: From Controversy To Common Strategy*, Bangkok: Focus on the Global South <http://www.focusweb.org/publications/2002/oxfam-debate-controversy-to-common-strategy.html>.
2. Charlene Barshefsky, speaking at a press briefing, Seattle, 2 December 1999.
3. Pascal Lamy, speaking at a press conference, Seattle, 2 December 1999.
4. Quoted in 'Deadline set for WTO reforms', *Guardian*, 10 January 2000.
5. Malhotra, K. (2002), 'Doha: Is it really a development round?', *Trade, Environment and Development*, 1, Washington, DC: Carnegie Endowment for International Peace.
6. See for example, Bello, W. (2000), *Why Reform of the WTO Is the Wrong Agenda*, Bangkok: Focus on the Global South; Bello, W. (2002), *Deglobalization: Ideas for a New World Economy*, London: Zed Books.
7. Nossiter, B. (1987), *The Global Struggle for More*, New York: Harper and Row, pp. 42–3.
8. Ibid., p. 45.
9. Bandow, D. (1985), 'The US role in promoting third world development', in D. Bandow (ed.), *US Aid to the Developing World: A Free Market Agenda*, Washington, DC: Heritage Foundation, p. xxii.
10. D. Mulford, speaking at the Asia-Pacific Capital Markets conference, San Francisco, 17 November 1987.
11. Testimony of Ambassador Charlene Barshefsky, United States Trade Rrepresentative, before the House Ways and Means Trade Subcommittee, US Congress, 24 February 1998.

12. Ibid.
13. Quoted in 'Worsening financial flu lowers immunity to US business', *New York Times*, 1 February 1998.
14. WTO (1998), *Annual Report*, Geneva: WTO, p. 12.
15. See <http://www.globalvision.org/program/globalization/nader.html>.
16. Coates, B. (2001), *Briefing from Doha*, 12 December, London: World Development Movement <http://www.wdm.org.uk/presrel/current/dejavue.htm>.
17. Lucas, C. (2001), 'Ill wind of trade', *Guardian*, 6 December.
18. Bello, W. (2001), 'Learning from Doha', presentation to the meeting of the Our World is not for Sale Coalition, Brussels, 7–9 December.

CHAPTER 8

1. Stiglitz, J. (2002), *Globalization and its Discontents*, London: Allen Lane/Penguin, p. 197.
2. WTO (2002), 'UNCTAD-ITC-WTO chiefs agree to enhance cooperation', Press Release, 30 October <http://www.wto.org/english/news_e/news02_e/unctad_itc_30oct02_e.htm>.
3. Keynes's original proposals and their fate are described in Rowbotham, M. (2000), *Goodbye America! Globalisation, Debt and the Dollar Empire*, Charlbury, UK: Jon Carpenter.
4. Sadly, we cannot claim this is an original analogy. It is attributed to C. Fred Bergsten, Head of the Institute of International Economics (IIE).
5. Local Government Association (2002), 'Update on WTO General Agreement on Trade in Services (GATS) – Decisions and Action Required', paper prepared for the LGA European and International Affairs Executive <http://www.lga.gov.uk/Documents/Agenda/european/250602/item2.PDF>.
6. Monbiot, G. (2003), *The Age of Consent: A Manifesto for a New World Order*, London: Flamingo.
7. Buira, A. (2000), 'The governance of the International Monetary Fund', paper presented at the Group of 24 meeting, Vienna, 29–30 September.
8. UNDP (2002), *Human Development Report 2002: Deepening Democracy in a Fragmented World*, New York: Oxford University Press.
9. Streck, C. (2001), 'The global environment facility – a role model for international governance?', *Global Environmental Politics*, 1, pp. 71–94.

SECTION 4 INTRODUCTION

1. Intermediate Technology Development Group (undated), *ITDG Energy Strategy*, Rugby: ITDG.
2. Standing Advisory Committee on Trunk Road Assessment (1999), *Transport and the Economy*, London: DETR, para. 40, p. 22.
3. Maddison, D., Pearce, D., Johansson, O., Calthrop, E., Litman, T. and Verhoef, E. (1996), *The True Costs of Road Transport*, London: Earthscan.

4. Sewill, B. (2003), *The Hidden Costs of Flying*, London: Aviation Environment Federation.

CHAPTER 9

1. Quoted in Goldsmith, E. (2001), 'Development as colonialism', in E. Goldsmith and G. Mander (eds), *The Case Against the Global Economy and for a Turn Towards Localization*, London: Earthscan.
2. Carroll, R. (2003), '40 million starving "as world watches Iraq"', *Guardian*, 9 April.
3. Food and Agriculture Organisation (2003), *World Agriculture 2003: Main Finding*, Rome: FAO.
4. Gordon, D. et al. (2000), *Poverty and social exclusion in Britain*, York: Joseph Rowntree Foundation/York Publishing Services.
5. Audit Commission (2001), *Tackling Obesity in England*, London: The Stationery Office.
6. Food and Agriculture Organisation, *World Agriculture 2003*.
7. Watkins, K. (2002), 'Greed in action: US farming subsidies will hit world's poor', *Guardian Society*, 5 June.
8. Oxfam (2002), *Milking the CAP: How Europe's dairy regime is devastating livelihoods in the developing world*, Oxfam Briefing Paper No. 34, Oxford: Oxfam.
9. Watkins, 'Greed in action'.
10. Lord Whitty, speaking at the Royal Smithfield Show, 25 November 2002.
11. This data is drawn from FAO (2001), *Food Balance Sheet Database*. Rome: Food and Agriculture Organisation. More details and analysis can be found in Lucas, C. (2001), *Stopping the Great Food Swap: Relocalising Europe's Food Supply*, Brussels: The Greens/European Free Alliance in the European Parliament <http://www.carolinelucasmep.org.uk/publications/greatfoodswap.html>.
12. Lucas, *Stopping the Great Food Swap*.
13. Council for the Protection of Rural England (1999), *Meadow Madness: Why the Loss of England's Grasslands Continues Uncontested*, London: CPRE.
14. US Food and Drug Administration (2000), *Residue Monitoring Report*, Rockville, MA: Center for Food Safety and Applied Nutrition Pesticide Program <http://vm.cfsan.fda.gov/~dms/pesrpts.html>.
15. See <http://themes.eea.eu.int/Sectors_and_activities/agriculture/indicators/nutrients/index_html>.
16. Lal, R. and Stewart, S. (1990), *Soil Degradation,*. New York: Springer Verlag.
17. Pimentel, D., Harvey, C., Resosudarmo, P., Sinclair, K., Kunz, D., McNair, M., Crist, S., Shpritz, L., Fitton, L., Saffouri, R. and Blair, R. (1995), 'Environmental and economic costs of soil erosion and conservation benefits', *Science*, 267, pp. 1117–23.
18. Jones, J.A. (1999), 'The environmental impacts of distributing consumer goods: A case study on dessert apples', unpublished PhD thesis, Centre for Environmental Strategy, University of Surrey, Guildford, UK.

19. Simms, A., Kumar, R. and Robbins, N. (2000), *Collision Course: Free Trade's Free Ride on the Global Climate*, London: New Economics Foundation.
20. Department of Environment, Transport and the Regions (2000), *The Future of Aviation: The Government's Consultation Document on Air Transport Policy*, London: DETR.
21. Sustain (1999), *Food Miles – Still on the Road to Ruin?*, London: Sustain.
22. Whitelegg, J. (1993), *Transport for a Sustainable Future: The Case for Europe*, London: Belhaven Press.
23. Ministry of Agriculture, Fisheries and Food (2000), *Agriculture in the UK, 1999*, London: MAFF.
24. Wintour, P. (2001), 'Extent of farm crisis revealed', *Guardian*, 11 April.
25. Countryside Agency (1999), *The State of the Countryside: Summary of Key Facts*, Cheltenham, UK: Countryside Agency.
26. Ainger, K. (2003), 'The new peasants' revolt', *New Internationalist*, 353, pp. 9–13.
27. Ibid.
28. Ainger, K. (2003), 'The market and the monsoon', *New Internationalist*, 353, pp. 22–7.
29. Comments in response to Policy Commission on the Future of Farming and Food (2002), *Farming and Food – a Sustainable Future*, London: Cabinet Office.
30. Quoted in 'Extent of farm crisis revealed', *Guardian*, 11 April 2001.
31. Quoted in Ainger, 'The market and the monsoon', p. 26.
32. US Department of Agriculture (1998), *National Commission on Small Farms: A Time to Act*, Washington, DC: USDA.
33. Policy Commission on the Future of Farming and Food (2002), *Farming and Food: A Sustainable Future*, London: Cabinet Office, p. 34.
34. North, R. (2001), *The Death of British Agriculture*, London: Gerald Duckworth.
35. DEFRA, 'Economic evaluation of the APRC' <http://www.statistics.defra.gov.uk./esg/evaluation/aprc/chapter3.pdf>.
36. Sustain, *Food Miles*.
37. Bennett, R., Henson, S., Harper, G., Blaney, R. and Preibisch, K. (2000), *Economic Evaluation of Farm Animal Welfare Policy: Final Report to MAFF*, Reading: University of Reading, Department of Agriculture and Food Economics.
38. Meadows, D. (2000), 'Can organic farming feed the world?', *Organic Farming Magazine*, USA, May.
39. Egziabher, T.B.G. (2003), 'How (not) to feed Africa', *New Internationalist*, 353, pp. 14–15.
40. Food and Agriculture Organisation (2000), *The State of Food Insecurity in the World*, Rome: FAO.
41. Kwa, A. (2003), *EU CAP 'Reform'? Let Us Not Be Fooled*, Geneva: Focus on the Global South.
42. Institute of Grocery Distribution (2001), *Grocery Retailing 2001*, Letchmore Heath, UK: IGD Research.
43. Institute of Grocery Distribution (2001), *European Grocery Retailing Now and in the Future*, Letchmore Heath, UK: IGD Research.

44. Department for Environment, Food and Rural Affairs (2002), *Sustainable Food and Farming: Working Together: The Future*, London: DEFRA, Chart 1, p. 35.
45. Box 9.1 is based on Friends of the Earth research reported in 'Ten reasons supermarket mergers are bad for consumers', 13 January 2003 <http://www.foe.co.uk/resource/press_releases/20030113134910.html>.
46. In October 2002, Friends of the Earth surveyed 151 supermarkets, 58 greengrocers and 29 markets: the results revealed that the average price for a kilogram of Cox apples was just £1.02 at market stalls and £1.07 at greengrocers, while at Morrisons or Asda-Walmart it would cost £1.27 and at Sainsbury as much as £1.44.
47. Sustain (2000), *A Battle in Store: A Discussion of the Social Impact of the Major UK Supermarkets*, London: Sustain.
48. NOP conducted the poll on 8–10 November 2002. See the Friends of the Earth press release of 18 November 2002, 'New poll shows public back farmers v supermarkets' <http://www.foe.co.uk/resource/press_releases/20021118000102.html>.
49. Friends of the Earth (2002), 'British apples for sale', media briefing, November.
50. Competition Commission (2000), *Supermarkets: A Report on the Supply of Groceries from Multiple Stores in the United Kingdom*, London: Competition Commission.
51. Ibid.
52. *Grocer Yearbook*, 2002.
53. Simms, A., Oram, J., MacGillivray, A. and Drury, J. (2002), *Ghost Town Britain: The Threat from Economic Globalisation to Livelihoods, Liberty and Local Economic Freedom*, London: New Economics Foundation.
54. Porter, S. and Raistrick, P. (1998), *The Impact of Out-of-Centre Food Superstores on Local Retail Employment*, Occasional Paper No 2, London: National Retail Planning Forum.
55. Jones, A. (2001), *Eating Oil: Food Supply in a Changing Climate*, London: Sustain/Elm Farm Research Centre.
56. Reported in *The Grocer*, 4 January 2003.
57. Friends of the Earth (2002), 'Supermarkets and Great British Fruit', media briefing, November.
58. Edwards, R. (2001), 'Slaughter of the innocents: The global meat market', *Sunday Herald*, 4 March.
59. Quoted on <http://www.npa-uk.net> 21 February 2001, National Pig Association.
60. Quoted in Vidal, J. (2001), 'Global disease on the rise – finger pointed at illegal trade', *Guardian*, 23 February.
61. National Audit Office (2002), *The 2001 Outbreak of Foot and Mouth Disease*, London: NAO.
62. Institute of Directors, quoted in *Daily Telegraph*, 20 April 2001.
63. Henley, J. (2001), 'First case identified in France', *Guardian*, 14 March; Vidal, J. (2001), 'Global disease on the rise', *Guardian*, 23 February; Bowdler, N. (2001), 'Virulent new strain sweeps the world', *Independent*, 25 February.

64. UK Creutzfeldt-Jakob Disease Surveillance Unit (2003), 'CJD Statistics' <http://www.cjd.ed.ac.uk/>.
65. Agra Europe (2001) 2 February <http://www.agra-europe.de/>.
66. Edwards, 'Slaughter of the innocents'.
67. Eurostat, <http://europa.eu.int/comm/eurostat/>.
68. Wallach, L. and Sforza, M. (1999), *Whose Trade Organisation: Corporate Globalisation and the Erosion of Democracy*, Washington, DC: Public Citizen.
69. Pretty, J.N., Brett, C., Gee, D., Hine, R.E., Mason, C.F., Morison J.I.L., Raven, H., Rayment, M.D. and van der Bijl., G. (2000), 'An assessment of the total external costs of UK agriculture', *Agricultural Systems*, 65 (2), pp. 113–136. Organic farming has, by contrast, only one-third of the hidden costs of non-organic agriculture, thus reducing the external costs by £1.6 bn, or £120–140 per hectare. In 1999, the UK was 15th, bottom of the EU league in terms of support for green farming (including organic) and rural schemes, spending 18.7 euros/ha (£12/ha) compared to 264.8 euros/ha (£158/ha) in Finland and 67.9 euros/ha (£40/ha) in Portugal.
70. European Parliament Economic and Social Committee (2002), *Opinion on the Future of the CAP*, Brussels, 21 March (NAT/122), Brussels: EP.
71. Kloppenberg, J., Hendrickson, J. and Stevenson, G.W. (1996), 'Coming in to the foodshed', *Agriculture and Human Values*, 13 (3), pp. 33–42.
72. National Farmers' Union (2002), *Farmers' Markets: A Business Survey*, London: NFU Public Affairs.
73. European Commission (2003), 'EU fundamentally reforms its farm policy to accomplish sustainable farming in Europe', press release, Luxembourg, 26 June.
74. Uhlig, R. (2003), '"Historic" CAP reform praised by Beckett', *Daily Telegraph*, 27 June.
75. Ibid.
76. National Farmers' Union (2003), 'Ministers reach agreement on CAP reform', press release, 30 January.
77. World Development Movement (2003), 'Shoddy CAP deal increases chance of Cancun collapse', press release, London, 26 June.
78. Oxfam (2003), 'EU CAP reforms a disaster for the poor', press release, 27 June <http://www.oxfam.org/eng/pr030627_eu_cap_reform.htm>.
79. Kwa, A. (2003) *EU CAP 'Reform'? Let Us Not Be Fooled*, Geneva: Focus on the Global South.
80. Lucas, C., Hart, M. and Hines, C. (2002), *Look to the Local: A Better Agriculture is Possible! A Discussion Document*, Brussels: The Greens/European Free Alliance in the European Parliament.
81. Wood, P. (2002), *A Better CAP*, Kingsbridge, South Devon: Family Farmers' Association.
82. Competition Commission (2000), *Supermarkets: A Report on the Supply of Groceries from Multiple Stores in the United Kingdom*, London: Competition Commission.
83. Friends of the Earth (2003), *Farmers and the Supermarket Code of Practice*, London: FoE <http://www.foe.co.uk/resource/briefings/farmers_supermarket_code.pdf>.

84. For further information, see Watson, A. (2001), *Food Poverty: Policy Options for the New Millennium*, London: Sustain.
85. Ghosh, A. (2001), *Economic Reforms in India: A Critical Assessment*, New Delhi: Centre for the Study of Global Trade Systems and Development.
86. See <http://www.mindfully.org/WTO/Indian-WBJA-Against-WTO.htm>.
87. For further details see Murphy, S. and Suppan, S. (2003), *An Introduction to the Development Box: Finding Space for Development Concerns in the WTO's Agriculture Negotiations*, Winnipeg: International Institute for Sustainable Development. <http://www.iisd.org/pdf/2003/trade_intro_dev_box.pdf>.
88. Green, D., Murphy, S., Tripathi, R. and Charveriat, C. (2002), *An Introduction to the Development Box*, London: CAFOD, Action Aid, Oxfam and IATP <http://www.cafod.org.uk/policy/devbox_02.shtml#1>.
89. Vandana Shiva, quoted in Hines, C. (2000), *Localization: A Global Manifesto*, London: Earthscan, p. 207.
90. Pretty, J.N., Morison, J.I.L. and Hine, R.E. (2003), 'Reducing food poverty by increasing agricultural sustainability in developing countries', *Agriculture, Ecosystems and Environment*, 95, pp. 217–34.
91. Quist, D. and Chapela, I.H. (2001), 'Transgenic DNA introgressed into traditional maize landraces in Oaxaca, Mexico', *Nature*, 414, pp. 541–3.
92. Orton, L. (2003), *GM Crops – Going Against the Grain*, London: ActionAid.
93. Meziani, G. and Warwick, H. (2002), *Seeds of Doubt*, London: Soil Association.
94. According to English Nature, 'untested introduction of GM crops could be the final blow for such species as the skylark, corn bunting and the linnet, as the seeds and insects on which they feed disappear', English Nature news release, 8 July 1998: 'Government Wildlife Advisor Urges Caution on Genetically Modified Organisms – The New Agriculture Revolution'.
95. This concept was first proposed in Hines, C. and Shiva, V. (2002), *A Better Agriculture is Possible: Local Food, Global Solution*, San Francisco, CA: International Forum on Globalization.
96. Lucas, *Stopping the Great Food Swap*, p. 26.
97. Institute for Agriculture and Trade Policy (2002), 'New WTO agriculture trade text reveals wide differences: Structural changes needed to fix market distortions', IATP press release, 18 December <http://www.iatp.org/iatp/library/admin/uploadedfiles/New_WTO_Agriculture_Trade_Text_Reveals_Wide_Di.htm>.
98. Ibid.

CHAPTER 10

1. Woodin, M.E. (2001), *Reach for the Future: Green Party Manifesto*, London: Green Party of England and Wales.
2. Ravi Bulchadani, quoted in 'The euro – special report', *Business Week*, 27 April 1998.

3. European Roundtable of Industrialists (1991), *Reshaping Europe*, Brussels: ERT, quoted in Balanya, B. et al., (2000), *Europe Inc: Regional and Global Restructuring and the Rise of Corporate Power*, London: Pluto Press, p. 50.
4. Speech by Jacques Santer to the board of directors of the AMUE, 26 February 1998, quoted in Balanya et al., *Europe Inc.*, p. 50.
5. Phone interview with Bertrand de Maigret, 11 March 1997, quoted in Balanya et al., *Europe Inc.*, p. 52.
6. Interview with John Russell, 16 December 1998, quoted in Balanya et al., *Europe Inc.*, p. 45.
7. Ibid., p. 46.
8. UNICE (1997), *Benchmarking Europe's Competitiveness: From Analysis to Action*, Brussels: UNICE, quoted in Balanya et al., *Europe Inc.*, p. 40.
9. Interview with Christophe de Callatäy, Communications Director, UNICE, 18 November 1998, quoted in Balanya et al., *Europe Inc.*, pp. 40–41.
10. Article 108 of the amended Treaty of Rome.
11. Quoted in *Le Monde*, 18 October 2002.
12. See <http://www.no.euro.com>.
13. In an interview on BBC Television's *Breakfast with Frost*, December 2002.
14. Crow, B. (2002), Letter in *The Times*, 24 August.
15. Michie, J. (2002), *Public Services Yes, Euro No*, London: New Europe Research Trust.
16. Reported in the *International Herald Tribune*, 20 December 2001.
17. Reported in the *Berliner Zeitung*, 9 August 2002.
18. Forder, J. (2002). *Democracy and the European Central Bank*, London: New Europe Research Trust.
19. Smith, R. (1999), 'PFI: perfidious financial idiocy', editorial, *British Medical Journal*, 319, pp. 2–3.
20. Quoted in 'PFI hospitals "cost NHS more"', BBC News Online, 17 May 2002 <http://news.bbc.co.uk/1/hi/health/1991037.stm.>.
21. Pollock, A.M., Shaoul, J. and Vickers, N. (2002). 'Private finance and "value for money" in NHS hospitals: a policy in search of a rationale?', *British Medical Journal*, 324, pp. 1205–9.
22. Reported in Elliott, L. (2002), 'Blair faces big problem in currency debate', *Guardian*, 26 August.
23. Achieving high levels of international trade, inward investment and economic growth, as measured by GDP, are not economic priorities we would set for a sustainable economy. They are however the principal goals of every government within the EU and therefore provide a useful measure of those governments' ability to meet the economic objectives they have set themselves.
24. No Campaign (2003), *The Euro isn't Working: A Year of Instability*, London: No Campaign.
25. Elliott, L. (2003), '"Economic crisis" forces German call for lower rates', *Guardian*, 2 July.
26. Forfas (2003), *Statement on Inflation*, Dublin: National Competitiveness Council.

27. Eurostat quarterly national statistics <http://europa.eu.int/comm/eurostat/Public/datashop/print-catalogue/EN?catalogue=Eurostat>.
28. Ernst and Young (2003), *European Investment Monitor: 2003 Report*, London: Ernst and Young LLP.
29. Mundell, R.A. (1961), 'A theory of optimum currency areas', *American Economic Review*, November.
30. Norman Tebbitt, a minister in Margaret Thatcher's government during the 1980s, famously used a speech to urge the unemployed to follow the example of his own father, who 'got on his bike' to look for work.
31. Michie, J. (2002), 'The currency that spells cuts', *Guardian*, 10 September.
32. European Commission (2003), 'Regional GDP per capita in the EU and candidate countries in 2000', Eurostat press release No. 10/2003, 30 January.
33. European Commission (2002), 'Unemployment in the EU and the Central European candidate countries', Eurostat press release No. 93/2002, 5 August.
34. Thirwall, A. (2000), *The Euro and 'Regional' Divergence in Europe*, London: New Europe Research Trust.
35. Elliott, L. (2002), 'Blair faces big problem in currency debate', *Guardian*, 26 August.
36. Office of National Statistics (2001), *Regional Gross Domestic Product* <http://www.statistics.gov.uk/pdfdir/rgdp0201.pdf>.
37. House of Commons ODPM: Housing, Planning, Local Government and the Regions Select Committee (2003), *Reducing Regional Disparities in Prosperity*, London: The Stationery Office.
38. Perrons, D. (1999), 'Deconstructing the Maastricht myth? Economic and social cohesion in Europe: regional and gender dimensions of inequality', in R. Hudson and A.M. Williams (eds), *Divided Europe: Society and Territory*, London: Sage.
39. HM Treasury (2003), *EMU and labour market flexibility*, London: The Stationery Office <http://www.hm-treasury.gov.uk/documents/the_euro/assessment/studies/euro_assess03_studworcestershire.cfm>.
40. Jacobs, J. (1986), *Cities and the Wealth of Nations*, London: Penguin.
41. For a review of regional currencies see Boyle, D. (2003), *Beyond Yes and No: A Multi-Currency Alternative to EMU*, London: New Economics Foundation.
42. Adapted from ibid.
43. It is advocated in ibid., and in Robertson, J. (2002), *Forward with the Euro and the Pound,* Research Study 17, London: Economic Research Council.
44. The Foundation for the Economics of Sustainability, *Feasta* <http://www.feasta.org/>.
45. See, for example, Monbiot, G. (2003), 'The bottom dollar', *Guardian*, 22 April.
46. Douthwaite, R. (1999), *The Ecology of Money*, Schumacher Briefing No. 4, Totnes: Green Books, on behalf of The Schumacher Society.

CHAPTER 11

1. Roberts, A. and Kingsbury, B. (1993), 'Introduction: the UN's roles in international society since 1945', in A. Roberts and B. Kingsbury (eds), *United Nations, Divided World*, Oxford: Oxford University Press.
2. UN Development Programme (2003), *Human Development Report 2003. Millennium Development Goals: A Compact among Nations to End Human Poverty*, New York: Oxford University Press. The Millennium Development Goals were adopted by 189 countries at the UN Millennium Summit in September 2000. The eight Goals are to be met by 2015 and range from halving extreme poverty to halting the spread of HIV/AIDS, to enrolling all boys and girls in primary school by 2015.
3. Green Party (1999), *European Election Manifesto*, London: Green Party of England and Wales.
4. Prodi, R. (2001), 'Looking towards Laeken', speech to the plenary session of the European Parliament, Brussels, 28 November.
5. European Environment Agency (1998), *Europe's Environment – The Dobris Assessment*, Copenhagen: EEA.
6. European Commission (2001), *A Sustainable Europe for a Better World: A European Union Strategy for Sustainable Development*, Brussels: European Commission <http://europa.eu.int/eur-lex/en/com/cnc/2001/com2001_0264en01.pdf>.
7. Lucas, C. (2001), 'The Heart Bleeds', *Guardian*, 27 June.
8. Lucas, C. (2002), *Draft Opinion of the Committee on Industry, External Trade, Research and Energy for the Committee on Employment and Social Affairs on Promoting a European Framework for Corporate Social Responsibility*, Brussels: European Parliament, 19 February <http://www.europarl.eu.int/meetdocs/committees/itre/20020325/460794en.pdf>.
9. Coates, B. (2002), *The World's Biggest Summit – So What? Making Sense of the World Summit on Sustainable Development*, London: World Development Movement <http://www.wdm.org.uk/cambriefs/wssd_wrap_up.pdf>.
10. Plenary on globalisation, 27 August 2002.
11. Anderson, S. (2001), *Seven Years Under NAFTA*, Washington, DC: Institute for Policy Studies <http://www.ips-dc.org>.
12. Ibid.
13. Center for Environmental Public Advocacy/Friends of the Earth Slovakia (2000), *Ten Years of Policies of Bretton Woods Institutions in Slovakia*, Slovakia: CEPA/FoES, p. 33.
14. Ibid., pp. 23–4.
15. Solga, H., Diewald, M. and Goedicke, A. (2000), 'Arbeitsmarktmobilität und die Umstrukturierung des ostdeutschen Beschäftigungssystems' (Employment Careers and the Restructuring of the Employment System in East Germany), *Mitteilungen aus der Arbeitsmarkt und Berufsforschung*, 33 (2), pp. 242–60.
16. Garton Ash, T. (2002), 'The grim wedding', *Guardian*, 27 June.
17. James Tutak, R. (2000), 'A slow lane from factory to forecourt', *Financial Times Survey*, 24 October.
18. Mokhiber, R. and Weissman, R. (2000), 'General Electric's global assault: How one huge company is giving the shaft to tens of thousands of

workers around the world – and even its own suppliers', *Mother Jones*, 26 May.
19. Quoted in Balanya, B. et al. (2000), *Europe Inc.: Regional and Global Restructuring and the Rise of Corporate Power*, London: Pluto Press.
20. The Rt Hon. Helen Liddell MP, Minister for Energy and Competitiveness in Europe, in the Department of Trade and Industry (2000), *EU Enlargement and the Single Market: Opportunities for Business*, London: DTI.
21. Speaking in Warsaw, 6 October 2000.
22. Arguably, the shift to 'yes' in the second referendum was a result of the question being spun into pro- or anti-enlargement.
23. European Commission (2003), *Eurobarometer 59*, Brussels: European Commission <http://europa.eu.int/comm/public_opinion/archives/eb/eb59/eb59_en.htm>.
24. EU Council (2001), *Laeken Declaration*, Brussels: European Commission.
25. MORI (2001), 'Britain turning against globalisation', 11 October <http://www.mori.com/polls/2001/globalisation.shtml>.
26. UN Development Programme (2003), *Human Development Report 2003. Millennium Development Goals: A Compact among Nations to End Human Poverty*, New York: Oxford University Press.

CONCLUSION

1. See note 21, Chapter 1.
2. See Box 1.1.

Bibliography – Principal Sources

Ainger, K. (2003). The new peasants' revolt. *New Internationalist*, No. 353, Jan-Feb.
Anderson, A. & Cavanagh, J. (1998). The rise of global corporate power, *Third World Resurgence*, no 97.
Anderson, S. (2001). *Seven Years under NAFTA*. Washington, DC: Institute for Policy Studies. <http://www.ips-dc.org>.
Audit Commission (2001). *Tackling Obesity in England*. London: The Stationery Office.
Babylonian Talmud, Shabbat 31.
Balanya, B. et al. (2000). *Europe Inc., Regional and Global Restructuring and the Rise of Corporate Power*. London: Pluto Press.
Bandow, D. (1985). The US role in promoting third world development, in D. Bandow (ed.), *US Aid to the Developing World: A Free Market Agenda*. Washington, DC: Heritage Foundation. p. xxii.
BBC News Online (2002). *PFI hospitals 'cost NHS more'*. 17 May. <http://news.bbc.co.uk/1/hi/health/1991037.stm>.
Bello, W. (1999). Architectural blueprints, development models, and political strategy. Paper presented at Conference on Economic Sovereignty in a Globalised World. Bangkok, 23–26 March.
Bello, W. (2000). *Why Reform of the WTO is the Wrong Agenda*. Bangkok: Focus on the Global South.
Bello, W. (2000). WTO: Serving the wealthy, not the poor. In S. Retallack (ed). *Globalising Poverty: The World Bank, IMF and WTO – Their Policies Exposed*. London: The Ecologist Report, pp. 36–39.
Bello, W. (2001). *Learning from Doha*. Presentation to the meeting of the Our World is not for Sale Coalition. Brussels, Belgium: 7–9 December.
Bello, W. (2002). *Deglobalization: Ideas for a New World Economy*. London: Zed Books.
Bennett, R. et al. (2000). *Economic evaluation of farm animal welfare policy, Final report to MAFF*. University of Reading, Department of Agriculture and Food Economics, December.
Bhattarai, M. & Hammig, M. (2001). Institutions and the environmental Kuznets curve for deforestation: a cross-country analysis for Latin America, Africa and Asia. *World Development* 29, 995–1010.
Blackwell, B. (2002). Argentina and the IMF – the art of falling apart. *Ecologist*. July 2002.
Blecker, R. (1999). *Taming Global Finance: A Better Architecture for Growth and Equity*. Washington, DC: Economic Policy Institute.
Bottari, M., Wallach, L. & Waskow, D. (2001). *NAFTA Chapter 11 Investor-to-State Cases: Bankrupting Democracy. Lessons for Fast Track and the Free Trade Area of the Americas*. Washington DC: Public Citizen and Friends of the Earth.
Boyle, D. (2003). *Beyond Yes And No: A Multi-Currency Alternative To EMU*. London: New Economics Foundation.

Bruges, J. (2001). *The Little Earth Book*. Barrow Gurney: Alastair Sawday Publishing Co. Ltd.

Buira, A. (2000). The governance of the International Monetary Fund. Paper presented at the Group of 24 meeting, Vienna: 29–30 September.

Butler, D. & Kavanagh, D. (2002). *The British General Election of 2001*. Basingstoke: Palgrave.

Carroll, R. (2003). 40 million starving 'as world watches Iraq'. *Guardian*, Wednesday April 9.

Cavanagh, J., Welch, C., & Retallack, S. (2000). The IMF formula: generating poverty. In S. Retallack (ed). *Globalising Poverty: The World Bank, IMF and WTO – their Policies Exposed*. London: The Ecologist Report. pp. 23–25.

Center for Environmental Public Advocacy/Friends of the Earth- Slovakia (2000). *Ten Years of Policies of Bretton Woods Institutions in Slovakia*. Slovakia: CEPA/FoES. September, p.33.

Center for Voting and Democracy (2002). Early 9/11 Political Returns In: *Primary Turnout Trending Towards Record Low*. Washington DC: CVD.

Chandrika, B. (2001). *TRIPS, HIV/AIDS and Access to Drugs*. UNDP.

Chossudovsky, M (1997). *The Globalisation of Poverty: Impacts of IMF and World Bank Reforms*. London and Atlantic Highlands, N.J.: Zed Books/Penang, Malaysia: Third World Network.

Clarke, T. (2001). Mechanisms of corporate rule. In E. Goldsmith and J. Mander (eds), *The Case Against the Global Economy*, Earthscan, London.

Coates, B. (2002). *The World's Biggest Summit – So What? Making Sense Of The World Summit On Sustainable Development*. London, World Development Movement. <http://www.wdm.org.uk/cambriefs/wssd_wrap_up.pdf>.

Cobb, C., Halstead, T. & Rowe, J. (1995). *The Genuine Progress Indicator: Summary of Data and Methodology*, San Francisco, Redefining Progress.

Collin, S., Fisher, T., Mayo, E., Mullineux, A. and Sattar, D. (2001). *The State of Community Development Finance 2001*. London, New Economics Foundation.

Competition Commission (2000). *Supermarkets: A Report on the Supply of Groceries from Multiple Stores in the United Kingdom*. London, Competition Commission.

Countryside Agency (1999). *The State of the Countryside: Summary of Key Facts*. Cheltenham, UK.

Dale, R. (2001). Terrorists exploit anti-globalization. *International Herald Tribune*, 22 September.

Daly, H. & Goodland, R. (1992). *An Ecological-Economic Assessment of Deregulation of International Commerce Under GATT*. Washington, DC, World Bank (Environment Department), unpublished.

Daly, H.E. (1973). *Toward a Steady State Economy*. San Francisco, W. H. Freeman.

Department of Environment, Transport and the Regions (2000). *The Future Of Aviation: The Government's Consultation Document On Air Transport Policy*. London, DETR.

Desai, M. (1998). A basic income proposal. Paper 4 in *The State of the Future*. London, Social Market Foundation.

DETR (2000). *The Future of aviation: the Government's consultation document on air transport policy*. London, Department of Environment, Transport and the Regions.
DfID (2000). *Eliminating World Poverty: Making Globalisation Work for the Poor. White Paper on International Development*. London, Stationery Office.
Dollar, D. & Kraay, A (2000). *Growth Is Good for the Poor*. The World Bank Development Research Group.
Dollar, D. & Kraay, A. (2001). *Trade, Growth, and Poverty*. Development Research Group, The World Bank.
Douthwaite, R. (1996). *Short Circuit: Strengthening Local Economies for Security in an Unstable World*. Devon, Green Books.
Douthwaite, R. (1999). *The Ecology of Money. Schumacher Briefing no 4*. Totnes, Green Books on behalf of The Schumacher Society.
Eckes, A.E. Jr. (1995). *Opening America's Market: US Foreign Trade Policy Since 1776*. Chapel Hill.
Ecologist (1999). *Beyond the Monoculture: Shifting from Global to Local*, 29(3), May/June.
Edwards, R. (2001). Slaughter of the innocents: The global meat market. *Sunday Herald*. 4 March.
Egziabher, T.B.G. (2003). How (not) to feed Africa. *New Internationalist*, 353, 14–15. Jan-Feb.
Elliott, L. & Atkinson, D. (1998). *The Age of Insecurity*. London, Verso.
Elliott, L. (2002). Blair faces big problem in currency debate. *Guardian*, 26 August.
Elliott, L. (2003). 'Economic crisis' forces German call for lower rates. *Guardian*, Wednesday 2 July.
Elliott, L. (2003). Third-way addicts need a fix. *Guardian*, 14 July.
Ernst and Young (2003). *European Investment Monitor: 2003 Report*. London, Ernst and Young LLP.
EU Council (2001). *Laeken Declaration*. Brussels, EC.
European Commission (1999). *Report from the European Union's Scientific Committee on Veterinary Measures Relating to Public Health*. Brussels, EC.
European Commission (2000). *Opening World Markets for Services, Towards GATS 2000*. Brussels, EC.
European Commission (2001). *A Sustainable Europe for a Better World: A European Union Strategy for Sustainable Development*. Brussels, EC. <http://europa.eu.int/eur-lex/en/com/cnc/2001/com2001_0264en01.pdf>.
European Commission (2001). *White Paper. European Transport Policy for 2010: Time to Decide*. Brussels, EC. <http://europa.eu.int/comm/energy_transport/en/lb_en.html>.
European Commission (2002). Unemployment in the EU and the Central European candidate countries. *Eurostat Press Release* No. 93/2002, 5 August.
European Commission (2003). *EU fundamentally reforms its farm policy to accomplish sustainable farming in Europe*. Press Release, Luxembourg 26 June.
European Commission (2003). Eurobarometer 59. Brussels, EC. <http://europa.eu.int/comm/public_opinion/archives/eb/eb59/eb59_en.htm>.

European Commission (2003). Regional GDP per capita in the EU and candidate countries in 2000. *Eurostat Press Release* No. 10/2003, 30 January.
European Environment Agency (1998). *Europe's Environment – The Dobris Assessment*. Copenhagen, EEA.
European Environment Agency (2002). *Environmental Signals 2002 – Benchmarking the Millennium: Environmental Assessment Report No 9*, Copenhagen, EEA.
European Parliament Economic and Social Committee (2002). *Opinion on the Future of the CAP*. Brussels, 21 March (NAT/122).
Fairtrade Foundation (2002). *Annual Review 2000/2001*.
FAO (1999). *The State of the World's Fisheries and Aquaculture 1998*. Rome, Food and Agriculture Organisation.
FAO (2000). *The State of Food Insecurity in the World*. FAO, UN.
FAO (2003). *World Agriculture 2003: Main Findings*. Food and Agriculture Organisation.
FoE, ACE, GMB & UNISON (1998). *Green Job Creation in the UK*. <http://www.foe.co.uk/resource/reports/green_job_creation.pdf>.
Forder, J. (2002). *Democracy and the European Central Bank*, London, New Europe Research Trust.
Forfas. (2003). *Statement on Inflation*. Dublin, National Competitiveness Council.
Forster, E.M. (1910). *Howard's End*.
Friends of the Earth (2000). *The Citizens Guide to Trade, Environment and Sustainability*, FoE, London.
Friends of the Earth (2003). *Farmers and the Supermarket Code of Practice*. London, FoE <http://www.foe.co.uk/resource/briefings/farmers_supermarket_code.pdf>.
Garton Ash, T. (2002). The grim wedding. *Guardian*, 27 June.
Ghosh, A. (2001). *Economic Reforms in India: a Critical Assessment*. New Delhi, Centre for the study of Global Trade Systems and Development.
Goldsmith, E. (2001). Development as colonialism. In E. Goldsmith and G. Mander (eds) *The Case Against the Global Economy and a Turn Towards Localization*. London, Earthscan.
Gordon, D. et al. (2000). *Poverty and Social Exclusion in Britain*. York. Joseph Rowntree Foundation/York Publishing Services.
Gray, J. (1998). *False Dawn: The Delusions of Global Capitalism*. London, Granta Books.
Green Party (1999). *European Election Manifesto*. London, Green Party of England & Wales.
Greider, W. (2000). *One World Ready or Not: The Manic Logic of Global Capitalism*. Simon and Schuster.
Greider, W. (2001). A new giant sucking sound. *Nation*, 31 December.
Gwartney, J.T., & Tideman, N.S.O. (1996). The Jerome Levy economic institute conference: Land, wealth, and property. *American Journal of Economics and Sociology*, 55(3), 349–56.
Harding, J. (2001). The anti-globalisation movement, *Financial Times*, 15 October.
Harker, D. et al. (1996). *Community Works! A Guide to Community Economic Action*. London, New Economics Foundation.

Hertz, H. (2001). *The Silent Takeover: Global Capitalism and the Death of Democracy.* London, William Heinemann.
Hines, C. (2000). Globalisation's cruel smokescreen. In S. Retallack (ed). *Globalising Poverty: The World Bank, IMF and WTO – their Policies Exposes.* London, Ecologist Report.
Hines, C. (2000). *Localization: A Global Manifesto.* London, Earthscan.
Hines, C. and Vandana, S. (2002). *A Better Agriculture is Possible: Local Food, Global Solution.* USA, International Forum on Globalization.
HM Treasury (2003). *EMU and Labour Market Flexibility.* London, Stationery Office. <http://www.hm-treasury.gov.uk/documents/the_euro/assessment/studies/euro_assess03_studworcestershire.cfm>.
House of Commons ODPM: Housing, Planning, Local Government and the Regions Select Committee (2003). *Reducing Regional Disparities in Prosperity.* London, The Stationery Office.
ILO (2003). *Global Employment Trends.* Geneva, International Labour Office.
IMF (2000). *Debt Relief, Globalization, and IMF Reform: Some Questions and Answers.* IMF Issues Brief. <http://www.imf.org/external/np/exr/ib/2000/041200b.htm>.
IMF (2000). *Globalization: Threat or Opportunity?* IMF Issues Brief. <http://www.imf.org/external/np/exr/ib/2000/041200.htm#X>.
Ingram, P., & Davis, I. (2001). *The Subsidy Trap: British Government Financial Support for Arms Exports and the Defence Industry.* Oxford, Oxford Research Group/Safer World.
Institute for Agriculture and Trade Policy (2002). *New WTO Agriculture Trade Text Reveals Wide Differences: Structural Changes Needed to Fix Market Distortions Slighted.* IATP, December 18. <http://www.iatp.org/iatp/library/admin/uploadedfiles/New_WTO_Agriculture_Trade_Text_Reveals_Wide_Di.htm>.
Institute of Grocery Distribution (2001). *European Grocery Retailing now and in the future.* Letchmore Heath: IGD Research.
Institute of Grocery Distribution (2001). *Grocery Retailing 2001.* Letchmore Heath: IGD Research.
International Federation of Red Cross and Red Crescent Societies (2002). *World Disasters Report.* Geneva.
International Federation of Red Cross and Red Crescent Societies (2001). *World Disasters Report 2001: Focus on Recovery.* Geneva.
International Forum on Globalization (2002). *Alternatives to Economic Globalization*, Berrett-Kohler, San Francisco.
International Society for Ecology and Culture (1999). *From Global to Local: Resisting monoculture, rebuilding community*, Devon, ISEC.
ITC (2002). *Overview World Markets for Organic Food & Beverages.* Geneva, International Trade Centre, UNCTAD/WTO. <http://www.intracen.org/mds/sectors/organic/overview.pdf>.
Jacobs, J. (1986). *Cities and the Wealth of Nations.* London, Penguin.
James Tutak, R. (2000). A slow lane from factory to forecourt. *Financial Times Survey*, 24 October.
Jones, A. (2001). *Eating Oil, Food Supply in a Changing Climate.* London, Sustain/Elm Farm Research Centre.

Jones, J.A. (1999). *The Environmental Impacts of distributing Consumer Goods: a Case Study on Dessert Apples*. Unpublished PhD Thesis. Centre for Environmental Strategy, University of Surrey, Guildford, UK.

Karliner, J. (2001). *Where Do We Go From Here? Challenging Corporate-Globalization After September 11*. San Francisco, CA. CorpWatch.

Keet, D. (1999). *Globalisation and Regionalism – Contradictory Tendencies? Counteractive Tactics? Or Strategic Possibilities?* Alternative Information and Development Centre, Cape Town, SA.

Khor, M. (2001). *Globalisation and the Crisis of Sustainable Development*. Penang, Third World Network.

Kloppenberg, J., Hendrickson, J., & Stevenson, G.W. (1996). Coming in to the foodshed. *Agriculture and Human Values*, 13:3 (Summer), 33–42.

Korten, D. (1995). *When Corporations Rule the World*. London, Earthscan.

Korten, D. (1999). *The Post-Corporate World: Life After Capitalism*. Kumarian Press. Connecticut.

KPMG (1999). *Unlocking Sharholder Value: The Keys to Success. Mergers and Acquisitions Global Research Report*. <http://www.kpmg.co.uk/kpmg/uk/image/m&a_99.pdf>.

Kwa, A. (2003). *EU CAP 'Reform'? Let us not be fooled*. Geneva, Focus on the Global South.

Lal, R., & Stewart, S. (1990). *Soil Degradation*. New York, Springer-Verlag.

Lang, J. & Lake II, C.D. (2000). The first five years of the WTO: General Agreement on Trade in Services. *Law & Policy in International Business*, 31.

LGA (2002). *Update on WTO General Agreement on Trade in Services (GATS) – Decisions and Action Required*. Paper prepared for the LGA European and International Affairs Executive, 25 June. <http://www.lga.gov.uk/Documents/Agenda/european/250602/item2.PDF>.

Lombard, M. (2000). Restrictive macroeconomic policies and unemployment in the European Union. *Review of Political Economy*, 12, 317–332.

Lópes, R. (1994). The environment as a factor of production: The effects of economic growth and trade liberalization. *Journal of Environmental Economics and Management*, 27, 163–84.

Lozada, C. (2001). Trading in Terror. *Christian Science Monitor*, 6 November.

Lucas, C. (1999). *The Greens' 'Beef' with the WTO*: London, The Green Party.

Lucas, C. (2001). *Swapping the Great Food Swap: Relocalising Europe's Food Supply*. Brussels, The Greens/European Free Alliance in the European Parliament. <http://www.carolinelucasmep.org.uk/publications/greatfoodswap.html>.

Lucas, C. (2001). Ill wind of trade. *Guardian*, 6 December.

Lucas, C. (2001). *Swapping the Great Food Swap: Relocalising Europe's Food Supply*. Brussels, The Greens/European Free Alliance in the European Parliament.

Lucas, C. (2001). The Heart Bleeds. *Guardian*, Wednesday 27 June.

Lucas, C. (2002). *Draft Opinion of the Committee on Industry, External Trade, Research and Energy for the Committee on Employment and Social Affairs on Promoting a European framework for Corporate Social Responsibility*. Brussels, European Parliament, 19 February. <http://www.europarl.eu.int/meetdocs/committees/itre/20020325/460794en.pdf>.

Lucas, C., Hart, M. & Hines, C. (2002). *Look to the Local: A Better Agriculture is Possible! A Discussion Document*. Brussels, The Greens/European Free Alliance in the European Parliament.

Lucas, C. & Hines, C. (2001). *Time to Replace Globalisation: A Green Localist Manifesto for the World Trade Organisation Ministerial*. Brussels, The Greens/European Free Alliance in the European Parliament.

Lundberg, M. & Squire, L. (1999). *The Simultaneous Evolution of Growth and Inequality*. World Bank.

MAFF (2000). *Agriculture in UK*, 1999. London, MAFF.

Magnusson, P. (2002). The highest court you've never heard of: Do NAFTA judges have too much authority? *Business Week*, April 1. McGraw-Hill.

Malhotra, K. (2002). Doha: Is it really a development round? *Trade, Environment and Development, Issue 1*, May. US, Carnegie Endowment for International Peace.

Mander, J. & Goldsmith, E. (1996). *The Case Against the Global Economy and for a Turn Towards the Local*. San Francisco, Sierra Club Books.

Mander, J. (2001). Facing the rising tide, in E. Goldsmith and J. Mander (eds) *The Case Against the Global Economy*, Earthscan.

Matthews, E., et al. (2000). *Pilot Analysis of Global Ecosystems: Forest Ecosystems*. Washington DC, World Resources Institute.

Mayer, A. (2000). *Contraction & Convergence: The Global Solution to Climate Change. Schumacher Briefing, 5*. Totnes, Green Books.

Mayo, E. & Moore, H. (2001). *The Mutual State: How Local Communities can run Public Services*, London, New Economics Foundation.

McGurn, P. (2002). California bans tax dodgers. *BBC News Online*, 26 July, <http://news.bbc.co.uk/1/hi/business/2152923.stm>.

Meadows, D. (2000). Can organic farming feed the world? *Organic Farming Magazine*. USA. May.

Meadows, D.H., Meadows, D.L., Randers, J. and Behrens III, W.W. (1974). *The Limits to Growth: A Report for the Club of Rome's Project on the Predicament of Mankind*, 2nd edn. New York, Universe Books.

Meziani G. & Warwick, H. (2002). *Seeds of Doubt*. London, Soil Association.

Michie, J. (2002). *Public Services Yes, Euro No*. London, New Europe Research Trust.

Michie, J. (2002). The currency that spells cuts. *Guardian*, 10 September.

Migration News (2002). *China: Migrants, North Korea, Economy*. August 9, 8.

Migration News (2002). *Trends: Population, Migration, Food*. 9, 11, November.

Milanovic, B. (2002). True world income distribution, 1988 and 1993: First calculation based on household surveys alone. *Economic Journal*, 112, 51–92.

Mokhiber, R. & Weissman, R. (2000). General Electric's global assault: How one huge company is giving the shaft to tens of thousands of workers around the world – and even its own suppliers. *Mother Jones*, 26 May.

Monbiot, G. (2000). *Captive State: The Corporate Takeover of Britain*. London Macmillan.

Monbiot, G. (2003). I was wrong about trade. *Guardian*. 24 June.

Monbiot, G. (2003). *The Age of Consent: A Manifesto for a New World Order*. London, Flamingo.

Monbiot, G. (2003). The bottom dollar. *Guardian*. 22 April.

MORI (2001). *Britain Turning Against Globalisation*. 11 October. <http://www.mori.com/polls/2001/globalisation.shtml>.
MORI (2001). *Labour Supporters and Public Services: 'But Don't Give Money To Private Sector', Says Survey*. <http://www.mori.com/polls/2001/gmb-011129.shtml>.
Mundell, R.A. (1961). A theory of optimum currency areas. *American Economic Review*, November.
Murphy, R., Hines, C. & Simpson, A. (2003). *People's Pensions: New thinking for the 21st Century*. London, New Economics Foundation. <http://www.neweconomics.org/gen/z_sys_PublicationDetail.aspx?PID=131>.
Murphy, S. and Suppan, S. (2003). *An Introduction to the Development Box: Finding Space for Development Concerns in the WTO's Agriculture Negotiations*. Winnipeg, International Institute for Sustainable Development. <http://www.iisd.org/pdf/2003/trade_intro_dev_box.pdf>.
National Audit Office (2002). *The 2001 Outbreak of Foot and Mouth Disease*. London, NAO. 21 June.
National Intelligence Council (2000). *Global Trends 2015: A Dialogue About the Future with Nongovernment Experts*. Washington DC, CIA. <http://www.cia.gov/nic/pubs/index.htm>.
New Economics Foundation (2001). *Mergerwatch*, Issue 3. London, NEF.
New Economics Foundation (2003). *Mergerwatch*, Issue 6. London, NEF.
New Internationalist (2000). *Restructuring the Global Economy*. 320.
NFU (2002). *Farmers' Markets: A Business Survey*. NFU Public Affairs, September.
NFU (2003). *Ministers Reach Agreement on CAP Reform*. <http://www.nfu.org.uk/>.
No Campaign (2003). *The Euro isn't Working: A Year of Instability*. London, No Campaign.
Norberg-Hodge, H. (2001). Ladakh – development as destruction. In A. Roddick (ed) *Globalization: Take it Personally*. London, Thorsons. pp. 112–115.
North, R. (2001). *The Death of British Agriculture*. Gerald Duckworth.
Nossiter, B. (1987). *The Global Struggle for More*. New York, Harper and Row. pp. 42–43.
OECD (1997). *Freight and Environment: Effects of Trade Liberalisation and Transport Sector Reforms*. OECD.
Office of National Statistics (2001). *Regional Gross Domestic Product*. <http://www.statistics.gov.uk/pdfdir/rgdp0201.pdf>.
Orton, L. (2003). *GM Crops – Going Against the Grain*. London, ActionAid.
Oxfam (2002). Milking the cap: how Europe's dairy regime is devastating livelihoods in the developing world. *Oxfam Briefing Paper*, No. 34. Oxford.
Oxfam (2002). *Rigged Rules and Double Standards: Trade Globalisation and the Fight Against Poverty*. Oxford, Oxfam.
Palast, G. (2000). An internal IMF study reveals the price 'rescued' nations pay: dearer essentials, worse poverty, and shorter lives. *Observer*, 8 October.
Palast, G. (2001). The fast track trade Jihad. *Observer*. Sunday, 14 October.
Panos (1999). *Globalisation and Employment, New Opportunities, Real Threats*. *Panos Briefing* 33, May.

Perkins, A. (2003). Hewitt links world poverty with terror *Guardian* 31 January.

Perrons, D. (1999). Deconstructing the Maastricht myth? Economic and social cohesion in Europe: regional and gender dimensions of inequality. In R. Hudson & A.M. Williams (eds), *Divided Europe: Society and Territory*. London, Sage.

Pettifor, A. (2002). *Resolving International Debt Crises – The Jubilee Framework for International Insolvency*. London, New Economics Foundation.

Pimentel, D., Harvey, C., Resosudarmo, P., Sinclair, K., Kunz, D., McNair, M., Crist, S., Shpritz, L., Fitton, L., Saffouri, R. and Blair, R. (1995). Environmental and economic costs of soil erosion and conservation benefits. *Science* 267, 1117–1123.

Policy Commission on the Future of Farming and Food (2002). *Farming and Food: A Sustainable Future*. London.

Pollock, A.M., Shaoul, J. & Vickers, N. (2002). Private finance and 'value for money' in NHS hospitals: a policy in search of a rationale? *British Medical Journal*, 324, 1205–1209.

Pomeroy, R. (2002). *Earth Summit Failure Could Imperil Trade Talks – EU*. Soenderborg, Denmark, Reuters. 23 July.

Porter, S. & Raistrick, P. (1998). *The Impact of Out-of Centre Food Superstores on Local Retail Employment: Occasional Paper No 2*. London, National Retail Planning Forum.

Pretty, J.N., Brett, C., Gee, D., Hine, R.E., Mason, C.F., Morison J.I.L, Raven, H., Rayment, M.D., van der Bijl., G. (2000). An assessment of the total external costs of UK agriculture. *Agricultural Systems* 65(2), 113–136.

Pretty, J.N., Morison, J.I.L., & Hine, R.E. (2003). Reducing food poverty by increasing agricultural sustainability in developing countries. *Agriculture, Ecosystems and Environment* 95, 217–234.

Roberts, A. & Kingsbury B. (1993). Introduction: the UN's roles in international society since 1945. In A. Roberts & B. Kingsbury (eds), *United Nations, Divided World*. Oxford, Oxford University Press.

Robertson, J. (2002). *Forward with the Euro and the Pound. Research Study 17*. London, Economic Research Council.

Robins, N., Meyer, A., & Simms, A. (1999). *Who owes Who? Climate change, Debt, Equity and Survival*. London, Christian Aid.

Rodrik, D. (2000). Comments on *Trade, Growth, and Poverty* by D. Dollar and A. Kraay, Harvard University. <http://ksghome.harvard.edu/ per cent7E. drodrik.academic.ksg/Rodrik per cent20on per cent20Dollar-Kraay.PDF>.

Rodrik, D. (2001). Trading in illusions, *Foreign Policy*, March/April.

Rowbotham, M. (2000). *Goodbye America! Globalisation, Debt and the Dollar Empire*. Charlbury, UK, Jon Carpenter.

Scott Cato, M. (2004). The watermelon myth exploded: Greens and anti-capitalism, in J. Carter and D. Morland (eds.), *Anti-Capitalist Britain*. London, New Clarion Press.

Selden, T.M. and Song, D. (1994). Environmental quality and development: Is there a Kuznets curve for air pollution emissions? *Journal of Environmental Economics and Management* 27, 147–62.

Shiva, V. (2001). *Yoked to Death: Globalisation and Corporate Control of Agriculture*. New Delhi, Research Foundation for Science, Technology and Ecology.

Shiva, V. (2002). *Export at Any Cost: Oxfam's Free Trade Recipe for The Third World.* <http://www.maketradefair.com/>.
Shuman, M. (1998). *Going Local: Creating Self-Reliant Communities in a Global Age.* New York, Free Press.
Simms, A. (2001). Climate change: the real debtors. *The Ecologist Magazine*, October 2001.
Simms, A., Kumar, R., and Robbins, N. (2000). *Collision Course: Free Trade's Free Ride On The Global Climate.* London, New Economics Foundation.
Simms, A., Oram, J., MacGillivray, A. & Drury, J. (2002). *Ghost Town Britain: The Threat from Economic Globalisation to Livelihoods, Liberty and Local Economic Freedom.* London, New Economics Foundation.
Smith, A. (1776). *The Wealth of Nations.*
Smith, R. (1999). PFI: perfidious financial idiocy. Editorial, *British Medical Journal*, **319**, 2–3.
Solga, H., Diewald, M., & Goedicke, A. (2000). Asbeitsmarktmobilitat und die Umstrukturierung des ostdeutschen Beschaftigungssystems. (Employment Careers and the Restructuring of the Employment System in East Germany). *Mitteilungen aus der Arbeitsmarkt und Berufsforschung*, **33**(2), 242–60.
Soros, G. (1995). *On Soros.* New York, John Wiley.
Soros, G. (2002). *On Globalization.* Oxford, Public Affairs Ltd.
Spencer Chapman, K. (2002). *The General Agreement on Trade in Services (GATS): Democracy, Public Services and Government Regulation.* Published by Jean Lambert MEP/The Greens & European Free Alliance in the European Parliament. <http://www.jeanlambertmep.org.uk>.
Stern, D.I. & Common, M.S. (2001). Is there an environmental Kuznets curve for sulphur? *Journal of Environmental Economics and Management*, **41**, 162–78.
Stewart, H. (2002). Brown dismisses Tobin tax plan. *Guardian*, 23 July.
Stiglitz, J. (2002). *Globalization and its Discontents.* London, Allen Lane.
Streck, C. (2001). The global environment facility – a role model for international governance? *Global Environmental Politics* **1**, 71–94.
Sustain (1999). *Food Miles: Still On The Road to Ruin?* London, Sustain.
Sustain (2000). *A Battle in store. A discussion of the social impact of the major UK supermarkets.* London, Sustain.
Thirwall, A. (2000). *The Euro and 'Regional' Divergence in Europe.* London, New Europe Research Trust.
Uhlig, R. (2003). 'Historic' CAP reform praised by Beckett. *Daily Telegraph* 27 June.
UNCTAD (2001). *FDI-Linked Cross Border M&As Grew Unabated in 2000*, UNCTAD Press Release TAD/INF/PR16, 27 June.
UNCTAD (2002). *UNCTAD Predicts 27% Drop in FDI Inflows this Year.* Press Release TAD/INF/PR/63. 24 October.
UNCTAD (2002). *World Investment Report.* <http://r0.unctad.org/wir/contents/wir02_dl.htm>.
UNCTAD (1997). *Trade and Development Report.*
UNCTAD (2002). *Trade and Development Report.*
UNDP (1999). *Human Development Report.*
UNDP (2002). *Human Development Report 2002: Deepening Democracy in a Fragmented World.* New York, Oxford University Press.

UNDP (2003). *Human Development Report 2003 Millennium Development Goals: A compact among nations to end human poverty*. New York, Oxford University Press.
UNEP (2000). *Report of the Twelfth Meeting of the Parties to the Montreal Protocol*. UNEP Ozone Secretariat.
UNEP (2002). *Global Environment Outlook 3*. Geneva, UNEP/Earthscan.
US Department of Agriculture (1998). *National Commission on Small Farms: A Time to Act*. Washington DC.
US Food and Drug Administration (2000). *Residue Monitoring Report*. Center for Food Safety and Applied Nutrition Pesticide Program. <http://vm.cfsan.fda.gov/~dms/pesrpts.html>.
Vidal, J. (2001). Global disease on the rise- finger pointed at illegal trade. *Guardian*, 23 February.
von Weizsäcker, E., Lovins, A.B., & Lovins, L.H. (1997). *Factor Four: Doubling Wealth, Halving Resource Use*. London, Earthscan.
Wackernagel, M. et al. (2002). Tracking the ecological overshoot of the human economy. *Proceedings of the National Academy of Science*, 99, 9266–9271.
Wade, R. and Wolfe, M. (2002). Are global poverty and inequality getting worse? *Prospect Magazine*, 72, March.
Wade, R. (2001). Is Globalization Making World Income Distribution More Equal? LSE-DESTIN Working Paper, No.01–01. <http://www.lse.ac.uk/Depts/destin/workpapers/wadeincome.pdf>.
Wallach, L., & Sforza, M. (1999). *Whose Trade Organization? Corporate Globalization and the Erosion of Democracy*. Washington DC, Public Citizen. <http://www.citizen.org>.
Watkins, K. (2002). Greed in action: US farming subsidies will hit world's poor. *Society Guardian* 5 June.
Watkins, K. (2002). Money talks. *Guardian*, 24 April.
Watkins, K. (2002). The Oxfam debate. *The Ecologist Magazine*, July 2002.
Watson, A. (2001). *Food Poverty: Policy Options for the New Millennium*. London, Sustain.
Weisbrot, M. (2001). Tricks of Free Trade. *Sierra Magazine*. Sept/Oct.
Weisbrot, M., Baker, D., Kraev, E., & Chen, J. (2001). *The Scorecard on Globalization 1980–2000: Twenty Years of Diminished Progress*. Centre for Economic Policy Research. Washington DC.
Whitelegg, J. (1993). *Transport for a Sustainable Future: The Case for Europe*. Belhaven Press, London.
Willmore, I. (2002). How to make corporations accountable. *Global economy: Observer Special* Sunday 14 July.
Wintour, P. (2001). Extent of farm crisis revealed. *Guardian*, 11 April.
Wood, P. (2002). *A Better CAP*. Family Farmers' Association.
Woodin, M. (2001). *Reach for the Future: Green Party Manifesto*. London, Green Party of England and Wales.
World Bank (2000). *World Development Report: Attacking Poverty*. Washington DC, World Bank.
World Bank (2001). *Annual Report*. Washington DC, World Bank.
World Council of Credit Unions (2001). 2001 Statistical Report. <http://www.woccu.org/pubs/publist.htm#stats>.

World Development Movement (2003). *Shoddy CAP deal increases chance of Cancun collapse. Press Release*, London. 26 June.
WTO (1988). *United States – Import Prohibition of Certain Shrimps and Shrimp Products (WT/DS58/R), Final Report*. Geneva, WTO.
WTO (1996). *United States – Standards for Reformulated and Conventional Gasoline (WT/DS2/R), Report of the Panel*, 29 January. Geneva, WTO.
WTO (1998). *Annual Report*. Geneva, WTO.
WTO (2001). *Communication from Cuba, Senegal, Tanzania, Uganda, Zimbabwe and Zambia – Assessment of Trade in Services*. 6 December, WTO reference S/CSS/W/132. Accessible through European Services Forum website, <http://www.esf.be/f_e_negotiations.htm>.
WTO (2001). *International Trade Statistics 2001*. Table II.1. Geneva, WTO.
WTO (2001). *WTO Policy Issues for Parliamentarians*. Geneva, WTO.
WTO (2002). UNCTAD-ITC-WTO chiefs agree to enhance cooperation. 30 October. <http://www.wto.org/english/news_e/news02_e/unctad_itc_30oct02_e.htm>.
WTO (undated). *Trade and the Environment in the WTO*. Geneva, Switzerland.
WWF (2002). *The Living Planet Report 2002*. WWF-The Global Environment Network.
Zoellick, R.B. (2001). Countering terror with trade. *Washington Post*. A35, 20 September.

Index

abattoirs 146, 156, 160
Africa 145
Agreement on Agriculture (AOA)
  attachment of 'Development Box' *see* WTO
Agreement on Sanitary and Phytosanitary Standards (SPS) 80
Agreement on Technical Barriers to Trade (TBT) 79–80
Agreement on Trade-Related Investment Measures (TRIMS) 81
agribusiness (TNCs) 154, 159, 162
agriculture 144, 148–9
  in Eastern Europe 208
  in India 110, industrialisation of 114
  intensive 148–9, 156–9, 164
  in Mexico 206
  and The Quad 136
  loss of jobs in sector *see* rural decline
aid 83–6, 97, 120, 125, 130, 139
  food aid 145, 153, 154
AIDS 28–9, 112
air freight 150, 162
Algiers Declaration of the Non-Aligned Movement (1973) 121
Atkinson, Dan 17, 113
aluminium 73, 74
American Chamber of Commerce (AmCham) EU Committee 178
Andhra Pradesh, India 151, 152
animal welfare 78, 79, 158–9, 160, 164, 165–6, 172, 212
  and GAST 78
anti-globalisation movement *see* global justice movement
anti-globalisation protest 4, 12, 17, 107
  Cancun 129
  Genoa 108
  Gothenburg 108
  Nice 108
  Prague 108
  Seattle 67, 108
apartheid 115
Argentina, economic crisis 118
Arla Foods 146
Asda-Walmart 155, 156, 166
Asian Financial Crisis (1997) 9, 72, 100, 109, 123
Association for the Monetary Union of Europe (AMUE) 177–8

Balls, Ed 113
bananas 20, 78
Bangladesh, textile workers 99
Bank of England 180, 198
bankruptcy of sovereign nation 85, 86, 113, 139 *see also* debt
bans on imports and exports
  prohibited under GATT Article XI 79
  of beef produced with growth hormones 80
barriers to trade 21, 25
Barsefsky, Charlene 117
Basle Convention 78
bauxite 74
Beckett, Margaret 163
benefits *see* welfare benefits *see also* Citizen's Income
Bello, Walden 100, 111, 117, 118, 125
Berlusconi, Silvio 4
biodiversity 35, 233 n94, 148, 159, 202 *see also* environmental degradation
biotechnology 80, 148, 169–71
Blair, Tony 11, 20, 75, 91, 210
Boeing 123
BP (British Petroleum) 21
Brazil
  G22 Membership 136
  desertion of land by farmers 151

Bretton Woods institutions 105
    118–19, 197, 120–3, 130–3,
    137–41, 200–1
  shares of votes 137
  accountability 137–9
  abolition of *see* revolution *see also*
    IMF *and* World Bank
British Airways 20
Brown, Gordon 183
BSE 114, 157–8
Bush, George W. 3, 91, 107, 145
Business Council on National Issues
    (Canada) 10
Business Roundtable of TNCs (US)
    10
Byers, Stephen 117

California, action of state treasurer's
    office 112
Cambodia, membership of WTO
    127
Campaign for the Protection of
    Rural England 163
Canada
  NAFTA 22–3
  cotton T-shirt quota removal 99
Cancun *see* WTO 5th Ministerial
    Assembly
CAP *see* EU
Capital
  mobility 8–10, 70
  in eurozone 188
  deregulation of 8
  flight of 71
capital advantage 8–10
capitalism 14–16
carbon budget 84
carbon credit 84
carbon debt 84
carbon dioxide emissions 149–50,
    156, 203
cartels 94
CBI 75
CDFIs (community development
    finance initiatives) 72, 111
Centre for the Study of Global Trade
    Systems and Development 167
CFCs 73
Cham Prasidh 127

China 99–100
  and textile industry 115
  G22 membership 136
  membership of WTO 100
  rural workers 100, 151, 154
Chiquita 20
Chossudovsky, Michel 30
CIA 4
CITES 78
Citigroup 20
citizen's income (CI) 92–3, 167
climate change 33, 84, 88, 89, 202
climate change levy 112
climate debt 131, 141
Clinton, Bill 11, 20
Coates, Barry 163
Codex Alimentarius 80–1
Cold War 85, 118, 119, 122
colonialism 7
community economic action 111
    see also CDFIs
community enterprises 111 *see also*
    CDFIs
comparative advantage 6–10, 190
competition policies 75
Contraction and Convergence
    (C&C)
  method of cutting emissions 87,
    198
cooperation 65, 68, 165, 192, 200–
    1, 210, 212
corporate accountability 204
corporate investment 65, 68
corporate lobbying 203–4
  at EU 209–10
  at Johannesburg Summit 204–5
corporate power 6, 11, 73, 81, 94,
    97, 107–9, 203–5, 154, 174 *see*
    also TNCs
Council for Economic and Financial
    Affairs *see* ECOFIN
credit sanctions 6
credit unions 72, 111
Creutzfeldt-Jakob Disease (CJD) 157
Crow, Bob 183
Currency
  as token of identity 192
  as symbol of control 192, 198

Index

as regulatory mechanism 192–6
  see also Ebcu
currency crises 71, 72
currency devaluation 71, 122
currency trading 71, 72

Daly, Herman 13, 103
DDT 73
De Maigret, Bertrand 178
debt 71, 83–6, 113, 117, 122, 130, 139–40, 168 *see also* sovereign nation bankruptcy
Debt crisis (1982) 122
deforestation 33
democracy xvi, 12, 17–32, 214
  and TNCs 17–29, 108
  and GATS 26–7
  and electoral turnout 31
  and economic localisation 70, 87 *see also* electoral politics; electoral systems
depression (1930s) 95, 102, 118
Desai, Meghnad 92
devaluation of currency 71, 122
development 6, 70, 82, 86, 97, 125–7
  export-led 99–101
  terminology 219n25 *see also* WTO and Agreement on Agriculture; WTO Ministerial Meeting in Doha
'Development Box' *see* WTO and Agreement on Agriculture
Development Round *see* WTO Ministerial Meeting in Doha
development trusts 111
DfID, UK 152
dioxins 73
diversification of local economies 70, 94, 95
  in poor South 84
Diversification of risk 8
Doha, WTO Ministerial meeting 3, 67, 113, 117, 125–7, 133, 136, 139
dollar, as global currency 196–8
dot.com bubble 9
Douthwaite, Richard 198
Drayson, Paul 20

East Asia Financial Crisis 30
East Germany, economy post-reunification 208
Ebcu (Emissions-backed Currency Unit) 198, 214
ECB (European Central Bank) 176, 179, 180, 181, 185, 190, 191
Ecclestone, Bernie 20
ECOFIN (Council for Economic and Financial Affairs) 182
ECOSOC 124
ecological footprinting 35
ecology 12
economic convergance 189
economic globalisation *see* globalisation
economic growth 12–15
  and globalisation 17
economic localisation 65–103, 109, 139
  and agriculture 145–73 *see also* foodsheds
  and currency 195–6
  and democracy 70, 87
  and energy supply 143
  and food security 145–73
  and money 174–99
  and multilateralism 213
  and transport 143–4
  as alternative to economic globalisation 97, 111, 200
  route to achieving 111–16 133, 143–4, 214
economies of scale 7
electoral politics 31, 107, 108, 116, 140, 210
electoral systems 91
Elliott, Larry 17, 113
emissions 150, 156, 159, 203
  emissions-trading scheme 87
  see also greenhouse gas emissions; carbon dioxide emissions
Emissions-backed Currency Unit (Ebcu) 198
EMU 10, 174–99
  and democracy 179–81
energy supply 143
enlargement *see* EU
Enron scandal 109, 112

environment 33–45
  and GAST 78
  environmental sustainability 129
    see also sustainability
  environmental degradation 4, 84, 149, 153, 159
Environmental Kuznets curve 13
environmental regulation 80, 90 see also standards
environmental taxation 75
environmentalism xx–xxi
equity ixx–xx, 12, 218 n.37 see also inequality
ERM 181, 190
Ethiopia, food distribution 171
EU (European Union) 10, 67, 90, 174–99, 201–12
  and energy taxation 112
  agreement with Bangladesh 126, 205
  ban on imports of beef with growth hormone 80, 158–9
EU Common Agricultural Policy (CAP) 145–6, 160, 165, 172–3
  and Eastern Europe 208
EU Economic and Social Committee Sustainable Development Strategy 160
EU enlargement 189, 192, 207–10, 237n22
EU Environmental Agency 202
euro 10, 144, 174–210
  as challenge to US hegemony 197
EU Summit in Gothenburg (2001) 211
Euroland see euro-zone
European Central Bank see ECB
European Commission 24, 27, 183
European Constitution 181
European Council of Ministers 202–3
European Investment Bank 207
European Parliament 90
European Roundtable of Industrialists (ERT) 10–11, 21, 177–8
European Single Currency see EMU; euro

European Single Market 10 see also EMU; euro; eurozone
eurozone 176, 179–82, 185–91
  unemployment 186–9
  inflation 186
  investment 187
  mobility of labour 187–90 passim.
exports 7, 10, 69, 79, 115, 99–103
  and reliance on subsidies 85, 102
exports, live see transportation of livestock

fair trade 74, 82, 88, 95, 96, 98, 100, 107, 113
'Fair Trade Miles' 171
Family Farmers' Association 161, 165
farmers' markets 161
FDI (foreign direct investment) 77
finance, international 6, 71
first-past-the-post electoral system 91
Fitzpatrick, Maurice 186
Focus on the Global South 136
food, intensive production see agriculture, intensive
food aid 145, 153, 154
food safety 158, 160
food security 86, 96, 125, 145–61
food sovereignty 159, 161 see also security, food
food swap 147, 153, 154, 159
food trade 114–15
foodsheds 161, 164
foot-and-mouth epidemic (UK 2001) 151, 156
foreign exchange markets 71–2
fossil fuel tax 162 see also fuel protests
fossil fuels 76, 77
France
  breach of Stability and Growth Pact 183
free trade 7, 11, 65, 98, 101–2, 117–18, 207, 124, 144, 160
Free Trade Area of the Americas 24, 205
fuel protests 114

Index 255

G22 136
G7 83, 84
G77 139
G8 137
   protest 108, 140
G90 136
Garten, Jeff 123
GATS *see under* WTO
GATT Article I Most Favoured Nation (MFN) Treatment 78
GATT Article III National Treatment 78
GATT Article III Process and Production Methods 78
GATT Article XI Elimination of Quantitative Restrictions 78–9
GATT Article XX General Exceptions to WTO Rules 79
Gaymard, Hervé 163
General Agreement of Sustainable Trade (GAST) 77–82
General Agreement on Tariffs and Trade (GATT) 77
   creation of WTO 119, 200
   Uruguay Round 10, 27, 124 *see also* WTO
General Electric (GE) 209
genetic modification 21, 159, 169–71, 233n94
Germany, breach of Stability and Growth Pact 183, 190
Gill, Ben 157
global constitution 5
global currency 196–8
Global Environment Facility 139
global food movement 159
global justice movement xx, 3–5, 67, 96, 132, 136, 144, 165, 216n4
global parliament 88, 89
global warming 73, 113 *see also* climate change
globalisation 4
   agriculture and 145–73
   environment and 33–45
   definition of 6, 18
   democracy and 17–32, 87–9
   economic growth and 17
   impacts of 105, 114, 213
   in comparison to economic localisation 68, 70, 87, 161
   inevitability of 11–12
   insecurity and conflict caused by 4–5
   public opinion of 211–12
   reformist critique 98
   theory of 6–10
   'with a human face' 68, 96
'Golden Rice' 170
Gore, Al 91, 107
Gothenburg, EU Summit (2001) 211
Graefe zu Baringdorf, Friedrich Wilhelm 172
green economics
   and anti-capitalism 15–16
   and economic growth and 14
   principles of 12
Green Marshall Plan (*see* UN) 77, 82, 84, 86, 87, 95, 99, 101, 130, 141, 168, 214
Green Party of England & Wales xxii, 174, 201
Green politics xix, 12, 140, 214
   democracy xx
   principles of xix–xxi
   social justice xix–xx
   subsidiarity xx
   sustainability xix–xx
greenhouse gas emissions 73, 84, 87, 89, 90, 150
   see also Contraction & Convergence
Greens in the European Parliament 207, 201
Greider, William 110
gross domestic product (GDP) 14, 234n23
gross national product 14
Group of 77 119, 125

Haiti, rice and self-sufficiency 147
Haskins, Lord 151
Hertz, Noreena 107
Hewitt, Patricia 4
Highly Indebted Poor Countries Initiative (HIPC) 83, 84, 95, 112, 139
Hillel, Rabbi 12

Hines, Colin 77 *see also* GAST
HIV 28–29
homezones 89
House of Lords 21
housing in South East (UK) 185
Human Development Index 14
human rights 6, 78, 79

ICC (International Chamber of Commerce) 10
IDA (International Development Agency) 120 *see also* World Bank
ILO (International Labour Organisation) 113, 130, 141
IMF (International Monetary Fund) 6, 17, 89, 99, 120, 122, 131, 129, 200
  and capital deregulation
  and democracy 30–1
  and Haiti 75, 147
  and HIPC 67, 83, 85
  and SAP (Structural Adjustment Programmes) 122–3, 127, 197
  and TNCs 94, 101, 112
  and World Bank meeting (1999) 117
IMF *see* International Monetary Fund
import of goods 7, 74, 77, 78, 79
Index of Sustainable Economic Welfare (ISAW) 14
India 100
  membership of WTO 110
  malnourishment 145
  membership of G22 136
Indian People's Movement against WTO 110, 167
Indonesia, IMF assistance 123
inequality 4–5, 7–8, 68, 98, 126, 189, 192, 221n2, 208
  and capitalism 15
  and citizen's income 92
  in taxation 77
  as a supposed pitfall of localisation 82 *see also* equity
infant industry protection 101–3
inflation 181–2
insecurity 4

Institute for Agricultural Trade Policy (US) 173
Institute for Policy Studies, Washington 70
Institute of Social and Economic Culture 18
Intellectual Property Rights 27–9, 81
intensive agriculture *see* agriculture, intensive
intensive food production *see* agriculture, intensive
International Bank for Reconstruction and Development (IBRD) *see* World Bank
international competitiveness 11, 19, 65, 68, 75
international finance 6
internationalism xxii, 6, 65, 68, 218n12, 174, 191–2, 200–15
investment 8–9, 71, 72, 81, 101, 188
investment controls 120
Iraq
  US led invasion 5, 200
  protest against invasion 107
Issing, Otmar 187
ITO (International Trade Organisation) 124

Jacobs, Jane 193
Johannesburg Summit on Sustainable Development (2002) 67, 83, 204–5, 212
Jowell, Tessa 20
Jubilee 2000 83, 140

Kennedy, Robert 14, 115–16
Keynes, John Maynard 69, 111, 131
Khor, Martin 37–8
Kloppenberg, Jack 161
Korten, David 16
KPMG 20
Kunast, Renate 172
Kuznets, Simon 14
Kyoto Protocol on Climate Change 5, 33, 109, 141, 150, 200, 201, 205, 212

Index 257

La Via Campensina 159
labour 7, 71, 75, 103, 122
   mobility in Europe during enlargement 208
   mobility of in euro-zone 187–8, 189, 190
   redistribution of 159
   tax on 76
Labour Party (UK) 20
Laeken, Belgium, Summit (2001) 211
Lafontaine, Oskar 19
laissez-faire 102
Lamy, Pascal 3
land
   access to 154
   enclosure of 7
   redistribution of 159
Land Value Tax (LVT) 93
Lang, Jeffrey 27
left, groups on traditional hard xx
LETS 72, 111, 195
liberalisation
   of capital accounts 8–10, 30
   of investment 71, 122
   of public sector 25–6
   of service sector 26
   of trade 96
   of trade markets 8–10
   of trade to combat terrorism 3
   under SAP 30, 122
limits to growth hypothesis 12
live exports *see* transportation of livestock
lobbying *see* corporate lobbying
local, definition of 69
local bonds 72, 112
local competition policies 75
local currency 195–6
   see also economic localisation of money
local democracy 91
local economies 65, 70, 94, 95
Local Government Association 137
local shops 156
localisation *see* economic localisation
localisation of money 71
localisation of production 74

Luxembourg
   currency union with Belgium 193

Maastricht *see* Treaty of Rome
MAFF (Ministry for Agriculture, Fisheries and Food, UK) 152
Malhotra, Kamal 118
Mandela, Nelson 29
market economies 16
market forces 8
Marshall Plan 20
Mexico
   EU bilateral agreement 205
   loss of jobs to and from 110
   NAFTA membership 22, 206
Millennium Development Goals *see* UNDP
Mississippi Supreme Court 23
Monbiot, George 20, 21, 88, 89, 90, 101, 225n22,n36, 226n46
money, localisation of 71, 174–99
monopolies 93
Monterrey Conference on Financing for Development (2002) 83
Montreal Protocol on Ozone-depleting substances 5, 33, 78
Moore, Mike 11
Morris, Bill 183
Most Favoured Nation (MFN) Treatment *see* GATT Article I
Multilateral Agreement on Investment (MAI) *see* OECD
multilateral environment agreement 5
Multilateralism 144, 200–15
Mundell, Robert 187
Munich, Re 84
Murdoch, Rupert 174
Murphy, Sophia 173
Museveni, President of Uganda 205

Nader, Ralph 124
National Farmers' Union of England and Wales 163
National Treatment *see* GATT Article III
nationalism 102, 192
Neilson, Poul 67

neo-colonialism 138
New Economics Foundation 69, 73, 111, 156
New International Economic Order 119
  adoption by UN 121
  Newly Industrialised Countries (NICs) of South and South East Asia 122–4
Nice Treaty 210
nitrate pollution 149
Non-Aligned Movement 119
Norberg-Hodge, Helena 67
North American Free Trade Agreement (NAFTA) 10, 22–4, 205, 206, 207
  Chapter II 22–4
  investor-to-state cases 22–4
  Loewen v Canada 23
  national treatment principle 22–4
  UPS v Canada 23
North, Richard 153

obesity epidemic 145
OECD 24, 133, 139
  MAI (Multilateral Agreement on Investment) 24, 136
  aid 83
oil 149
oil shocks 121–2
OPEC 119, 121
optimal currency area 187–91
organic farming 159, 162, 165
organic food 107, 162, 232n69
Oxfam 24, 163

packaging 149, 162
Panitchpakdi, Supachai 29, 130
patent rights see WTO, TRIPS
PCBs 73
pension funds 112
pensions 73, 92, 118, 178
Perot, Ross 110
POD (Programme of Obstruction and Deconstruction) 132–41
political donations 20, 92, 112
Poverty Reduction and Growth Facilities 117
PowderJect 20

Prebisch, Raul 119
precautionary principle 80
Pretty, Professor Jules 169
PRGF (Poverty Reduction and Growth Facility) 83
private finance initiatives 25, 26, 73, 184–5
privitisation 26, 122, 204
Process and Production Methods (PPMs) see GATT Article III
procurement 71
Prodi, Romano 183, 202
protection of infant industries 97, 101–2
protectionism 7, 21, 95, 101–3, 120
protest 67, 107–8, 110, 11, 114, 116, 129, 131
  against G8 May 1998 140
  against GATS 136–7
  against MAI 136
  against public spending cuts 182
  Cologne 140
  Gothenburg 210, 211
  Prague 140
public services
  and capital liberalisation 9
  and CDFIs 73
  and GATS 25–6
  currency crises 71
  education 25
  NHS (UK) 25
public spending cuts and the euro 182–5
PWC 20

Quad, The 125, 134, 135, 136
quotas
  as part of Green Marshall Plan 87
  foodshed specific 164–5
  prohibited under GATT Article XI 79
  removal by Canada on cotton T-shirts 99
  to protect standards 95
  to regulate trade 96

'race to the bottom' 19
Reagan, Ronald 122

Index

redistribution of wealth 82, 97–9, 119
Reebok International 177
reform 133
regional disparities 185, 188–9, 191, 192–6
regulation *see* standards
revolution 105, 128, 129–41, 214
'revolving door' appointments 21
Ricardo, David 7–10
Rio Earth Summit (1992) 83
RMT (Rail, Maritme and Transport Union) 183
RSPB (Royal Society for the Protection of Birds) 163
Ruggiero Renato 11
rural decline and loss of jobs in agricultural sector 115, 150–67
  Brazil 151
  Canada 151
  China 151
  India 167
  Poland, and enlargement of EU 151
  US 151
Russell, John 178
Russia
  default on debts 1998
  Kyoto Protocol 200

Safeway 155, 166
Sainsbury's 155, 156, 166
Santer, Jacques 177
SAP 83, 117 *see also* IMF
Schroder, Gerhard 20
Seattle see WTO Ministerial Meeting (1999) 67, 96, 129 *see also* protest
Second World War 102, 118, 174, 191, 200
security 5
  economic security 174–99
  economic security in South 95
  energy security 86
  see also food security
self-build housing 111
self-determination 90
self-reliance 69, 77, 86, 96, 98, 129, 161, 165, 198

self-sufficiency 69, 82, 88, 132, 147, 171
September 11, 2001 3, 4
Shiva, Vandana 99, 136, 167
Short, Clare 6, 68
Shuman, Michael 70
Simon of Highbury, Lord 21
single currency *see* euro
Single Market (EU) 10, 177
'site here to sell here' 74, 75, 87, 94, 214
slavery 7
Slovakia and EU Enlargement 207–8
Slovakia Centre for Environmental Policy Advocacy 207
Small and Family Farmers Alliance 161
Smith, Adam 6–10, 16
social justice xix–xx, 12 *see also* equity; inequality; human rights
soil erosion 148–9, 159, 202
Solans, Domingo 183
Solvak Railway Company 207–8
Soros, George 107, 113
South Africa 112, 115
South East (UK)
  economy 185
sovereign nation bankruptcy 85, 86, 113, 139
soya bean production 154
Spahn, Paul Bernd 72
speculation 71, 72, 196
SPS *see* Agreement on Sanitary and Phytosanitary Standards
Sri Lanka 100
Stability and Growth Pact (Dublin 1996) 180, 182–3
standards 213
  animal welfare 78, 79, 160, 164, 165–6, 212
  as 'technical barriers to trade' 79
  environmental 78–82 *passim*, 94, 101, 133, 160, 165–6, 176, 212
  food 79, 80, 164
  health 79, 80, 212
  human rights 79
  labour 78, 79, 82, 101, 133
  social 79, 81
  see also regulation

Stiglits, Joseph 30, 113, 129
structural adjustment 131, 139–40, 147, 207, 209
SAP (Structural Adjustment Programmes) *see* IMF
structuralism 119–20
subsidiarity xx
  trade 69, 74
subsidies under EU CAP 162–5
subsidised exports 146, 147, 162–5, 167–71 *passim*
Sultan of Brunei 20
supermarkets 114–15, 231n45,n46, 154–6, 161–2
  Code of Practice 166–7
surpluses *see* subsidised exports
sustainability xix, xx, 65, 68, 70, 77, 175
sustainable development 13, 72, 78, 86, 109, 117, 130 *see also* Johannesburg Summit
Sutherland, Peter 17
swine fever 157, 158

tariffs
  to protect standards 95, 102, 120
  and self-reliance 165
  to regulate trade 96
  and The Quad 136
taxation of employment 76 *see also* ecological taxation
TBT (Agreement on Technical Barriers to Trade) 79, 80
terrorism 3–5, 212
  liberalisation of trade to counter 3
Tesco 30, 155, 166
Thailand, and structural adjustment 123
Thatcher, Margaret 174
Third World Network 136
Thirwall, Tony 189
Tietmeyer, Hans 19
TNCs (Transnational Corporations) 10–11, 15, 18, 73, 74, 75, 99
  and Eastern Europe 209–10
  and IPRs 94
  Code of Conduct on 73
  Codex Alimentarius 81
  democracy and 17–29, 108
  environment and 73, 75
  GATS and 26–7
  regulation of 75
  regulation under NIEO 121
  UN Centre on 73
  see also agribusiness TNCs; corporate power; corporate lobbying; WTO TRIPS
Tobin tax 72, 113, 224n10
Toepfer, Klaus 5–6
trade 3, 6, 7, 70, 77, 88
  in emissions 87
trade subsidiarity 69, 74, 195–6
Trans-European Networks (TEN) programme 203
transportation
  environmental impacts of 75, 76, 143, 203
  of food 149–50, 156, 162, 171
  of goods 70, 143–4, 177
  of livestock 157–60
  of resources 74, 76
Treaty of Rome (Maastricht) 180–1, 191, 204
TRIMS (Agreement on Trade-Related Investment Measures) 81, 113
TRIPS *see under* WTO

UK Policy Commission on Food and Farming 150
UN 72, 133, 134, 200, 201
  as sponsors of Green Marshall Plan 95, 99
  role in sovereign nation bankruptcy 86
  target for aid 83
  see also Green Marshall Plan
UN Centre on Transnational Corporations 73, 124
UN Declaration of Human Rights 141
UNDP (United Nations Development Programme) 120, 137–8, 139
  Millennium Development Goals 141, 200, 204
UN Economic and Social Council *see* ECOSOC

Index 261

UN General Assembly 119, 124
  Special Session 1974 121
UN Security Council 5
UNCTAD 130, 73, 119, 121, 124
  Code of Conduct on Technology Transfer 73
  Set of Principle in Restrictive Business Practices 73
Unemployment
  in eurozone 186-7
  see also rural decline
UNEP (United Nations Environment Programme) 5, 33, 84, 139
  GEO 3, 33-4, 35-7, 130
UNICE (Union of Industrial and Employers' Confederations of Europe) 178-9
United States
  and Iraq 5
  and NAFTA 22-3
  Bretton Woods strategy of economic control 137-8, 197
  Department of Agriculture 152
  farming 151-2
  hegemony 197
Unwin, Brian 207
Uraguay Round see GATT
US Business Roundtable of TNCs 10

violence, increase caused by globalisation 4
Vision 2020 151, 152
von Wiezsäcker, E. 76

War
  on terror 3, 5
  on Iraq 5 see also Second World War
Washington Consensus 118 see also WTO; IMF; World Bank; Bretton Woods
Watkins, Kevin 24, 103
weapons proliferation 6
welfare benefits 75, 77, 92, 167, 190
Welteke, Ernst 183
Whitty, Larry 147
Whitty, Lord, 20
World Bank 6, 24, 8, 99, 117-18, 122, 200
  and campaign to boycott bonds 139
  and HIPC 83
  and IMF meeting (1999) 117
  and Vision 2020 152
  Compliance Advisor/Ombudsman's office 138
  growth in lending 121
  IBRD (International Bank for Reconstruction and Development) 120
  protest against 108
World Environment Conference, Stockholm (1972) 33
World Food Programme 145
World Trade Center 3
WTO (World Trade Organisation) 3, 6, 89, 117-41, 200
  5th Ministerial Assembly, Cancun (2003) 117-18, 124-6, 129, 135, 200
  agriculture 160, 162, 166, 172, 173
  creation of 124
  destabilising of 135-7
  economic localisation 77
  emergence from GATT 119
  GAST 78-82
  Indian People's Movement Against 110
  internal reform 105
  like product rule
  non-tariff barriers to trade 103
  replacement of 133-7
  view on comparative advantage 10
  Complaints to
    US pharmaceuticals v South Africa, AIDS drugs 29
    US v EU, bananas 20, 78
    US v EU, beef 159
    US v Indian import barriers 110
  Doha Ministerial meeting of 3, 67, 113, 117-18, 124-7, 129, 133, 135, 136, 173

WTO
  Doha Ministerial meeting of *continued*
    Agreement on Agriculture 82, 125, 132, 146
    proposal for 'Development Box' 87, 92, 96, 97, 125, 132, 167–9
  General Agreement on Trade in Services 24–7, 82
  democracy 26–7, 108
  development 26
  domestic regulations 25, 78
  liberalisation of investment 71
  local government 26
  Market Access 25
  Ministerial Meeting in Seattle 67, 96, 117, 129, 135
  protest against 136–7
  public Services 25
  reform 109 *see also* GAST

TNCs 26–7
women 26–7
TRIPS Agreement on trade related aspects of IPRS 27–9, 81
  democratic governance 29–30
  EU beef import ban 80
  General Exceptions to Rules 79
  and Agreement to Technical Barriers to Trade 80
  generic drugs 28–9
  HIV/AIDS 28–9, 94, 112
  innovation 94
  precautionary principle 80
  private sector 27–9
  replacements for CFCs 94
  the South 28–9, 94
WWF Living Planet Index 35

Young, Don 4

Zambia, food distribution 171
Zoellick, Robert 3